THE PUBLIC INTELLECTUAL IN CANADA

This illuminating, entertaining, and timely volume examines the place and impact of public intellectuals in our rapidly changing and diverse society. Boasting an all-star cast of contributors – including some of Canada's most prominent writers, journalists, and academics – it probes the role of public discourse and intellectual persuasion in shaping Canada's past, present, and future.

The Public Intellectual in Canada examines how individuals have come to assume this role, how they are received by various publics, and what they have been able to accomplish. The pieces cover topics ranging from the potential and perils of advocacy to the influence of think tanks on public policy. Many pieces also delve into the roles of pollsters, political actors, pundits, social activists, economists, and ethicists, among others.

Broad in scope and stylistically diverse, these essays offer a fascinating overview of the links between thought, public exposition, and action in the fields of politics, science, and culture.

NELSON WISEMAN is an associate professor in the Department of Political Science at the University of Toronto. A columnist for *The Hill Times*, he is also the author of the CHOICE Outstanding Academic Title *In Search of Canadian Political Culture*.

The Public Intellectual in Canada

EDITED BY NELSON WISEMAN

UNIVERSITY OF TORONTO PRESS
Toronto Buffalo London

ISBN 978-1-4426-4526-4 (cloth)
ISBN 978-1-4426-1339-3 (paper)

Printed on acid-free, 100% post-consumer recycled paper with
vegetable-based inks.

Library and Archives Canada Cataloguing in Publication

The public intellectual in Canada / edited by Nelson Wiseman.

Includes bibliographical references.
ISBN 978-1-4426-4526-4 (bound). – ISBN 978-1-4426-1339-3 (pbk.)

1. Intellectuals – Canada.   2. Canada – Intellectual life.
I. Wiseman, Nelson, 1946–, editor of compilation

FC95.5. P82 2013   305.5'520971   C2013-902086-1

University of Toronto Press acknowledges the financial assistance to its
publishing program of the Canada Council for the Arts and the
Ontario Arts Council.

Canada Council   Conseil des Arts
for the Arts   du Canada

ONTARIO ARTS COUNCIL
CONSEIL DES ARTS DE L'ONTARIO
50 YEARS OF ONTARIO GOVERNMENT SUPPORT OF THE ARTS
50 ANS DE SOUTIEN DU GOUVERNEMENT DE L'ONTARIO AUX ARTS

University of Toronto Press acknowledges the financial support of the
Government of Canada through the Canada Book Fund for its
publishing activities.

Contents

THE PUBLIC INTELLECTUAL IN CANADA

Introduction

Caught up in a small-pond syndrome, Canadians can be self-deprecatingly modest. Invited to contribute to this book showcasing some of Canada's prominent public intellectuals, David Suzuki – whose syndicated television series *The Nature of Things* has been broadcast in over forty countries – asked: "Could you tell me what a public intellectual is so I can decide whether I'm competent enough to write something?" Denys Arcand – the winner of three dozen film awards including an Oscar for *The Barbarian Invasions*, which revisits the aging intellectuals of *The Decline of the American Empire* – responded with similar self-effacement: "You have been misinformed. I am not an intellectual. I am an old film director. I tell tales that I don't always understand. The exact opposite of an intellectual who tries to make sense of the surrounding reality." Protesting that he too was "uncomfortable" self-identifying as a public intellectual, for that would suggest he was taking on "airs," pollster Michael Adams, whose best-selling books chart the values and value differences of Canadians and Americans, opted initially to write about "why Canada has no public intellectuals." Somewhat less hesitantly Conrad Black, who had renounced his Canadian citizenship to accept a British peerage, responded from a prison cell in the United States: "I am not comfortable bandying about the phrase 'public intellectual' in reference to myself, not that I would contest its accuracy, just that it is un-Canadian in its portentousness."[1]

For many Canadians, like Suzuki, the public intellectual is a formless and vaguely amorphous notion, a barely recognizable creature. For others, like Adams and Black, the term carries the burden of pomposity. However disinclined they are to use the term to describe themselves, Suzuki, Arcand, Adams, and Black qualify as public intellectuals precisely because they forsake excessive professionalization. They favour capturing a public culture in a world of ever-increasing hyper-specialization and an increasingly fragmented public space, communicating their ideas on an array of public issues to a wider audience beyond their narrow fraternity of peers.

In Canada, intellectually fertile periods have fluctuated with periods of arrested intellectual development. Unlike American, British, and French public intellectuals, who usually take for granted the worth of their work and the sturdy cultural foundations of their societies, Canada's public intellectuals have had to negotiate the shoals of Canadian identity as they have striven to reconfigure it. Labouring in the cultural shadow of the United States, they have resisted the pull of their neighbour and have helped to guide their country along a distinctive trajectory in its constant struggle with its identity. Their ideas about Canada and its future anticipate its fulfilment.

Because of their stronger European roots, and perhaps because of their native politeness and relative deference to authority, Canadians exhibit more respect for intellectuals than do Americans. In the United States, a deep-seated, easily tapped anti-intellectualism has infused political life.[2] English Canada's public intellectuals, however, have never evoked the reverence that Russians have for their intelligentsia nor have they become the media phenomenon they are in France, where the spectacle of television effectively conjoins information, entertainment, and opinion. As transmission belts between the public intellectual and her public, a country's media may transform a public intellectual – think of essayist John Ralston Saul, the first Canadian president of International PEN, or novelist Margaret Atwood – into a media personality, a celebrity intellectual.

In common with the continental French, francophone Quebeckers have demonstrated a greater receptivity to public intellectuals than have English-speaking Canadians. Where in English Canada could a newspaper with the cerebral heft of *Le Devoir* attract an elite crowd including the provincial premier, the prime minister, and Quebec's captains of industry, as *Le Devoir* did in 1990, to a fund-raiser for the paper? (See Gregory Baum's essay in this collection.) Radio Canada's *"Tout le monde en parle"* – the name and format borrowed from its European forerunner – is another example of Quebeckers' greater respect for intellectuals; they are not dismissively cast as eggheads. The program, featuring unrehearsed exchanges among artists, intellectuals, and politicians, attracts a million and a half viewers in a province with fewer than seven million francophones, the equivalent of an Academy Awards–sized audience in the rest of Canada tuning in every week.[3]

As an independent critic, the public intellectual is a free-ranger who offers a breadth of vision that transcends any one particular branch of a science, art, or vocation; as such, he is much more than a scholar in a single field or a professional specialist. Unlike those who theorize narrowly or technically about their specific branch of learning or expertise, the public intellectual taps and channels the critical, contemplative, and creative sides of his audience's minds. Expressing himself in a publicly accessible manner on issues of general public concern, the public intellectual has no manual or reference guide to lead him.

Popularizing one's science is insufficient to qualify as a public intellectual unless an ethical or political dimension propels the message. Grounded and engaged with his world, the public intellectual is no alienated or disconnected dilettante hobbyist, no private intellectual content to toy leisurely with ideas. Driven by an audacious sense of obligation to himself and to society, he tells the truth the way he sees it, and in a democracy, dispelling ignorance is perhaps his first duty. Social commitment and civil courage delineates him from other intellectuals.

Today, most intellectuals – many in this collection – are ensconced as academics within universities. Professors research what interests them as they teach students, and like other public intellectuals are an elite privileged class with an ability to influence mass opinion. Karl Mannheim, the path-breaking theorist who founded the field now known as the sociology of knowledge and who criticized the overspecialization of academic disciplines, recognized that universities imposed certain status expectations of their professors and would frown on them adopting the role of a public intellectual. (Stephen Clarkson pursues this theme in his essay.)

An increasing number of public intellectuals work in ideologically driven think tanks and policy institutes such as the right-wing, Vancouver-based, Fraser Institute and Winnipeg's Frontier Centre for Public Policy and the left-leaning Ottawa-based Canadian Centre for Policy Alternatives and Caledon Institute of Social Policy. Some public intellectuals, such as John Richards (who writes on Aboriginal policy in this collection), has a foot in the university as well as at a think tank (C.D. Howe Institute). Pleading their positions, think tanks aspire to be policy "do tanks." Some public intellectuals occasionally toil as government intellectuals, at various times and among others in this collection, Tom Flanagan, Hugh Segal, and Pierre Fortin. In doing so, they are often required to set aside and subordinate their critical and creative sides to the goals of the leader or the institution that recruits them. As well, there are social movement intellectuals, such as Baum and Maude Barlow who are more radical than government intellectuals, but who – with an intellectual temperament archetypally Canadian – disavow extremism. And there are public intellectuals such as Michael Adams, who hails from the worlds of business, and those like Doug Saunders, the widely read and honoured journalist.

Any selection of Canada's public intellectuals is arbitrary if not randomly chaotic. One man's public intellectual is another man's propagandist and what public intellectuals produce varies in quality and appears in an imperfect market. Best-sellerdom or temporal currency is not sufficient: rejected or overlooked in his own time, a public intellectual may have his ideas embraced in a subsequent era. Alternatively, they may exhaust themselves. Harold Innis, the only non-American to have served as president of the American Economics Association, shunned popular media and severely criticized academics who appeared therein. Others, however, extrapolated from his thesis regarding the exploitation of Canada's natural resources and the links those resources engendered between imperial and colonial cultures, and these students of Innis stimulated a broader public consciousness of his thinking about Canada's political and economic development. The widespread transmission of Innis's ideas – Canada's citizenship guide now refers to him[4] – qualifies him as a public intellectual, although during his lifetime relatively few Canadians beyond the academy knew of him. His path-breaking theorizing and that of Marshall McLuhan, who built on his work, qualifies both of them as public intellectuals, for they helped Canadians and others to understand themselves and their society.

Where do Canadians stand among those considered the leading global public intellectuals today? This is a matter of promotion as well as discriminating taste. Sorties in classification are perilous and inevitably flawed, but they reflect a growing demand to make available relevant informed learning in an increasingly global knowledge society. A list of the world's "top 100 current public intellectuals" selected by editors of *Foreign Policy* magazine in 2005 and 2008 transcended a nation-based approach, but revealed the journal's own bias: a disproportionate number of those it listed had contributed to its pages.[5] Asked by the magazine to weigh in on their choices via the Internet, many respondents succumbed to organized campaigns; in 2008 they voted ten Muslims as the world's top ten public intellectuals.[6] Some on *Foreign Policy*'s list, such as Christopher Hitchens, advertised themselves and offered links on their websites to facilitate voting for them. Partisans of others, such as Michael Ignatieff, solicited votes on their behalf.

Five persons somehow linked to Canada appeared on *Foreign Policy*'s 2008 list. Two, pop sociologist and journalist Malcolm Gladwell (slapped down by Mark Kingwell in his contribution here) and Harvard linguist and experimental psychologist Steven Pinker, were listed as "Canada/United States." Another, theoretical physicist Lee Smolin (who came to Canada in 2001), is recorded as "United States/Canada." The other two Canadians on the list, philosopher Charles Taylor and Ignatieff, appeared as unhyphenated Canadians, although Ignatieff had lived longer outside of Canada than in it. As evidence of the fickle nature of determining the reputations of public intellectuals, Canadian Naomi Klein, who was listed fifth in *Foreign Policy*'s 2005 inventory and whose book *No Logo*[7] became a manifesto of the anti-corporate globalization movement (and to whom Sylvia Bashevkin draws particular attention in this collection), was absent from the magazine's 2008 list.

This book brings together a wide range of exceptional figures, some of Canada's most thoughtful, knowledgeable, and prominent contemporary public intellectuals, both academics and non-academics. Original thinkers with inventive ideas, their voices are rich, their perspectives diverse. The result is an idiosyncratic eccentric compilation, surprisingly and invitingly eclectic. The thread that binds the various issues addressed – from underpopulation and Aboriginal policy to the travails of ethicists and the impact of economists, to the roles of pollsters, political actors, pundits, and social activists – is the place of the public intellectual in Canadian society. Some contributors assume the mantle of the public intellectual, others hesitate to adopt it, and most are content to identify the work of public intellectuals, what they do and who they are. With verve and panache, the authors meditate in one way or another on the role of the public intellectual and his societal responsibilities.

This book appears at a time of revolutionary change in the arenas available to public intellectuals and their audiences for public thought. In today's brave new technological world, where the electronic systems and digital products of modern communications such as the Internet permit anyone to publish widely and scream loudly, public intellectuals continue to serve as salutary antidotes to the simplification and trivialization of public debate. The authors of the essays here reflect on how well public intellectuals fare in Canada, on the functions they fulfil, and on how the conditions and forums for the widespread public debate of ideas might be improved.

Some essays offer highly personal insights and accounts; others present empirical scholarly studies. Together the essays touch on intellectual history, the sociology of knowledge, philosophy, and public policy. Issues addressed include the media as filters of public thought, the changing university environment, advocacy, influence in public policy, and the rise of think tanks.

These essays cover social and political thought more comprehensively than science and culture. From the world of science, only metallurgist Ursula Franklin receives sustained treatment (in Bashevkin's essay) although Franklin and other scientists such as Suzuki, Nobel Prize–winning chemist John Polanyi, neurosurgeon Wilder Penfield, and those associated with the Pugwash Institute, for example, have certainly given an ethical or political cast to their public interventions. Many outstanding figures from the world of literature, such as novelists Atwood and Mordecai Richler and literary critic Northrop Frye, who appear only fleetingly in these essays, also indisputably qualify as public intellectuals.

The figures that appear in these essays are but a sampling of those who could have appeared. One could list many more of Canada's distinguished men and women of letters who are not referred to, including Robertson Davies, Al Purdy, Roch Carrier, and poet Dorothy Livesay, a two-time winner of the Governor General's Award who exhibited a lifelong concern for women's issues and rights. From the worlds of art and music, those not mentioned include the eccentric and brilliant colourist Greg Curnoe, known for his hyperbolic anti-Americanism outbursts, and Bruce Cockburn, whose passionate devotion to human rights found expression in *If I Had a Rocket Launcher*, inspired by his visit to a Guatemalan refugee camp in Mexico. An unmentioned and generally unheralded Canadian whose primary public arena was global is John Humphrey, who penned a draft of the Universal Declaration of Human Rights, dubbed by Eleanor Roosevelt as "the international Magna Carta of all mankind."[8]

The relative absence of women voices (four of sixteen) in this collection speaks to the historical inability of women to claim equal space and attention in public forums. Women have faced daunting cultural and social barriers and their participation will continue to be underplayed if only issues traditionally considered properly in the public sphere, as opposed to those deemed personal and private, define the work of public intellectuals. Equal Voice, an organization which has attracted media attention with its mission to promote the election of more women to all levels of government, focuses on the political because it believes the election of more women will produce public policies more sensitive to women's concerns. Paradoxically, as the women's movement has declined, more women have gained recognition for their contributions as public intellectuals.

The all-star cast of contributors in this collection is a truly impressive assembly. Many are widely known and will be familiar to the reader. All of them have influenced public affairs in Canada as doers as well as thinkers and they span the ideological spectrum. With them, we explore and examine the place of the public intellectual in the context of a rapidly changing and diverse Canadian society in an increasingly interdependent world.

NOTES

1 David Suzuki, email to author, 10 Aug. 2009; Denys Arcand, letter to author, 9 Sept. 2009; Michael Adams, email to author, 9 Sept. 2009; and Conrad Black, emails to author, 31 July and 3 Aug. 2009.

2 Philip Resnick, *The European Roots of Canadian Identity* (Peterborough: Broadview, 2005), Edgar Z. Friedenberg, *Deference to Authority: The Case of Canada* (White Plains, NY: M.E. Sharpe, 1980), and Richard Hofstadter, *Anti-Intellectualism in American Life* (New York: Vintage Books, 1966).

3 Andrew Chung, "Tout le monde en parle," *Toronto Star*, 29 Sept. 2008, http://thestar.blogs.com/notebook/2008/09/liberal-party-l.html, and "Charest in hot seat on TV talk show," *Toronto Star*, 6 Dec. 2010, p. A8.

4 Citizenship and Immigration Canada, *Discover Canada: The Rights and Responsibilities of Citizenship* (Ottawa: Minister of Public Works and Government Services, 2009), 26.

5 Accessed 29 Dec. 2009.

6 "Survey says world's top 10 intellectuals are Muslims," *Reuters*, http://blogs.reuters.com/faithworld/2008/06/25/survey-says-worlds-top-10-intellectuals-are-muslims/.

7 Naomi Klein, *No Logo: Taking Aim at the Brand Bullies* (London: Flamingo, 2000).

8 Henry J. Steiner, Philip Alston, and Ryan Goodman, *International Human Rights in Context: Law, Politics, Morals* (Oxford: Oxford University Press, 2008), 146.

PART ONE

What Are Public Intellectuals For?

1 The Public Intellectual and the Democratic Conversation

JANICE GROSS STEIN

1. A "Public Intellectual"?

A friend recently introduced me to a colleague whom he described as a "serious public intellectual." Pausing for a moment, he then went on to say, "And I mean that as a compliment." I was puzzled. What was he suggesting? Was it insulting to be described as a public intellectual?

As a polite Canadian, I did not pursue the issue there and then, but the comment niggled. Is "public" the troubling part of the description? Is it acceptable to be a private intellectual, engaging in the life of the mind behind closed doors where prying eyes cannot see? Or is it that "intellectual" is an unflattering category, laden with subtle meanings that become apparent when we examine it in the light of popular culture, however we understand that term. Or possibly, could this be a particularly Canadian issue, a discomfort with any public display of prowess, one more instance of the "tall poppy" syndrome that some commentators charge bedevils Canada.

I understand the term "intellectual" to refer to someone who uses her intellect. That is, however, an obviously tautological statement. What does it mean to use one's intellect? It means to draw on reason and analysis to put arguments forward. The trouble with this definition, of course, is that it encompasses almost everyone. Farmers use reason and analysis to make arguments about what is appropriate to plant and when it is appropriate to harvest. Physicians use reason and analysis to diagnose patients and recommend treatments. Lawyers use reason and analysis to defend their clients within a publicly constituted legal framework. Virtually every skilled problem solver uses reason and analysis in many different ways in their lives, regardless of what else they might do. Clearly, there is more to being an intellectual than the use of reason and argument. But what? What sets the intellectual apart from other reasoning and thoughtful people?

An intellectual may be someone who devotes her life to the search for truth, who uses her power of reason and analysis to strip away falsehood and clarify and illuminate what is true. This understanding of the intellectual does not take us much farther. Scientists of all kinds search for truth in their laboratories, in the field, in the research that they do. Physicists seek to know the universe, its deep and underlying truths that are 'hidden from the naked eye. Sociologists seek to understand why societies are stable and why they change. In my own field, scholars have tried for the last two millennia to understand the causes of war. Yet we generally do not think of these truth seekers as intellectuals. We call them scientists, researchers, social scientists, philosophers, or even scholars, but the search for truth for its own sake does not seem to be the defining attribute of an intellectual. What then?

I suspect that we reserve the term "intellectual" for someone who plays with abstract ideas for the sheer fun of it. Like jugglers, intellectuals initially have no ulterior motive other than to play with concepts and abstractions, for the pleasure that it gives. Like artists who are driven to make art, even when no one appreciates what they create, intellectuals may have no instrumental purpose other than to enjoy and enhance the elegance of ideas. Unlike the stereotype, then, intellectuals are not generally desiccated people. On the contrary, they are passionate about ideas. No matter how disciplined and meticulous they are in the making of their arguments, when they argue they do so with feeling, at times mesmerized by the beauty of the idea, dazzled by the elegance of the argument. Intellectuals are creatures of both reason and passion and the two are inseparable. Indeed, the newest research in neuroscience tells us convincingly that without emotion, we cannot reason. The two are not opposites, as philosophers long argued, but integral one to the other.

If I am right, it is no shabby thing to be an intellectual, to be passionate about thinking and reasoning, about abstract ideas and concepts. No apologies necessary. Much follows, however, from this description of intellectuals as passionate thinkers.

If the argument that intellectuals are passionate thinkers bears thinking about, then it is the passion that pushes intellectuals to share the excitement of their ideas with others. Like artists, they want to communicate their vision, their understanding of the world. They want others to read what they write, to hear what they are saying, to understand what they understand. Michael Cunningham, a writer of fiction, rejected the myth that writers write for themselves and described his ongoing mental dialogue with his readers. There is always a reader with him, he insisted, even if the reader is only in his imagination. In this sense, intellectual activity is not a private activity for long. The life of the mind is intensely personal and passionate, but sooner or later spills over and becomes a public activity. Intellectuals need an interlocutor, even if that interlocutor is imaginary. The passion drives the ideas and the arguments out into the world, at times even before these ideas are ready to be born.

My interest is in a subspecies of these intellectuals, those who believe in the possibility of dialogue with the public. Working within a democratic tradition, they are committed to an informed and engaged citizenry. Indeed, they believe that only if citizens are informed and knowledgeable about the issues can democratic debate flourish and democracy be deepened. It is their commitment to engagement with the public that justifies the term "public intellectual."

2. Public Intellectuals and the Democratic Conversation

A thinker's commitment to engagement with the public is somewhat different from one who seeks truth for its own sake. Scientists who seek truth, for example, who do research, are not always driven to communicate that truth to the public in their societies. They are not because the knowledge they create will often not be used directly by citizens themselves, but by others who are intermediaries between the scientist and the citizen. Some kinds of knowledge, moreover, are especially abstract or technical and extraordinarily difficult to communicate in a meaningful way. The field of quantum information, for example, is much more difficult to speak about with a group of citizens than are some of the acute dilemmas that bioethicists have explored. People experience and live these bioethical dilemmas – end of life care, euthanasia, genetic engineering – and are often open, at times eager, to join in public conversation about these issues. They want the opportunity to learn and to argue.

Certainly some subjects are inherently very difficult technically and require advanced levels of expertise to comprehend. But I argue that generally as a society we are failing to engage and that we need to find new and imaginative ways to do so if our democracy is to flourish. To this process of democratic engagement, I argue, intellectuals must contribute.

3. Obstacles to Public Conversation

Critics currently bemoan the state of debate in contemporary democratic societies. They write of the "dumbing down" of public discussion, the growing presence of the quick quip and the superficial sound bite, and the rise of demagogues who dominate talk radio shows and the blogospheres. All of these, they argue, are a threat to the quality of our democratic life. Without a well-informed citizenry, vigorously debating the future, our democratic institutions atrophy, becoming the preserve of a political class and privileged elites. Our public space empties out and private interest replaces public concerns and a shared sense of a common future and the collective good.

This, of course, is not a new concern. In ancient times, when democracy was direct and intimate, philosophers still worried about the quality of public debate. Roman leaders put on circuses to distract restless publics from the issues of collective concern. It is not unusual, therefore, that each generation worries anew about the quality of conversation in public space. That is as it should be.

If we are worrying more than usual at this moment, if we are bemoaning hyper partisanship, superficial debate, and sound bites that displace serious, substantive conversation, we have good reason. Several trends have converged to debase the quality of public debate in our democratic lives.

Foremost among these is the revolution in communication technologies and the creation of digital public space. In the early, heady days of the nineties, democratic theorists held out great hope that the new technologies would build a platform for a new kind of civic engagement, for a public discussion which would be wide-ranging and open to everyone. The possibilities were limited only by the cost of a computer and the availability of a connection. In retrospect, this hope was overwhelmingly naive and impossibly optimistic. Revolutionary changes in technology, as they always have and always will, enabled new kinds of communication, some of it very good but some of it deeply discouraging. From the perspective of civic engagement and public conversation, the most important consequence was the levelling effect on knowledge, reasoning, and argument.

In the Internet era, the age of Twitter and blogs, everyone who writes is an instant expert. The distinction between disciplined knowledge and opinion is elided and, indeed, at times disappears. Every one's opinion is of equal merit and there are very limited ways to distinguish the deeply knowledgeable, the well-informed, from those who simply have opinions. The sceptic may well interrupt at precisely this moment and say, with some aggravation: This sounds like a rationalization for an unhealthy elitism, a defence of the intellectual steeped in knowledge and practised at reasoning from the true hero or heroine of this story, the democratic citizen. We have long ago abandoned the fantasy of the philosopher king, if we ever had it at all.

This, I respond, is a fundamental misreading of the most basic processes of democratic society. All opinions are equal when we come together to choose our leaders, when we exercise our most basic democratic rights at the ballot box. Knowledge, argument, and reason do not have special prerogative or special privilege on voting day, nor should they. Any such contention would indeed be elitism, rightly suspect and discredited by citizens. The question I am asking is, rather: how are opinion of citizens formed before voting day? What opportunities do they have to learn about the issues that are most important to them?

This is not a trivial question. As our societies have become more globalized and more specialized, it has becoming increasingly challenging for citizens to navigate their way through a rich, but noisy and confusing, environment. Standard and familiar places to go – the local newspapers, for example, and public broadcasters – have become increasingly fragile as they compete for attention and resources in our multimedia digital environment.

The benefits of this hyper active, rich, multimedia digital universe are well known. As citizens, we can find what we want, when we want it, and how we want it. We range far and wide, download what appeals, and read, watch, or listen when it is convenient. A new, wonderfully rich world is open to all of us, there for the asking, except in the growing number of societies where governments now rigorously control and limit access to the digital universe.

This rosy picture is, of course, not the whole story, not even in democratic societies where access to the digital world is unimpeded. Print and electronic media compete for the attention of the public in a hyper-competitive environment. In this world, traditional media are being squeezed financially. Newspapers in Canada, for example, have reduced their foreign correspondents over the last decade and, counter-intuitively, generally pay less attention to global issues than they did a decade ago. More space – and resources – are devoted to human interest stories, to lifestyle sections, and to stories designed to attract younger readers who have largely left the print world behind for the digital world. With a few outstanding exceptions, such as the *Globe and Mail*, our newspapers are no longer the essential resource for engagement on civic issues that they once were.

Nowhere is this change more evident than in our public broadcaster. In the last few years, leadership at the CBC has set as their top priority to increase their audience share. In their flagship news programs, they have shortened the length of news items, reduced the coverage of international issues, cut the number of foreign correspondents, introduced glitzy graphics and snippet items that flash on and off the screen, and quickened the pace of items to produce a faster-moving program for viewers who are used to multitasking and tweeting in 140 characters or less. All this to appeal to easily distracted people living in a noisy, fractious, crowded, busy environment.

Surprisingly, these changes at the CBC provoked significant controversy. That they did is encouraging, for it suggested that there was still a constituency that cared about the public broadcaster, that believed that it had a special role in civic education that private broadcasters would not fill. These loyalists decried the deliberate "dumbing down" of news and current affairs by the leadership of the CBC to increase its viewership, the subtext of many of the changes.

I am one of those who mourned the loss of the CBC radio that I treasured, was profoundly aggrieved by the debasement of the talented CBC news team, who were forced into an awkward and at times silly framework, and deeply regretted the shrinking of shared space that the CBC historically has provided for public discussion. It is with no *Schadenfreude*, therefore, that I read that the readership of the *Globe and Mail*, which by and large refused to compromise on the quality of its content, has increased. By contrast, at the CBC, which provided video snippets to attract the video generation, the viewership has declined. These asymmetrical results are momentarily comforting for people who are concerned about the shrinking space for civic engagement.

This new digital world generally contributes to the shrinking of shared space for civic engagement. Digital technology enables division of space into ever smaller and smaller slices. No longer do citizens gather around their radios to listen to the same broadcast, as they once did, nor do they watch the same newscasts on their televisions, as they once did. There is less and less shared conversation around the water cooler about something people all saw or read the night before. Now it is about a two-minute video that went "viral" on YouTube. This makes it more difficult to have a conversation about common issues, even when we differ in perspectives. If we are not reading, listening, or watching the same content, we have less and less to talk about together.

The story becomes even more difficult if we believe the evidence that people increasingly read newspapers that agree with their views, watch television shows on networks that affirm their pre-existing beliefs, and go to websites of like-minded people. As public space fractures and choice multiplies, conversations become less, not more, diverse. In the most pessimistic account, conversations no longer involve the exchange of ideas and a discussion of differences, but rather a gathering of the faithful to exchange views with others who think like they do. When the faithful gather, attitudes are reinforced rather than challenged. Thinking congeals. The opportunities for education through the discussion of differences become fewer and fewer and the voices more shrill. When there is little opportunity to bridge differences, this shrillness puts democratic debate and discussion at risk.

It is no accident that we are seeing a dramatic increase in partisanship, an inability to reach across the aisle, to bridge differences and find political compromise on important policy issues. On the contrary, debates are becoming vitriolic, laced with personal attacks, burdened with stereotypes. This hyper-partisanship is visible not only in the parliament of Canada, but also in the Congress of the United States and in the parliaments of Europe. As the capacity of the traditional "aggregators" – our media, our political parties – recedes and is replaced by a splintered digital world, political parties are finding it harder and harder to bridge differences and broker compromises, to grease the wheels of democratic processes. Collecting and bridging differences – aggregation – is essential to the smooth functioning of any democracy, and it is precisely this function which is being put at risk. It can hardly be a coincidence that we are seeing increasing partisanship as the media have splintered and lost their role of creating shared space for political discussion.

To this toxic stew we add the final element, the loss of respect for politicians and the progressive alienation of citizens from the political process. Citizens who listen to the vitriol and watch the antics of our elected representatives are disgusted by the partisanship, dismayed by the stereotyping, disheartened by the poor quality of debate and discussion, and disquieted by the lack of attention to serious challenges. It is no surprise that citizens are increasingly suspicious of the motives of politicians and distrustful of the leaders whom they elect. Most citizens no longer regard political life as honourable, and that is a sad commentary on our democratic societies.

The increasing vitriol amidst the partisanship of public debate, and the emergence of "infotainment" as a substitute for serious talk, shrink the space for democratic governance. If these trends deepen, democratic societies will not get the governments that we deserve. It is in this context that I explore a possible role for public intellectuals in pushing back against these trends, in broadening, even marginally, the space for civic engagement.

4. The Obstacles to a Role for the Public Intellectual

Why privilege any role at all for a public intellectual in this crisis of democracy? To put it bluntly, why place any confidence in people who live a life of the mind, who like to play with abstractions. As Mark Kingwell rightly points out in this volume, public intellectuals are subject to the same temptations and foibles as their fellow citizens. They can be vainglorious, enthralled by the sound of their own voices, attention seekers who are flattered by the attention that they receive. They can be co-opted by those in power, seduced by fame or benefits. They can succumb to the temptation of fifteen minutes of fame and, as Tom Flanagan notes, get drawn into sixty-second interviews on television, becoming advocates for partisan causes rather than interpreters of complex problems. They can use their intellect to debate rather than to consider, to quip rather than to analyse, to insult rather than to assess. Public intellectuals, in other words, are human, with all the temptations, foibles, and weakness of will that human beings struggle with all the time.

When public intellectuals succumb to these temptations, as some most certainly do some of the time, they abuse the authority that they implicitly carry as "thinkers." The risk of this kind of abuse merits a well-deserved caution to avoid elevating public intellectuals to a position of authority that they do not merit.

This kind of risk, however, applies to almost any category of human activity. Clerics have abused their religious authority. Some physicians have been known to abuse their authority in their dealings with patients, as have lawyers in their dealing with clients. Athletes, scientists, judges, artists can all misbehave at times and yet all engage with the public in different ways at different times. It makes no sense, then, to hold public intellectuals to a unique standard, one that is higher than any other group that has obligations to the public. It equally makes little sense to be more sceptical, more suspicious of public intellectuals than of any other group that engages with the public.

If we set perfection as the bar, no engagement with the public is possible at all. We consequently do not expect perfection, but generally evaluate by the strength and excellence of the contribution. In other words, we judge on the merits. We judge the fifty-home-run hitter by the fifty home runs, until and unless we find that the hitter was on steroids. We need to judge public intellectuals by the quality of the ideas they put on the table for public discussion, until and unless we find that they are a voice for special interests or an accomplice in intellectual fraud. We need, in other words, to be diligent, critical listeners. It is worth adding that intellectuals are especially likely to engage in self-flagellation, setting standards for their own participation which make it impossible for them to participate at all in public life. When the best is the enemy of the good, it is democratic conversation that suffers.

There is a more serious obstacle to the participation of intellectuals in public life. More and more, those who play with ideas, especially within the contemporary academy, do so in language that is "professional": dense, jargonized, obscure, impenetrable by those outside their narrow specialization. Schooled in this language which excludes rather than includes, some are unable to communicate with the public even if they wanted to do so. I recently asked an extraordinarily bright graduate student of mine, who is working on a problem that is of major public interest, to put the jargon aside and to explain to me, in a sentence or two, what she had found. She couldn't do it. I was troubled that she could not and resolved to look again at how we are educating our students. There is a serious and deep contradiction here: research that is motivated by a desire to serve the public interest is done in such a way that its results cannot be communicated to the public. In other words, ideas about inclusion are expressed in language that excludes.

If a charge of elitism can be levelled against intellectuals who try to engage with the public, it is not *because* they engage, but rather *how* they engage. Those who speak in ways that cannot be understood outside a narrow circle of initiates, who use language to establish authority rather than to clarify, who exploit their rhetorical and conceptual fluency to outflank others rather than to address the issues, do not expand the scope of democratic conversation. The first and cardinal rule of public engagement is modesty.

5. A Role for the Public Intellectual?

If intellectuals who engage in public conversation are prima facie no worse than others who do the same, the final questions are *why* should they engage and, when they do, *how* should they do so. Each of these questions is more complex than they first appear.

The "why" of engagement, it seems to me, is easier. A democracy cannot thrive without informed public debate. Intellectuals are one, only one but nevertheless one, group who, when they know something about something that matters, should contribute. Some who do earn their living directly or indirectly from the public purse and feel an obligation to give back to the public. Here too, no apologies are necessary. Many who support themselves from the books they write, the films they make, the magazines they publish, also feel an obligation to contribute what they know when the issue at stake is important. It is puzzling that this should even be an issue. Those who play with ideas, who have reasoned through a problem, who have mastered a body of knowledge, should certainly feel no more reluctant to engage in conversation than does the average citizen.

Intellectuals, as I have argued, do run a real risk. Because they have wrestled with the problem, they may not be patient enough to reason carefully again in public so that people can trace their reasoning. The temptation is to short-circuit, to share the conclusions but skip the argument, and to invoke authority to justify doing so. When they do so, they choke off conversation with those whom they think are less informed. Modesty and a duty of care can mitigate this risk significantly.

There is a second challenge. An acquaintance of mine, a regular columnist whom I admire enormously, once said to me critically, "I listen to you but when you're finished speaking, I often do not know where you stand." The rebuke stung, especially coming from him; it smarted so much that I thought about it carefully. Indeed, he was quite right: very often, when I am asked in public about an issue, I try to build in the complexities. On the one hand, but on the other hand … Occasionally important issues are so clear that the answer is glaringly obvious and it is a pleasure to give it. Most of the time, however, "on the one hand but on the other hand" better captures the grey of the issue. To speak of it as black or white is distorting, simplifying, patronizing … A rush to judgment feeds the culture of sound bites, of instant premixed answers to complex problems, of snappy opinion rather than careful analysis.

There is a deeper challenge here. Where I stand on an issue does not really matter at all. What I know about the issue does. This is a central distinction, one which separates the advocate from the analyst. The advocate selectively marshals evidence and argues forcefully for a position to convert the opposed or persuade the undecided. That is an entirely legitimate function in our society and it is performed by our political representatives, by advocacy organizations, by editorial writers who have a definite point of view, and often by columnists who have reached a judgment. In all these cases, it is clear to attentive listeners that these are advocates who have reached a judgment and are trying to persuade them.

The intellectual comes from a different place and presents a different face to the public. Playing with the idea, stretching it first one way and then the other, pushing it here and pushing it there, expands rather than simplifies the contradictions. Exercising the idea unearths the unexpected, the complex, the counter-intuitive, the unintended. That kind of play teaches us that usually there is no straight line from here to there, that the route is circuitous, that we can almost certainly not see the end, and if we do, we will be wrong. It teaches us to resist the simple, even when it appears to be simple, for it almost never is. Turning the idea around, pushing it backward and forward, up and down, allows us to look and see from multiple perspectives. Slowly, slowly, the greys push out and cover more and more of the black and white.

It is this sense of contradiction that intellectuals can bring to conversation in public space. Just as athletes and musicians bring a special set of skills when they play in public, so too does the intellectual. They are better equipped than others to resist the quick fix, to refrain from the quick quip, to try to stretch out the conversation, and to frustrate the listener by dragging their feet and refusing to rush to judgment. It is that hesitancy, the insistence that we might see the problem differently, that is the intellectual's stock in trade.

In today's hyper-ventilating world, in our frenetic, noisy, distracting public space, this slow deliberate pace is probably the most valuable asset that the intellectual can bring to public conversation. The refusal to be rushed, the detailing of an argument, step by painful step, mutes the frantic tempo of public – and private – life, with its relentless drumbeat. The best music, the best writing, music or writing that endures over time, alters its tempo to re-engage the eyes and ears. It occasionally says "Stop. Pay attention. Stop and listen. Stop and see. Stop and think. Stop and hear. Stop and feel." When intellectuals connect with the public, when the relationship is working, when it's right, the public stops, even for a moment, to listen, to think, to hear, to see. And that moment is magical.

2 The Public Intellectual and Politics: Why Choices Matter

HUGH SEGAL

Politics at its best is not only a debate about the ideal way ahead in a democracy, but also an engagement between proponents of differing agendas for the very debate itself. Whether it is an ideological debate between left and right, a methodological debate within a specific government or legislature, or a more arcane debate between different shades of the Keynesian economic spectrum on US campuses, is determined by the challenges and political context of the time.

At one level, where we are today in European, North American, and Asian economies – and parts of our present geopolitical circumstances both good and bad – are not unrelated to the roles key intellectuals have played in the politics and policies of our time. It is hard to look at America's foreign policy stance in today's world without reflecting on Henry Kissinger's immense contribution, both in office and outside of office, to the broad notion of balance of power between different key political and military forces, or Jean Kirkpatrick's stout defence of democracy and freedom as enduring foreign policy principles. The low-tax, highly leveraged nature of the American economy, the engineering in terms of derivatives, securitization, and diffusion of high-risk debt that has both spread debt-based excesses and imperilled international finance, is not unrelated to the impact during the Reagan, Bush, and Clinton years of the Chicago school of free-market economists such as Milton Friedman, who were both dominant and intellectually compelling. In the end, of course, it was politicians, congressmen and women, business leaders, senators, and parliaments that sustained or advanced policies tied to the ideas these public intellectuals advanced. This is not about blame – which is a topic for another essay. It is about influence and impact.

Thousands of mitigating particularities made the application of the ideas referenced above imperfect and not without distortion, as is the case with any eventful political or market context. Events often conspired to make the context around any idea's application very different from what the intellectual proponent had, in fact, proposed.

Suffice it to say for our purposes, the role of intellectuals, or, as the Oxford dictionary would have it, "persons possessing a highly developed intellect" has not been slight in the politics of the modern Western world. It is helpful, in the political context, to reflect on the middle-English and Latin roots of the word intellectual – namely, coming from "understanding" or intellectus.

It seems fair to suggest that there is a profound difference in today's politics between those whose presence, as public intellectuals, aids in public understanding of a complex issue or series of choices and a public intellectual assuming the role of advocate. Part of the challenge, of course, is sorting through the differences between "understanding" and "advocacy" in today's complicated, media-cluttered, and politically intense world.

Unhelpful to the discussion around what influence public intellectuals have on our politics is a lengthy debate on who exactly a public intellectual is and by what terms of performance or competence a public intellectual may be defined. That is the very kind of credentialist debate that speaks so eloquently to those battles of academic expertise that, in their insularity, reduce a public intellectual's relevance. To put the problem another way, is a young, relatively inexperienced post-doctoral fellow, with a new piece of social policy research on the structure of political dissent, a piece of research that is methodologically sound and peer-reviewed, less important to the public debate than Noam Chomsky – simply because the former is not well known and the latter is better known and utterly predictable in his anti-establishment narrative? To acquiesce in this "notoriety versus new ideas" construct in the structure of the public intellectual's role would be to argue in turn that new ideas matter less than established reputations, which, if true, would further suggest that the role of the public intellectual in politics is itself very much caught up in its own "path dependency" rut. That the same practitioners and intellectuals take the same paths on vital issues time and time again, differing only as to the speed and trajectory of predictable ideas within the policy rut is itself "path dependency." That the political powers that be, or civil service practitioners, often discount the views of public intellectuals, emerges logically from predictable path dependency on transient political controversies which inevitably dilutes the value of an intellectual's issue-specific value-added. The "familiarity breeds contempt" rule also applies.

Many of the toughest choices in democracies are not between good and evil but between competing public goods. It is important to reflect on how best, in the past, public intellectuals have played in this arena, how this has changed, and what challenges we face.

In the United States, it is hard to envision an American political and policy history without the involvement of intellectuals who were either in politics or advised those in politics from academe, and who were central to critical decisions at critical times. Dr Kissinger and Dr Friedman, Benjamin Franklin, Thomas Jefferson, Woodrow Wilson, Bernard Baruch, Jonas Salk, Arthur Hyak, Irving Kristol, Condoleezza Rice, Paul Krugman, are but a few names that suggest themselves as having had, or continuing to have, impact on politics in varied ways. We could all add more names to this list.

In Canadian politics and policy, figures such as O.D. Skelton and the creation of the federal public service; André Laurendeau on language policy; Claude Ryan on Quebec; Tom Courchene on equalization and currency; Tom Axworthy on democracy promotion; Jack Granatstein on history's impact on today's choices, especially on defence and security; Gad Horowitz on Red Tories; George Grant on technology and American exceptionalism; Blair Neatby on history; Marcel Trudel on the roots of French Canada; Tom Kierans on economics; Bill Watson on the size of the state; Pierre Fortin on economic and fiscal choices; Donald Savoie on the centralization of power; Keith Banting on social policy; Roger Gibbins on the West; Des Morton on Canadian history; Charles Taylor on multiculturalism; David Cameron on federalism; Harold Innis on culture and communication; Janice Stein on foreign policy; David Bercuson on defence policy; Tony Penikett on the North; Dennis Stairs on foreign policy – all come to mind easily, along with many others. With the new-found, post-Second World War political conceit that science and public programs can always reduce the likelihoods of debilitating illness, economic ruin, and diminished productivity, a new prominence for public intellectuals in the hard sciences, computer technology, business theory, medical research, and scientific ethics has appeared in both the political and political media frames.

Part of what shapes the real and perceived role of the "public intellectual" in our political and public policy debate is the media frame around that debate. And here, an enormously influential Canadian intellectual, Marshall McLuhan, shaped a media frame ("form is more important than content") that has had a compelling impact on reducing the role of the public intellectual in our public discourse. The other critical minimizing impact has come from the utter confusion between news, analysis, entertainment, and media formats that now routinely infect decisions made by most networks in programing decisions. And, as politics needs media to penetrate, stimulate, or sedate public consciousness just as much as media need politics as a cheap source of endless content to sustain their economic model, this mutual exploitation over time reduces the need for any intellectual debate that is about competing ideas, analysis, theories, or science.

This is occasioned by a media world that, with a few exceptions (PBS in the United States, TVO, Canal Savoire or CBC Radio in Canada), has become an acolyte of McLuhan's theory about the "medium" being "the message." This conclusion about his nuanced and vast philosophic reflections on the works of Harold Innis and on the role, shape, cultural force, and intervention of television in particular, is a huge oversimplification of his enormous intellectual reach and breadth. Be that as it may, that oversimplification has produced an enormous bias that favours form over content. Recent changes to the format of CBC TV News in Canada, mirroring CNN and similar formats, speak to the point. Room for the "public intellectual" in the news cycle has been diminished, if not eradicated entirely. Ideas and their proponents appear usually in the context of medical research breakthroughs or new horrors about food, product, drug, or climate safety. This is classically about the opposite of value-added public intellectuals, namely, an unbecoming obsession with instant factoids about relatively recent and often overstated risks, claims, hopes, or aspirations associated therewith. They are as unworthy of news-cycle prominence as car accidents but dominate coverage nonetheless.

Neil Postman describes this phenomenon in this way: "Together, this ensemble of electronic techniques called into being a new world – a peek-a-boo world, where now this event, now that, pops into news for a moment, then vanishes again. It is a world without much coherence or sense; a world that does not ask, indeed, does not permit us to do anything; a world that is like the child's game of peek-a-boo entirely self-contained. But like peek-a-boo it is also endlessly entertaining."[1] What he wrote here, in 1985, about the realities of the nineteenth and twentieth centuries, pressures for peek-a-boo style "newsertainment," has only worsened since. New obsession with email, Twitter, Facebook, the web generally, and handheld smart phones of one variety or another, plus the myriad applications associated with most of the above, have infected media management because passing fads are real market forces that cannot be ignored. Politics suffers now in all too many ways from a milder form of this "instrumentality über alles" bias. These mutually reinforcing infections reduce, in large measure, the constructive role in political debates available to even the most competent and articulate of public intellectuals, whatever their relevant area of expertise.

Beyond important events like the annual Massey Lectures or parliamentary hearings that are, absent scandal or partisan excess, rarely covered in the media, the chief use put to the public intellectual is usually when being arrayed by producers to sharpen a point/counterpoint take on a story, even if the counterpoint is utterly contrived. The emergence of "think tanks" or independent research organizations as relatively activist participants in the idea and analysis side of party politics and public policy is a refreshing counterbalance to these comparatively restrictive trends in the media/political dependency relationship overall.

In the United States, in the United Kingdom, and in Canada, think tanks such as the Brookings Institution, the Pew Center, the Policy Exchange, the Institute for Research on Public Policy, the Centre for Policy Alternatives, the Caledon Institute, the Canada West Foundation, and Montreal Economic Institute among others have deployed public intellectuals in the context of specific studies or research (usually, but not always, empirically reviewed before publication) that garner political, bureaucratic, and media interest.

C.D. Howe studies on productivity or taxes, IRPP studies on health care or defence or federal/provincial fiscal relations, Canada West Foundation's studies on resources or gambling, or the Canadian International Council studies on the Arctic or border management have all been part of the public policy debate over the last decade in Canada. University-related institutions such as the Munk School for Global Affairs, the Queen's Institute for Intergovernmental Relations, the McGill Centre for the Study of Canada, the Canadian Defence and Foreign Affairs Institute at the University of Calgary, the Centre for Global Studies at the University of Victoria, the Centre for Foreign Relations at Dalhousie, or the Institute for Regional Development Studies at the University of Moncton, to name but a few, have all been constructive participants in an intellectually-based policy debate agenda. This has thrust public intellectuals such as Tom Courchene, Donald Savoie, Jennifer Smith, David Bercuson, Janice Stein, Gordon Smith, Ron Watts,

Des Morton, Antonia Maioni, and Bill Watson into the media on serious and specific "deep dive" issues in ways that are complementary to their other respective areas of individual academic research and not generated by the agendas of the media or various political parties in or out of government. In a sense, think tanks, which are largely underfunded in Canada, have created a separate space where scholars involved in issues as diverse as day care, defence procurement, the effectiveness of foreign aid, border management, federalism, Canada–China relations, maritime security, or foreign relations can introduce and defend insights, findings, new formulations, and propose public policy options that bring the media and the political class out of their foxholes to look at agenda items not only of their own making. Recent federal government policy statements on the Arctic and negotiating border disputes[2] very much mirror empirically reviewed think tank studies on the Arctic by Franklyn Griffiths of the University of Toronto, Whitney Lackenbauer of Wilfrid Laurier, and Rob Hubert of the University of Calgary published in 2009 by the Canadian International Council. A recent IRPP study (2002) published on national security policy co-authored by Dr Ann Fitzgerald, then of the Royal Military College of Science at Shrivenham and Cranfield University, and General (retired) Donald Macnamara of Queen's School of Business[3] was mirrored closely in the federal government's National Security Policy Statement[4] eighteen months later. That this is a good thing is not diminished by the fact that think tanks are themselves not wholly beyond bias.

The Institute for Public Policy Reseach (IPPR) in the United Kingdom has been associated with the Labour Party, just as the Policy Exchange has a Tory frame. In Canada, the C.D. Howe Institute is rarely far from Bay Street on issues like taxes or regulation, and the Fraser Institute and L'Institut économique de Montréal are usually not very far from the more "small c," smaller government side of the Conservative Party. In the same way, the IRPP's rigorous use in Canada of data-based methodologies, empirically reviewed, implies a bias towards evidence-based public policy not necessarily welcomed in Ottawa since the long-form census controversy of the summer of 2010.

Both governments and opposition parties can be resentful, federally and provincially, in the United States and Canada, when think tanks seek to impact the agenda with new studies on challenging issues. The usual political view of this very public intellectual sort of event is "hijacking." The very term itself makes the case about the insularity and "control" mindset of those who would think to deploy it. (There is, in

my view, no conceit more reflective of political shallowness and bureaucratic self-reverence than the notion that, in a democracy, a government, minister, or department can be in control of anything. None
among us would want to live in a society where any government had
the competence or will, let alone the instruments, to actually control an
issue or debate.)

The challenge is not one of defining rules for public intellectuals, as
in an open society there should be very few rules on this front, or even
norms, because, as a telescope to scan the horizon, norms are relentlessly fogged and view-distorting. The challenge is trying to determine
where public intellectuals can have the most constructive impact with
value-added insights.

Part of the public discourse around policies these days is the general
disregard, and indeed contempt for, partisanship of any kind. Public intellectuals who allow a partisan halo to impact their media or learned-
journal presence pay a price. The most effective public intellectual is,
frankly, beyond partisanship or needs to be.

Often, intellectuals can be inside the partisan frame nominally, but
still be undiminished by it through the sheer force and intellectual
rigour of the work they do. Now retired from the senate, Dr Michael
Kirby chaired committees of the senate that produced deeply salient
and broadly acclaimed reports – one on health care overall[5] and one on
mental health.[6] They were seen by all parties as seriously constructive
contributions supported by partisans and non-partisans of all stripes.
As a PhD in mathematics, a member of the Trilateral Commission, a
professor at the Dalhousie School of Business, and associate clerk of
the federal cabinet during the constitutional negotiations of the 1980s,
Kirby's polymath skills were not unduly tainted by his Liberal partisan affiliations. Similar comments might well be made about the late
Dalton Camp and his role as chair of the Ontario Royal Commission
on Book Publishing and as a centrist political columnist who grew out
of his partisanship by reaching that point in his life where all partisans
seemed beneath him. Truth be told, he was influential as a public intellectual when he won the presidency of the Progressive Conservative
Party in 1966 by campaigning for the post on the issue of democratiza-
tion of the leadership process – a trend he started for all parties that
transformed the political process. Camp forced politics to face up to
the intellectual challenges of a modern, urbanizing society. This was a
most challenging task in Canada with its electoral map wildly skewed
towards the rural voter.

This is not a new narrative. Phrases such as "the Trudeau govern-ment" or the "Tory policy" tend to denote a news piece that will be critical, pejorative, if not condescending. The mere association of an idea or policy with a sponsorship deemed to benefit a partisan inter-est is to downgrade that policy as being, at some level, insensitive or insufficient or narrow – which in some cases is quite fair and in others, not so much. The association, through debate or the media, or search for corroborative or countervailing voices, of a public intellectual with this sort of story in broadcast, print, or digital media taints the intel-lectual with the political parties' back and forth on the issue, devaluing the perceived quality of the intellectual's contribution. Political party "thinkers" conferences are a particularly challenging contradiction and temptation in this area.

It is best for intellectuals who wish to sustain a larger truth about society, science, history, or philosophy, or even vital trends on economic or social policy, to, where possible, resist the temptation to be dragged into these sorts of transient, high-intensity, but essentially peek-a-boo melees. They usually do little good, generate no profound new understanding, and, aside from labelling academics, do not do very much to expand their influence, reach, wisdom, or impact. They serve the media interests which are, by definition, short term, hollow, and conflict-oriented.

Celebrity often associated with public intellectual engagements and especially media appearances can be both constructive and toxic in terms of expanding or diluting impact. Noam Chomsky is a celebrity among a certain mix of theorists on culture, language, media, and anti-establishment political theory and analysis. He is also an intellectual whose work is widely read and respected by many. His arguments are frequently cited and referenced by academics, polemicists, ideologues, and journalists who share a healthy scepticism about anything found in the mainstream media or in any statement by any elected leader or their minions. However I might profoundly disagree with his views and analysis, it would not be my conclusion that he has been defined by his celebrity or the self-reverential pressures that celebrity and its exigencies generate. These can sometimes make celebrity, its cultiva-tion, pursuit, or expansion, more important than the quality of the in-tellectual contribution a public intellectual might make and the nature of the value-added element of that contribution. It is unlikely that the overexposed public intellectual, caught in the sandal straps of celeb-rity, can have recurring and substantive impacts in ways that change the public debate or consistently inform the debate for the better. Celebrity, by its very nature, displays a form of typecasting which often moves the public intellectual into the advocacy frame. The ubiquitous panel discussion seems to breed this kind of typecasting. It is very unlikely that one might find a leading endocrinologist like Dr Henry Friesen, or outstanding historian such as Dr Margaret MacMillan, on a regular media issue-du-jour panel. And their relative impact when they do engage publicly is intensified because they do not do regular panels of the mundane "fill the timeslot" format so much preferred by the networks.

There is nothing wrong with celebrity, as long as it is not automatically confused with substantive intellectual contribution to the political process. It may, on occasion, produce just such a contribution, but as a dependable predictor of the public intellectual's role in policy or politics, it is limiting and capricious when not a serious constraint.

In the present multimedia universe, rapid overexposure for business, labour, or political leaders is a potentially negative problem. Welcomes can wear out quickly for even the most competent and well-meaning public figures, even if the mix of communication skills, humour, and overall persona are congenial and attractive. This is as true for a public intellectual as it might be for a politician or a journalist. Celebrities can produce larger viewership in the high-stakes media competition for share-of-voice in the marketplace of ideas. But it may not produce impact when it is most necessary or vital to the public interest. If, in this media frame, there is an enduring and desperately necessary role for the public intellectual, it relates directly to what William Fox wrote about so insightfully in his book *Spinwars: Politics and the New Media*,[7] where he explores the serious problem of the "congenial truth." This "truth," which is often a mix of what folks want to hear and what journalists want to say or advance, may or may not meet any real or contextually objective approximation of the actual facts or truth on the ground. Or, as Fox observes: "Congenial truths can take hold even in circumstances where the truth is not sustained by facts. In fact, 'congenial truth,' when combined with theories of dominant media frames, creates a version of the truth far removed from reality."[8] It is surely here, as elsewhere, that facts, insight, perspective, study, and expertise matter and where the role of the public intellectual is of greatest value. Piercing the "congenial truths," biases, fears, or complacency of any situation is surely what the expertise and reflective depth of the public intellectual should have as his or her highest purpose.

Recent contributions on the issue of parliamentary prorogation by Dr Ned Franks[9] of Queen's University or former professor Patrick Monahan[10] of the Osgoode Law School, while differing one from the other, had the value of adding context, precedent, history, and reflections on the "reserve" power of the Crown to a public debate that would have been about little else than who finds the prime minister cuddly and who does not.

Two wonderful, non-partisan examples of public intellectuals among many are Margaret Atwood and the late Mordecai Richler, both compelling, deeply talented, and highly awarded fiction writers of Canadian provenance and global acclaim. Mordecai Richler's remarkable novels, such as *The Apprenticeship of Duddy Kravitz* (1959), humorous yet reflective of the hypocrisies, joys, and ethnic foibles of Canadian and other societies, served many purposes that were enlightening, entertaining, and as small "p" political as any. His non-fiction articles and columns such as his famous piece in the *New Yorker* on anti-Semitism in Quebec, indulged in every stereotyped misrepresentation of legitimate French Canadian nationalism known to humankind. As a public intellectual, his contribution was through fiction and inspired humour. His weighing in on temporal peek-a-boo debates also had more to do with fiction and humour and very little with enlightenment. His role as commentator and citizen was no better or worse than that of many others. His deep Anglo roots in Quebec and inability to speak French informed and handicapped his non-fiction capacities. His irascibility and curmudgeonly stance made him no less lovable, even if the intellectual content added little.

Margaret Atwood, whose many novels bespeak a deep and abiding creative talent and a sensibility that reflect the very best of her craft, has had different interventions on issues as a public intellectual. Her Massey Lectures on debt[11] and the book that predated the great credit collapse, *Payback: Debt and the Shadow Side of Wealth*,[12] speak to the value-added contribution of a public intellectual at its best. In a way no ten news broadcasts or op-eds could, she added tone, history, sinews of civilizational development, human nature, and broad context to a discussion our shuffle-along society had avoided for too long. This is the sort of deep-dive, value-added engagement, diligence, and contribution that takes hard work, insight, judgment, and true due diligence of the kind missing from some institutions on Wall Street in recent times. By contrast, her championing of the "Save the Prison Farm" cause in Kingston in the spring of 2011, while a legitimate, no doubt sincere and heartfelt expression of opinion, does not serve any value-added public intellectual role of the kind someone with a doctorate that focused on prisoner rehabilitation or recidivism might have furnished. That she cheered fellow travellers in the cause is undeniable. But that was her reputation as a great novelist and writer at work – not as a relevant public intellectual with deep-dive insights to offer. As a citizen, she is of course to be commended for taking the time and effort to engage.

Politics diminish and ignore public intellectuals when the intellectual chooses to be less than discerning about how they engage. A public intellectual as a serious expert, academic, researcher, or teacher is not a call-up opinion source for the news channels – or at least he/she should not choose to be so branded. Public intellectuals are important to the public policy process when their depth and perspective allows them to broaden the debate and the policy options beyond the trench warfare of parliaments, where the contrived urgent always takes precedence over what is truly important. In a sense, the trivializing of the public intellectual and the dilution of the good and value they might add is a product of a joint and mutual hostage taking. The media and the partisan seek to kidnap, tame, and groom the public intellectual, while the intellectual may seek high-name recognition for other non-intellectual collateral purposes. A public intellectual at his or her best is no one's hostage and their freedom and intellectual insight is more than opinions du jour. Anything less and the public intellectual is merely another captive of both the media and the politics of the shallow and can become road kill on the highway of public debate and deliberation. Our democracy and our many superb public intellectuals deserve better.

NOTES

1 Neil Postman, *Amusing Ourselves to Death* (20th anniversary edition; Toronto: Penguin Books, Toronto, 2005), 77.
2 Foreign Affairs Canada, 20 Aug. 2010.
3 W.D. Macnamara and Ann FitzGerald, "A National Security Framework for Canada," Policy Matters monograph series (Montreal: Institute for Research on Public Policy, October 2002).
4 Public Safety Canada, *Securing an Open Society: Canada's National Security Strategy* (Ottawa, April 2004).

5 Standing Senate Committee on Social Affairs, Science & Technology, *The Health of Canadians: The Federal Role* (Ottawa, October 2002).
6 Standing Senate Committee on Social Affairs, Science & Technology, *Out of the Shadows at Last: Transforming Mental Health, Mental Illness and Addiction Services in Canada* (Ottawa, May 2006).
7 Bill Fox, *Spinwars: Politics and the New Media* (Toronto: Key Porter, 1999), 104–12.
8 Ibid., 105.
9 Professor at Queen's University in the Department of Political Studies; author or editor of thirteen books, including *The Parliament of Canada*, *The Canoe and White Water*, and *Dissent and the State*.
10 Dean of Osgoode Hall Law School from 2003–9, current vice-president academic and provost of York University.
11 Massey Lectures, CBC Radio, November 2008.
12 Margaret Atwood, *Payback: Debt and the Shadow Side of Wealth* (Toronto: House of Anansi, 2008).

3 Public Thought and the Crisis of Underpopulation

DOUG SAUNDERS

The jazz pianist Paul Bley, two decades after he had left Montreal's downstairs clubland for the frenetic experimentation of Greenwich Village, told an interviewer why it was necessary to leave Canada. There simply wasn't, in any Canadian city, the critical mass of musical inventors, not enough people around, to make the scene, and the difference was immediately, explosively apparent. "For us practicing our standards and sitting in and playing *well* and whatever, it just wasn't the same breed of animal. You thought you were playing jazz … But when you heard the amount of wind that came off these stands [in New York], you realized you would have to totally lose your reticent Canadian personality before you could even expect to keep up. That was the shock. That incredible power. And confidence."[1]

The architect Frank Gehry, five decades after he left the staid streets of post-war Toronto for the modernist foment of Los Angeles, told me that his radical reconfiguration of the public building into a new curvilinear form would never have taken place had he stayed in Canada. "I remember reading the final exam for first-year architecture – they had the exams there [in secondary school] so you could see what it was like – and you had to design a traditional little cottage. And I remember thinking, this is just terrible, boring, nothing to it. So based on that, if I had stayed there, I never would have gotten into architecture."[2] As it happened, his classmate at Harbord Collegiate, Morley Safer, made a similar discovery, about the world of television journalism, after spending a few years at the post-war CBC before fleeing to the greater creative possibilities of a larger country.

We have little trouble understanding why a great jazz pianist or architect, or perhaps even a TV personality, might find it necessary to leave Canada in order to achieve a full realization of their creative potential. While these pursuits and their attendant institutions all exist within Canada, it is widely appreciated that Canada does not yet have a sufficiently large population to provide the very big cities, major educational institutions, and large constellations of peers, audiences, funders, and tutors necessary to host these crafts in their most elevated and influential form. It hardly surprises us that a successful actor should relocate to Los Angeles or New York or London, or a tenor to Berlin or Milan, and in fact we tend to be suspicious, for good reason, of those who don't. This, we know, is just the nature of a place like Canada. To be something of an outpost, albeit one that exports a good number of future stars, is no source of shame; rather, it is accepted as a consequence of being a very sparsely populated country. Canada's underpopulation, for people in these fields, is an ever-present factor.

That is hardly a controversial point. Not, at least, when it is applied to the creative arts. When the subject turns to matters of public thought, national self-examination, and political development, though, we tend to look away. That Canada's political, intellectual, and rhetorical development is constrained by a crisis of underpopulation should be a self-evident fact, but it is one that is rarely admitted in public. Are we less intelligent because there are so few of us, spread over such a large piece of land? No, certainly not as individuals. But collectively, this sad confluence of demography and geography does leave us impoverished. We may indeed be able to think and imagine great things, but our sparsity renders us unable to articulate these thoughts, to build them into a network of reflection, to convey them to a wide public, to build a functioning national dialogue on a proper scale. The crisis of underpopulation is, in every important way, made manifest as a crisis of public thought.

The problem, in short, is that anglophone Canada[3] lacks the population and audience base to create and maintain the institutions that make public thought possible – periodicals, think tanks, institutes, publishers. The economies of scale simply do not exist, beyond a minimal level, to allow these institutions and venues to develop in sufficient size and for sufficient duration to create a body of influential and fully developed and debated public ideas. The history of Canada is one of such institutions endlessly being formed, sometimes with great ambitions, and then after a brief period either going out of business or failing to attain any more than a token size, staffing level, publication reach, or public influence. We have no place to put our thought, because we do not have enough people to support a container.

What do I mean here by "public thought"? While other authors in this collection will examine this question in detail, I am deliberately going to leave my definitions broad and general, because the nature of the thought is secondary to the question of its ability to exist. For the benefit of this argument, though, I will examine two widely used definitions of public thought: as a form of influential expression and analysis located in the publishing space between formal academia and mass-market journalism; and as a form of political and policy thought located in think tanks and institutes that support the political system and articulate both academic and ideological concepts in a public space. Both of these crucial forms of thought and the institutions that support them, I will argue, are severely underdeveloped in Canada, to the point that public intellectuals are largely absent from the most important debates on identity and policy. At root is the crisis of underpopulation, a concept that I will briefly discuss before examining its effects.

The Nature of Canada's Underpopulation

The fundamental reason why these institutions are so much less robustly developed in Canada – and therefore the reason why public thought has less voice and influence in Canada – is that the community meant to support and draw from these institutions consists of somewhere between twenty-one and twenty-four million English speakers scattered more or less sparsely over an area of land encompassing five time zones, several geographic and cultural regions, a dozen isolated political jurisdictions, and the second largest land mass on Earth.[4] Underpopulation is a basic fact in Canada, one whose challenges have played a major part in political and cultural debates throughout the country's history, but is hard to gauge precisely.

In 2001, I asked a group of demographers to assess Canada's "ideal" population on cultural, economic, and ecological grounds.[5] While this is a nebulous question, given the impossibility of defining "ideal" and the many factors beyond mere population that could influence a country's outcomes, there was a wide consensus that Canada's optimum point would involve a population in the broad area of 100 million people. It was around the 100 million mark, reached shortly before 1920, that the United States was first able to assert itself economically as a fully independent force and to master and export its own forms of literature, music, cinema, and theatre – it was this population level that turned America into the capital of the modern world. The demographer

Morton Weifeld made a comparison: If the tiny strip of land upon which most Canadians live – that is, less than a tenth of Canada's land mass – were to develop the population density of the Netherlands (a dense European state, but one with plenty of open spaces and park-lands), then Canada would have 400 million people. A population den-sity one-quarter that of the Netherlands would leave Canada's natural spaces untouched. (In fact, they would probably be far better protected: densely populated places like California and France tend to do better at conservation than empty zones like the Asian steppe, which produced such ecological catastrophes as the Aral Sea disaster unobserved.) It would give this narrow southern strip of Canada the population den-sity of Spain or Romania, two countries noted for their unspoiled tracts of nature. And it would expand Canada's major cities to a size capable of exerting true influence, in wake of the World Bank's well-supported conclusion that the very largest cities will be the ones that will prosper economically and culturally in this century's economy. Most important, of course, would be the effects on Canada's institutions: A tripling of the current population, giving Canada an anglophone or English-fluent allophone population of about 75 million, just more than Britain's, would be just enough to support the aforementioned public-thought institutions at a sustainable and influential scale.

The 100 million figure keeps popping up; it seems to be a constantly rediscovered benchmark of Canadian success. In 1968, a group of schol-ars, policy advocates, and business leaders formed the Mid-Canada Development Corridor Foundation, which argued, based on research into resource industries, that Canada required a population of at least 100 million in order to have a sustainable and independent economy (its goals were partly those of economic nationalism).[6] In 1975, a study by Canada's Department of Manpower found that economies of scale leading to "significant benefits to Canadian industry" would occur only after the population had reached the 100 million mark.[7] And more recently, in 2010, the journal *Global Brief* argued in detail that Canada will need a population of 100 million on geostrategic, defence, and dip-lomatic grounds:

A national population of 100 million – three times the current Canadian population – is a symbolic quantum. It could very well be 85 million or 130 million and yield the same desired effects. And these effects would be pincer-like: first, a far larger demographic base to build strong national in-stitutions and structures (east-west-north-south) across the vast territory of Canada – institutions that, while today often absent or weak, would eventually serve as a bulwark for international strategic influence; and second, a far larger talent pool to populate the strategic arms of the Canadian state – the military, diplomatic, general civil service and political branches of government – as well as connected sectors and organizations (business, cultural, educational, scientific) in Canadian society at large. In the process, the Canada of 100 million, through the force of new domestic structures, coupled with growing international impact (and prestige), undergoes an evolution of the national geist – one arguably appropriate for this new, more complicated, more international century. In short, Canada becomes a serious force to be reckoned with.[8]

Whether Canada's ideal population is 100 million or half that many is not important here; what is important is that it is not currently high enough to support fully functional institutions of public thought, given the costs of serving a minimum audience base across a very large area of territory joined by expensive transportation links and severed by linguistic and regional discrepancies.

The Effects of Underpopulation on Public Thought

The first category of public thought to consider – the one perhaps most commonly considered – is *public thought as a popular and influential form of expression and analysis located in the intellectual and media space between academic studies and journalism.* This is the critical, reflective public thought of the review essay, the intelligent magazine, the print-heavy weekly. The "public intellectuals" who work in this arena have traditionally been a prevalent and influential force in the English-speaking world and are the group most broadly discussed in the United States, in part because of the fame of such communities of public thinkers as the New York Intellectuals and the neoconservatives, all of whom worked in this intermediary publishing space. There are similar communities in Europe, notably the circle of German thinkers, writers, and journalists who contribute regularly to the feuilleton sections of the broadsheet newspapers. (In France, public thought is more heavily reliant on accredited academics, though the feuilletons and intellectual magazines serve a similar purpose.)

This class of public thinkers are sometimes university-based academics and sometimes independent thinkers drawn from literary and journalistic communities, writing generally in essay forms (including review essays and longer magazine think-pieces, as well as occasional newspaper essays, and more recently the highbrow blog post and on-line essay) that engage both intellectual concepts and current cultural and political debates, in a language and format accessible to educated non-specialist members of the general public. Their work is, for example, the subject of Richard Posner's provocative book *Public Intellectuals: A Study of Decline*.[9] The "decline" discussed by Posner is not a decline of public thought or its institutions in the United States per se, but rather a wilting of its quality caused by the shift of the mass of thinkers from the world of independent publishing into academia (causing them to resemble more their European counterparts), thus entrapping them in an increasingly micro-specialized disciplinary environment and damaging their ability to be universal, general-interest thinkers.

The crucial institutions of this sort of public thought are traditionally the political-essay weekly or fortnightly (the *Spectator* and *New Statesman* in Britain, and in the United States the *New Republic* and *Nation* on the left and the *National Review* and *Weekly Standard* on the right); the small political or intellectual magazine (the most famous being the New York–based magazines *Politics*, the *Partisan Review*, *Commentary*, *Dissent*, and the *National Interest*, some of which began as left-wing periodicals and became neoconservative in their later years); the review-essay weekly (the *Times Literary Supplement*, *London Review of Books*, and *Literary Review* in Britain, and the *New York Review of Books* in the United States); the "intelligent" mass-circulation monthly or sometimes weekly magazine (notably *Prospect* in Britain, and the *Atlantic Monthly*, *Harper's*, and *New Yorker* in the United States); and the book publishing company willing to engage in serious long-form policy or academic-based popular non-fiction – whether an academic publisher willing to publish more generalist, popular titles (like Oxford University Press or the University of Chicago Press), or a mass-market publisher willing to publish more serious and analytical titles. This sphere of public thought also extends into the more sophisticated broadsheet newspapers and their online offshoots in most countries.

In Canada, this sort of public thought has always struggled against a severe shortage of institutions suited to its publication. Compared to the British and American publications listed above, the space between the mass media and the academic journal in Canada has generally been a barren plain, with occasional sprouts of momentary creative activity punctuating a thin undergrowth of publications too small and limited to have any impact on the national debate.

Even in far larger countries, the variety of periodicals in which public intellectuals thrive have always struggled to remain viable, regardless their influence. In the United States, the political-intellectual weeklies that have tended to dominate debate on the right and left have long regarded their threshold of medium-term survival as being a circulation of 100,000 copies. This level is just enough to support a minimum staff (heavily bolstered by unpaid interns and backstopped by charitable contributions) and to commission the sort of writing that suits the magazine's goals. At the moment, the fortnightly *National Review* (203,000 copies) and the weekly *Nation* (158,000) are managing to break this threshold, while the fortnightly *New Republic* (54,000) and the *Weekly Standard* (81,000) are not, leaving their publication futures in jeopardy if they are to rely strictly on subscription and advertising revenues. Even at these circulation levels, however, these magazines are rarely able to remain solvent from their own resources. All four, to greater or lesser degrees, have relied on the ownership or largesse of wealthy individuals who have shared their political affinities. Indeed, the *Nation* has made this dependency a matter of pride, boasting in its advertising that it has lost money during every one of its 150-plus years of publication. The situation in the United Kingdom is similar, but the threshold smaller. There, magazines generally regard something in the circulation range of 30,000 to 50,000 to be the threshold of survival or failure, and even then they tend to rely heavily on volunteer efforts. The *Spectator*, the flagship of Britain's conservative public intellectuals, manages between 75,000 and 80,000 subscribers, while its left-wing counterpart the *New Statesman* has hovered around 30,000, its existence often threatened by its low numbers.

This may help explain why such publications play little or no major public role in Canada: the subscription levels are an order of magnitude lower than those in the United States, and less than half those in Britain. There are no public-thought weeklies or fortnightlies of this sort in Canada, and serious monthly or bimonthly periodicals have struggled to exist. If the threshold of survival is 30,000 in Britain and 100,000 in the United States, in Canada it is generally considered to be 10,000 by magazine professionals. In practice, the magazines that have tried to carry the flag of public thought have rarely managed to break the 5000 mark. This is the case for *This Magazine* on the left, which continues only because of its charitable status (and thus receipt of indirect state funding through charitable-donation tax deductions) and reliance on volunteer labour; and for the erstwhile *Western Report* and its various precursors and successors on the right, all of which fell below this threshold and failed. (It is striking that Canada today lacks a serious long-form periodical, in print or online, for public intellectuals on the right.) While some of these publications have nurtured journalistic careers, none can be said to have influenced public thought or policy in Canada to any notable degree in modern times.

There have been periods of glory for such small magazines. For a time in the 1960s, the *Canadian Forum*, under the editorship of Ramsay Cook and William Kilbourn, managed to exert some real influence on the Canadian centre-left, both in the Liberal Party and the newly formed NDP; it played a significant role in launching the career of its sometime contributor Pierre Trudeau (as did the francophone, highly influential, but rarely read Montreal counterpart *Cité Libre*). And the small magazine *Explorations: Studies in Culture and Communication* managed, under the editorship of Edmund Carpenter and Marshall McLuhan between 1953 and 1959, to have a considerable influence on the cultural politics and understanding of media at the time (as did McLuhan's subsequent books, whose widespread discussion, publication, and influence mark a high-water mark for this sort of public thought in Canada). Today there remain a number of small Canadian public-thought publications of good quality that are focused on small but wide-interest communities of educated citizens, including a reinvigorated *Queen's Quarterly* (which wielded some influence in the post-war decades), *Global Brief*, and *Policy Options*. Despite their importance, they do not have the influence or reach of their counterparts in other English-speaking countries, probably owing to the geographic and population challenges of Canada.

Without much chance of finding a home in viable single-focus publications, this sort of public thought in Canada has been left to the larger and more general-purpose weekly or monthly long-form magazine, which tends to balance entertainment and journalism with more serious fare that epitomizes public thought. This has been, especially in the United States, the most influential venue for the public intellectual, with publications ranging from the weekly *New Yorker* (with a circulation, however diminished, still exceeding one million) to *Harper's* (220,000) and the *Atlantic Monthly* (400,000). In Britain, this field is left largely to *Prospect* magazine, whose circulation of around 40,000 is balanced by its considerable influence on larger-circulation mass media. Also, the weekly glossy magazines of daily newspapers sometimes rise to the level of public thought, notably the *New York Times Magazine*, which frequently publishes influential essays by both academics and journalists, but also occasionally the magazines of the *Times* or the *Guardian* in Britain.

In Canada, the fate of such long-form magazines has been a matter of constant public interest and concern throughout the post-war decades, precisely because of their status in formulating public thought and constructive policy debates in a way that could bring together the academy, the media, and government in a neutral territory. For much of that period the lion's share of magazine advertising lineage in Canada was tied up in the Canadian editions of *Reader's Digest* and *Time*, which together accounted for more than half the Canadian magazine business in both circulation and staffing. In the 1960s, when the federal government began talking seriously about taxing these titles to produce a fund for Canadian magazines, the need for significant public-intellectual titles came to the fore. Robert Weaver, the editor of *Tamarack Review*, expressed a popular view when he wrote, in 1961: "This fund should then be used to assist magazines that need support to stay alive, but the bulk of it should be used to establish and subsidize indefinitely one national monthly of the type of *Harper's* or the *Atlantic Monthly*."[10]

That would never occur, of course. When the Canadian magazine industry did come to be protected by Ottawa in the 1970s, the largest recipient of funds in English Canada was *Maclean's*, which used the federal money (as much as $3 million a year in subsidies during the 2000s) to shift away from public thought – that is, to change from a long-form monthly resembling *Harper's* or the *Atlantic Monthly*, which it had occasionally been in the 1960s, into a newsweekly in the vein of *Time*, closed (until its recent resurrection) to the sort of public thought that Canada seemed to lack. For a period of three decades, this left the middle ground, largely unaccompanied, to the vicissitudes of *Saturday Night*, a magazine whose fortunes are often treated as synonymous with those of public thought in Canada; its collapse in 2005 was entirely a product of underpopulation, with both reading and advertising audiences far too small to support a serious monthly. Its successor the *Walrus*, formed by former staff with a greater interest in serious public thought, and with the backing of private individuals willing to risk their savings on a marginal title, has proved a lone outpost of a certain sort of public-intellectual writing in Canada during the past half-decade. There were other titles that briefly carried the torch: the *Imperial Oil Review*, which was serious and influential, if limited, between the 1950s and the 1970s; *Quest*, a large-circulation newspaper-insert title billed as "Canada's

urban magazine," which for a few years in the 1970s, under the editorship of Michael Enright, managed to be a genuine vehicle for serious
public thought, until it lowered its brow and then folded.

Review magazines have had a similarly spotty history, and this may
be why the review essay, so important to influencing public debate in
Britain and the United States, has never had much of a foundation in
Canada. *Books in Canada* and *Quill & Quire* have largely relegated themselves to consumer-oriented reviews rather than essays. In the 1980s
and until its demise in 1993, the *Idler* served as an important voice for
public thought on the right (and proved, in the end, to be something of
a test flight for the more intellectual incarnations of the *Ottawa Citizen*
and the *National Post*, both of which ran substantial essay sections in
the late 1990s and early 2000s). The one success story here is the *Literary
Review of Canada*, which from its inception in 1991 has been a small-
scale counterpart to the *New York Review of Books*, publishing important
essays on public affairs and academic developments. But, like other
publications, it is limited in scope by its government funding, which
requires it to stick exclusively to Canadian topics and titles, a restriction
that keeps it out of many important international debates.

Book publishing may appear to be one bright spot in Canadian
public thought – indeed, it could be credibly argued that there are too
many non-fiction titles published – but the effects of underpopulation
are tangible. Most of the important public-intellectual publishing in
Canada is done by the Toronto-based branches of the major New York
publishers (Random House, Penguin, and HarperCollins). There is a
good reason for this: independent Canadian publishers have failed to
remain consistently viable because the size of the publishing market is
simply too small. McClelland and Stewart, the flagship independent
publisher for English Canada, managed to retain a voice in the post-
war decades almost entirely because of large-scale government subsidies at every state of the book-writing and publishing process (that is,
so long as the contents of the books were largely Canadian, a fact that
has prevented Canadian publishers from having much international
influence), and occasional full-scale government bailouts, including
a rescue loan of almost $1 million from the Ontario government in
1971. None of that prevented M&S from folding in 2000; since then,
it has been operated on a near-charitable basis by the University of
Toronto and Random House. The limited scale of Canadian publishing can be felt in the range of important titles by Canadians that must
be published outside Canada. The most visible recent example was

the Toronto historian Margaret MacMillan's chronicle of the Versailles Treaty negotiations, *Paris 1919: Six Months That Changed the World*, a work that became a major part of public debate, but which failed to achieve publication in Canada until after it had been in print in Britain for almost two years and had won the two largest British non-fiction awards. As with many such books, it was likely absent from the Canadian book market because it did not directly concern Canada (despite being of central interest to Canadian debates about nationalism and culture), and therefore was ineligible for most forms of publication financing from federal and provincial governments. This, alas, remains a commonplace situation.

As Canada's population has increased, public thought has become more viable in general, and a generation of intellectuals (discussed throughout this volume) have been able to work in Canada; but the fact is that the population remains too small and sparse to support a full stable of institutions without frequent failures and bankruptcies. This form of public thought did have something of a golden age in the 1960s, albeit one confined to a small circle of people who tended to meet at the roof bar of Toronto's Park Plaza Hotel, propelled by the unlikely venue of the newspaper-published weekly magazine. For a brief moment, the rotogravure magazines, joined by *Maclean's* and *Saturday Night* during a moment of seriousness, served as a vehicle for public thought. The *Globe Magazine* carried policy-oriented essays from 1957 to 1971; the *Canadian* magazine, published by Southam and the *Toronto Star* from 1965, was substantial and serious for a while in the 1960s, until it started losing money; and very briefly, the *Star Weekly*, under the editorship of Peter Gzowski from 1967 to 1968, was a home to substantial content, though that ended after it lost $2 million on a circulation of 646,000. For a while, these glossy titles parried with the burgeoning academic modernism emerging from New York and Paris, held dialogues with the likes of Susan Sontag, Hanna Arendt, and Irving Howe, and provided a platform that allowed academics like McLuhan and Northrop Frye to achieve a genuine public significance and influence. But this seriousness was both a cause and a result of these magazines' lack of profitability: all these titles, with the exception of *Saturday Night*, would either shut their doors or abandon public thought by the mid-1970s. It is interesting that Gzowski and Enright, two key figures in this brief era of public-thought publishing, ended up in CBC Radio's current-affairs programs, which may have been Canada's sole consistent outlet for public intellectualism.

The second category to consider is *public thought as a means to support, renew, and provide a reliable intellectual policy basis and source of professional development for the major political parties through policy institutes or think tanks*. This group of thinkers overlaps with the first in that they tend to express themselves through the same media institutions (as well as by publishing reports and books through their own institutions which are then reported upon by these periodicals). But the "think tankers" play a different role in a nation's political life. Sometimes they are drawn from academia or the media, but just as often they come from the staff of the major political parties; these form the three poles of a triangle that tends to define the career movements of these public intellectu- als. When a party is in power, these think tanks serve as a source of policy advice, a test bed for renegade or experimental ideas within the party's sphere of policy interest, and a platform for acceptable dissent within the ideological parameters defined by the party. When the party is out of power, the major think tanks serve as a source of employment for political staff who would otherwise disperse into careers elsewhere, places where policies can be formulated and reconceived during pe- riods of opposition, and a set of competing institutions that serve to reinvent and renew the political thought of their respective ideological group. The large, successful think tank is a vital base for a nation's po- litical thought located between the academy, the political party and the media, and speaking to the public directly through all three.

In the United States, the think tank and the public thought it pro- duces have become as central to the political system as the parties themselves, if not more so. In his major study of these institutions, *Do Think Tanks Matter?*, Donald E. Abelson examines their role over three decades of election and administration. Jimmy Carter's "outsider" bid for the presidency was built on the authority of the Council on Foreign Relations and the Brookings Institution, which had served as intellec- tual redoubts for deposed Democrats during the Nixon and Ford years: after Carter's election victory, he appointed no fewer than fifty-four CFR fellows and more than a dozen Brookings staff to his administra- tion. Ronald Reagan took this an order of magnitude further, building his entire candidacy on the conservative think tanks that had served as the Republican retooling operation during the Carter interreg- num. During his campaign and transition to office, Reagan assembled 23 domestic- and economic-policy task forces with 329 advisers, and 25 foreign-policy and defence working groups with 132 advisers, all of them drawn from Washington's major conservative think tanks.

Individual think tanks used even more extensive resources to build the conservative revolution. In autumn of 1979 the Heritage Foundation drew on more than 300 staff and advisers to produce an 1100-page "blueprint for the construction of a conservative government," which the Reagan team relied upon heavily; the foundation estimated in 1982 that 60 per cent of its proposals had been adopted. When Reagan took office, the think tanks formed his cabinet and staff: in his first term, he appointed 55 Hoover Institution staffers, 36 from the Heritage foundation, 34 from the American Enterprise Institute, 32 from the Committee on the Present Danger, and 18 from the Center for Strategic and International Studies. This provoked a Democratic Party response: the candidacy of Bill Clinton, who virtually emerged from this world of public thought. Clinton had been a founder and later a chairman of the Democratic Leadership Council, created in 1985 as a source of economically liberal ideas for party renewal. And he had taken part in the 1989 creation of the centre-left Public Policy Institute. And George W. Bush, another "outsider," nevertheless relied heavily on the think tanks – especially the Hoover Institution, which provided most of his 100 campaign advisers. He also employed, and later appointed to cabinet, scores of officials from the American Enterprise Institute and the Center for Strategic and International Studies. His foreign- and defence-policy advisers (the "Vulcans" who devised the War on Terror) were drawn almost exclusively from the Project for the New American Century, a 1990s-era neoconservative think tank, and the AEI. And all the while the Democrats were biding their time in the Brookings, the CFR, and the PPI, waiting to create the core of Barack Obama's administration.[11]

In Britain, think tanks and their members have become increasingly crucial to political party development and election success during the past thirty years. While a number of venerable party-linked institutions had existed across the spectrum for a century or more, Margaret Thatcher made unprecedented use of a new constellation of large and well-financed institutes in her recreation of the Conservative Party during the 1970s, drawing heavily on the staff and resources of her own Centre for Policy Studies, which she co-founded with Sir Keith Joseph in 1974, and the very large and influential free-market think tank the Institute of Economic Affairs. Tony Blair's recreation of his party as the liberal-left New Labour depended heavily on the social-democratic think tanks Demos, the Institute for Public Policy Research, and Progress. When Gordon Brown launched his own reinvention of Labour in a more classically social-democratic mould in the first decade of this century, he relied on the venerable Fabian Society and the newly created Brownite think tank Compass as well as the IPPR. The Liberal Democrats, for their part, are increasingly reliant on the key liberal think tank Centre Forum. During their rise to coalition-government prominence, the post-Thatcherite "Notting Hill" Tories, under David Cameron, drew their current political staff and ideological framework overwhelmingly from the large conservative think tanks Policy Exchange and the Centre for Social Justice, the newer centre-right institute Reform, and the "red Tory" think tank Res Publica, launched a year before the 2010 election in an explosion of funding and attention. Together, the above institutions and a few others like them form the intellectual and staffing backbone for the three parties and their source of renewal.

Nothing of this sort has been able to materialize in Canada, because the economies of scale render such institutions uneconomical beyond a token level. There are think tanks in Canada – hundreds of them – but none are of sufficient size to fulfil the party-support and policy-formulation functions they do in larger countries. The threshold for permanent, sustainable influence in a think tank appears to be around 100 staff members. In the United States, the Brookings Institution has 250 staff and the Hoover Institution 320; others with more than 100 staff include the American Enterprise Institute (190), the Urban Institute (450), the Carnegie Endowment for International Peace and the Council on Foreign Relations (more than 100 each), the Hudson Institute (125), the Center for Strategic and International Studies (220), the Heritage Foundation (150), and the Carter Institute (160).[12] In Canada, only one conventional think tank, the conservative Fraser Institute, has more than 50 staff (it has 64 employees, and a budget of $10 to $15 million); the venerable center-right C.D. Howe Institute, which ought to be a Canadian version of the Hoover Institution or of Britain's Centre for Policy Studies, has only 21 staff and a budget of under $5 million, preventing it from playing a major role in any political party.[13]

Indeed, the organizations that have provided the most support to Canadian political-party development in recent years have not been conventional think thanks, but lobbying organizations. Prime Minister Stephen Harper built his political career, and honed his brand of conservatism, as president of the National Citizens' Coalition, a conservative lobbying and tax-campaign group with a budget of $2.8 million. Liberal prime minister Paul Martin built his leadership bid and drew some of his key staff from the Earnscliffe Strategy Group, a lobbying and policy-research firm with about twenty staff. While these organizations serve some of the party-continuity and staff-development functions of a think tank, they are missing the crucial element of public thought: as message-driven lobby groups, they do not produce the deep and independent supply of policy knowledge, or the continuous independent research into future tangents of policy and politics, that a real think tank could. They also are simply not large enough to serve as the "third leg" of the democratic stool.

The Osgoode Hall scholar and former Privy Council official Irvin Studin, writing in the public-intellectual journal *Policy Options*, identified this lack of comprehensive think tanks as the source of a "democratic deficit" in Canada, in which political parties become "captured" by a permanent bureaucracy which has intellectual resources at hand that are simply unavailable in the political realm due to think-tank economies of scale:

> Our political parties are in dire need of designated policy think tanks ... in order that they be able to form stronger, deeper and, most importantly, more consistently prepared governments when they come to power ... The political executive in our present political system and culture – one in which the civil service has the overwhelming policy advantage over the government of the day – is ill-equipped to meaningfully deliver on any large-scale, complex policy agenda of its own making ... If such a large-scale policy agenda is promised to the electorate in the course of a general election, all the worse: what is the point of a month-long series of national debates and convulsions over a series of policy promises or "directions" that can nary be delivered in any recognizable form? ... The democratic deficit lies in the fundamental asymmetry or incongruity or imbalance between the legitimacy of the elected political executive and the overwhelming policy-cum-administrative power of the modern unelected bureaucracy. This imbalance necessarily grows as the policy environment becomes more complex: files require increasing degrees of expertise, and the incumbency and division of power advantages of the bureaucracy become ever significant – *unless*, of course, the political executive itself becomes far more sophisticated. Rectification of this democratic deficit, it follows, must lie in a redressing of this imbalance.[14]

The rectification of this "democratic deficit" involves the same challenges, and involves overcoming or working around the same underlying demographic problems, as the cultural deficit chronicled earlier in this chapter. Studin advocates publicly funded think tanks, an idea that would not be unprecedented (they exist in other countries), but would be politically awkward given their role in partisan affairs. But this is the main solution that has been applied, in the post-war decades, to the cultural deficit: to the extent that institutions of public thought exist in Canada, it is because governments pay for them. There is, in itself, nothing wrong with this. Other, larger countries have publicly funded journals, magazines, newspapers, and book publishers. But, as we have seen, the need to rely entirely on state funding – that is, the lack of sufficient population to support any self-sustaining institutions – leads to nationally centred funding sources that tend to bias these institutions towards parochial and national issues and away from larger syntheses that might produce a larger international impact.

In both cases, Canada is unable to think. This does not mean that Canadians are unable to think; a very high literacy level and high education level tend to produce, and export, a great number of public intellectuals. But because public thought exists not in the individual mind but in the institutions that bond thinkers into a communication network linked to specific audiences, Canada remains intellectually crippled. Either the population will need to grow to a more viable level, or the institutions of public thought will have to rely on artificial support.

NOTES

1 Bill Smith, "Interview with Paul Bley," *Coda*, April 1979.
2 Doug Saunders, "Gehry's lament," *Globe and Mail*, 29 Sept. 2001, R1.
3 I am limiting this discussion to the three-quarters of Canada that uses English as its main language, and bracketing francophone Quebec out, because the terms of discussion are somewhat different. It might be argued that the Quebecois community has been better able to forge a "national conversation" at the public-intellectual level because its population is more tightly concentrated across a geographically limited and linguistically isolated space and because the dialogue around nationalism has both circumscribed the range of public-thought topics and forged a sufficient body·of publications and institutions to propel this conversation at a reasonably heightened level. On the other hand, there are many in Quebec who would argue that these very factors have impoverished Québécois public debate. Because of these very different terms of reference, I am relegating the francophone Canada discussion to another discussion.

4 Statistics Canada's 2006 census counts the total Canadian population as
   31,612,897; those for whom English is the "language spoken most often
   in the home" number 20,840,743, or 66.7 per cent of the population; those
   who speak a third language in a province where English is the sole official
   language number 3,118,142, or 9.9 per cent. We can assume that some proportion of bilingual francophones participate fully in the English-
   Canadian culture, but also that some percentage of third-language
   speakers and bilingual anglophones do not.
5 Doug Saunders, "Why Canada needs 100 million people," *Globe and Mail*,
   31 March 2001, F3.
6 Edward Cowan, "Vast development plan is urged for mid-Canada," *New
   York Times*, 15 Sept. 1968.
7 Study cited in Richard Gwyn, "Just what kind of country would you like
   Canada to be?" *Windsor Star*, 4 Jan. 1975.
8 Irvin Studin, "Canada – Population 100 Million," *Global Brief*, Spring/Sum-
   mer 2010.
9 Richard Posner, *Public Intellectuals: A Study of Decline* (Cambridge, MA:
   Harvard University Press, 2003).
10 Fraser Sutherland, *The Monthly Epic: A History of Canadian Magazines*
   (Markham, ON: Fitzhenry & Whiteside, 1989), 205.
11 Donald E. Abelson, *Do Think Tanks Matter? Assessing the Impact of Public
   Policy Institutes*, 2nd ed. (Montreal: McGill-Queen's University Press, 2009),
   127–49.
12 Ibid., 24–7.
13 One organization classed as a think tank, the Conference Board of Canada,
   has 200 staff, but despite the quality of its economic research, the Conference Board acts more as a policy-support organization for the corporate
   community than as a conventional political think tank.
14 Irvin Studin, "Revising the Democratic Deficit: The Case for Political Party
   Think Tanks," *Policy Options*, February 2008: 62–7.

4 What Are Intellectuals For? A Modest Proposal in Dialogue Form

MARK KINGWELL

Q: So who are considered the important ones in this country?

A: Any simple list will be controversial, a form of special pleading both for who's on and who's not. But Marshall McLuhan and Northrop Frye, obviously. And Harold Innis. You could add George Woodcock and George Grant. I think Glenn Gould should be in there. Jane Jacobs for sure, though she was actually American. Margaret Atwood. Charles Taylor, too, but he's different because he just did good scholarship and left it to percolate into the wider world. Not quite the same thing. Then he chaired that commission in Quebec, ran for office. Oh yeah, so also Michael Ignatieff.

Q: Is he the guy some people call The Torturer?

A: He never actually tortured anyone, and for the record when Americans are in charge it's not torture, it's "enhanced interrogation technique." But Ignatieff did defend the Iraq war, and its attendant depravities, over and over in the *New York Times Magazine*. Tony Judt, an important English public intellectual in his own right, who died not long ago, classed him with Thomas Friedman and Peter Beinart as the "useful idiots" of the Bush regime, "America's liberal armchair warriors."

Q: Whoops. That's when he was calling himself an American, right? What's he doing now?

A: Don't ask.

Q: Okay, but is there anyone younger?

A: Sure, but what's the point of mentioning them?

Q: Don't they do some interesting things, especially on television?

A: Television. Listen, a few years ago one of the national newspapers ran an extended poll to find the country's favourite public intellectual. The clear winner: Don Cherry.

Q: That deranged hockey guy with the, uh, special clothing sense? You're joking.

A: I wish I was. So there you go – the hockey guy, who is by any rational standards an incoherent blowhard, is the country's favourite intellectual. You can't blame television itself, though. It's no better or worse than the people who produce it. But anyone who tells you this country is less anti-intellectual than, say, the United States or Britain hasn't been paying attention. The hockey guy as public intellectual is a one-line joke on the country as a whole.

Q: I get it. It's an updated version of the egghead-meathead conflicts of times past. Instead of mocking eggheads as hopelessly inept, or domesticating them by having them, say, learn how to surf and dance to rock 'n' roll in a beach blanket movie, you just collapse the distinction.

A: Exactly.

Q: Where does that leave us?

A: It could leave us with a fairly interesting question, like what do we even think intellectuals are for, anyway? I mean, what do we imagine is the point of them? The newspaper poll assumed that the concept of "public intellectual" was clear enough to use without further ado. But then the generated answer actually begs the question, since it's clear that the concept is not clear.

Q: That's all a bit finely spun, isn't it? A sort of meta-intellectual question for intellectuals about intellectuals.

A: You started it. Anyway, there's something here for everyone.

Q: What do you mean?

A: Consider the standard defences of intellectuals. From the time of at least Socrates and Lao Tzu, they saw themselves as performing a necessary function, chiding those in power for their blindness and ambition, warning the rest of us about the dangers that cling to power. Intellectuals were, in this tradition, essential barriers to tyranny. And when they tried to work on the side of power, as Plato disastrously did when he accepted Dion's invitation to tutor Dionysius in Syracuse, things went badly wrong. Even Aristotle, an altogether more rational intellectual, was frustrated by Alexander the Great, an altogether greater ruler. Real kings are always a disappointment to philosophers.

Q: But wait! Didn't Plato actually advocate that there should be philosopher-kings? It's somewhere in the *Republic*.

A: Book 7, 473c–d. Socrates says this to his young friends, especially Glaucon and Adeimantus, the brothers: "Until philosophers rule as kings or those who are now called kings and leading men genuinely and adequately philosophize, that is, until political power and philosophy entirely coincide, while the many natures who at present pursue either one exclusively are forcibly prevented from doing so, cities will have no rest from evils, … nor, I think, will the human race." Socrates said it, but you have to see that Plato himself didn't mean it. There's all kinds of evidence in the text that the idea is being set up as a deliberate provocation. Some people even think the whole discussion about the philosopher-king is meant as a warning, to readers smart enough to catch on, that real philosophers shouldn't even think of ruling. It's a dialogue, not a treatise.

Q: Hey, is this why we're having a dialogue right now, instead of this being an essay? So we can toss ideas around without being bound to them?

A: I don't know. Sure.

Q: Back to Plato. So, despite his own project with Dionysius, Plato thinks philosophers should stay out of politics?

A: Despite, or maybe because of. Plato had also seen the Thirty Tyrants nearly destroy Athens, after all, not to mention witnessing the staged trial that convicted Socrates for corrupting youth and celebrating false gods. He knew exactly what happened to intellectuals when they got on the wrong side of politicians. But he also knew that, without intellectuals to harass and scold them, and to awaken at least some of the people, there would be no curb at all on power.

Q: So you're saying that people like Karl Popper, who blame Plato for initiating a utopian urge that always ends in totalitarianism, are wrong?

A: Not wrong that this happens, but wrong that Plato didn't realize that. He's not seriously calling for an ideal city in the *Republic*, he's telling us that any desire for an ideal city is going to entail force and deception – and hence will cease, by definition, to be ideal. Notice that even the basic claim about the philosopher-king is haunted by a spectre of force: philosophers are not going to be allowed to go on just philosophizing, any more than kings are going to be able to rule without philosophy. Elsewhere there are defences of lying for political purposes, and a blithe suggestion that all the adults of any actual society will need to be exterminated to begin creating an ideal one. And then we're told that philosophers are lovers of wisdom? No, Plato was too smart to miss the contradictions, or to be making them inadvertently. Popper wasn't paying enough attention to the text. It's all in there.

Q: Okay, but at one point Plato himself still felt "the lure of Syracuse," as Mark Lilla called it.

A: Yeah. I'm not sure any really great thinker can deny the temptation, even if they should always resist it. An intellectual looks at society and thinks: I could do better than that, for crying out loud.

Q: But not without some violence. And that would make them, and society, worse. Also, they're probably wrong. The basic building blocks of politics are people, not ideas. Of course ideas are in the mix, sometimes with real power, but it really all comes down to the mysteries of human desire. What do the miserable creatures want? They hardly know themselves.

A: That's it. The whole "crooked timber of humanity" business. No such thing as an ideal state, or even a very rational one, when you're dealing with the humans. They're pretty hopeless.

Q: So philosophers, or intellectuals, should not aspire to rule. But where does that leave them? Seems like depression, or cynicism, would be their natural fate. I mean, you're right, looking at the humans, trying to make them better or anyway not worse, constantly being disappointed, is bound to make anyone depressed.

A: It happens. We could say this, though: just as it is an intellectual's job not to rule, it's also his job not to be too cynical. Or, since we've been talking about ancient Greece, we could say they should be Cynical. The original Cynics were social critics, really, not defeatists. The used sarcasm and satire, but they never gave up. Hope for the best, expect the worst.

Q: I like that idea, and yet satire can become a bad habit. It seems to breed misanthropy.

A: I don't think you're right. Or maybe I believe there's a good kind of misanthropy, a humanistic kind. Frye himself defined satire as "militant irony," and that militancy is as important as the irony. You can be militant only if you believe in something, if you have a mission. You pursue the mission aslant, but you still pursue it.

Q: And what is the mission?

A: I guess the simplest way to put it would be to say that it's calling out the best of ourselves, our highest possibilities, while acknowledging that we are really sad and limited, even sometimes downright nasty. We invent astonishing art forms like contrapuntal music, with geniuses like Gould to play it, and then we use the same ingenuity and creativity to think up ways to torture each other.

Q: Misanthropic humanism. Isn't that a contradiction in terms?

A: It's not a contradiction, it's an irony. The tension contained in the phrase – how can one be saddened by human foible while celebrating

the value of the human? – wedges open a gap in the self-congratula-
tions typical of liberal humanism, its blithe confidence in the idea of
the individual. Misanthropic humanism is a Grenzbegriff, a limit concept. It asks us to question the illusions of human existence even as it
acknowledges that same existence as the only source of meaning in the
world.

Q: Can you give me some examples?

A: I could – Hobbes maybe, Nietzsche for sure, Michel Foucault at
times. But rather than discuss their specifics, or even try to define the
rigid extension of the concept of intellectual – a fool's errand – let's
consider four types of the modern public intellectual to see what they
tell us about their role today. The beginning of the modest proposal up
there in the title.

Q: I thought we had established that role: criticism of power, and
reflection on human possibilities.

A: But you're far too trusting! That sounds good, but it only sounds
good to intellectuals.

Q: To intellectuals? I don't think I understand.

A: Of course not! That's why I'm here. Look, most intellectuals, public or otherwise, assume what most ordinary people do not really see,
namely, that what they do is important. A public intellectual presum-
ably imagines that he or she is performing some useful, even indis-
pensable, service. That service may be to ideas themselves, to public
discourse, to democracy, or to some other large abstraction: in an excit-
able version of this, to justice, or humanity, or the future. The reality is a
lot more complicated, and depressing. These days, there are four forms
that public intellectual engagement typically takes.

Q: Four?

A: Yes, four. Stop repeating what I say. The four types are: (1) the
savvy media don, what Pierre Bourdieu dismissively labelled "le fast-
thinker"; (2) the political pundit or professional contrarian, with an
ideological axe to grind; (3) the tame cleric, selling soft soap on behalf
of the current arrangement; and (4) what I would like to call the persistent xenocyst.

Q: You're kidding.

A: No, really, it's the right term and I'll explain why.

Q: Okay, go on.

A: So le fast-thinker is the guy – it's usually a guy – who opines about
this, that, and everything at the drop of a chase producer's phone call.
Specializes in the near-instant generation of a TV "quote," mostly about

features of the passing scene: pop stars, movies, clothing and education trends, sexual mores, generational differences. And so on.

Q: Didn't you used to do this sort of thing all the time?

A: Nah, that was the smiley bald guy in the suit. He's gone now.

Q: Right. Okay, so this popular culture business is trivial and constant, but is it really bad? I mean, what's the problem?

A: The problem is that the producer always wants you to explain "what it means" or "what it says about us." And the only valid answer to these questions is, very little if not nothing. Meanwhile, the various answers offered to the questions only serve to torpedo themselves. We can call this the "white lipstick conundrum."

Q: How's that?

A: Here's Frye, in *The Modern Century*: "Thus if there appears a vogue for white lipstick among certain groups of young women, that may represent a new impersonality in sexual relationships, a parody of white supremacy, the dramatization of a death-wish, or the social projection of the clown archetype. Any number may play, but the game is a somewhat self-defeating one, without much power of sustaining its own interest. For even the effort to identify something in the passing show has the effect of dating it, as whatever is sufficiently formed to be recognized has already receded into the past."

Q: Sounds like he's mocking McLuhan there.

A: Yeah.

Q: Okay, so by this reasoning, today's vampire fixation, say, or obsession with celebrity drunkorexia, or, going back a bit, the metrosexual backlash – remember that? – are already yesterday's reality. It's like calling something "cool." As soon as you do, it no longer is, it no longer can be. Classic self-collapse of positional goods.

A: Which means that, as so often when it comes to the pursuit speed, you cannot succeed; le fast-thinker, no matter how nimble, can never be fast enough. His comments themselves consign cultural phenomena to the dustbin of so five minutes ago.

Q: Pundits surely are better, then?

A: Yes and no. The pundit, as I consider him – and again, they are usually guys – is essentially a shill for a particular position, or cluster of them. They are the ones you see on the Sunday morning television shows, being angry and interrupting each other.

Q: Sure. Again, though, what's wrong with that?

A: The word pundit is from Sanskrit, and means an expert in Sanskrit. The pundits we see now are not experts in anything, except punditry.

That is, they speak authoritatively but not necessarily, or at all, from a position of authority. Eric Alterman, who long ago lamented the rise of a "punditocracy" in American politics, even set out the rules for success in this sphere. The two most important are these: (a) remember that it is better to look right than to be right; and (b) blanket the media with a contrarian view about an argument already in progress.

Q: That's a bit reductive, isn't it?

A: That's the point! Reductionism rules! Shouting down your opponent is nobody's idea of valid argument, and yet that's precisely what most of these people do, even in print. Mockery goes a long way, passing itself off as satire even while being in the service of power. There is no external burden of proof: you can say anything, even if it's wrong, without fear of comeuppance. And most telling of all, simply assuming the stance of an aggrieved minority – the besieged conservative battling gamely against the mainstream liberal media that provides him with a stage and princely salary, the lone courageous supporter of an allegedly unpopular but massively funded war – is enough to generate an aura of moral righteousness.

Q: Stop shouting, I get it. That's why these people sometimes change positions so radically, no?

A: Yes, exactly. You can't be a contrarian when the wind shifts and your formerly outsider position is now widely held. That's the moment to cross the ideological floor, denounce your once courageous but now sadly sheep-like former comrades, and get some new fill in your disputatious sails.

Q: Christopher Hitchens.

A: Christopher Hitchens.

Q: Okay, so I agree that a blustering punditocracy is a danger to democracy. It hollows out public discourse by reducing all sallies to carriers of ideological position, and it probably erodes civility too, understood as a general willingness to engage in meaningful political dialogue. But surely it was ever thus?

A: Maybe. Television has been a huge enabler of these erosions, because it rewards certainty and appearance. But print is actually not much better, despite our romanticizing of written argument. When it comes to new media, who the hell knows? Lots of incivility and nonsense, to be sure, sometimes at a level hard to imagine among civilized people; but also some really smart and effective content-strategy interventions. No room for optimism, I'd say, but certainly room for hope.

Q: Huh. I want to get back to that distinction in a minute, but meanwhile explain category three, the tame cleric.

A: Obviously I borrow the noun from Julien Benda's 1927 polemic *La trahison des clercs*. It's usually translated as "The Betrayal of the Intellectuals" or "The Treason of the Learned," but I prefer the more general and suggestive idea of the taming of the clerics. The real treason comes when intellectuals accept their status as adjuncts to the order of things, and today that almost always means accepting a system whereby they are warehoused in institutions dedicated to the "training" of the "workforce" of "tomorrow."

Q: I've heard you rant about this before, but explain "clerics" first.

A: Cleric just means someone in holy orders, eventually contracted to "clerk" and expanded to mean any learned person. The French *clercs* means intellectuals or academics, but I like to translate it as "clerics" because it reminds us, even if we're secular, that scholarship is a kind of holy order. We don't wear those gowns for nothing.

Q: What about Benda then?

A: Benda's point was both specific and general. He attacked certain French and German intellectuals of his day, especially Charles Maurras and Maurice Barres, for their abandonment of Enlightenment ideals of intellectual life, embracing instead toxic forms of nationalism and racism. These articulate men had reduced themselves, and their learning, to being mouthpieces for power. Benda considered this move, which certainly brings prestige and even the double-edged gift of influence, a crime against the true vocation of intellectuals.

Q: Which is?

A: Benda was an optimist. For him, intellectuals were "all those whose activity essentially is not the pursuit of practical aims, all those who seek their joy in the practice of an art or a science or a metaphysical speculation, in short in the possession of non-material advantages." Because such people existed, he said, "humanity did evil for two thousand years, but honored good. This contradiction was an honor to the human species, and formed the rift whereby civilization slipped into the world." According to him, this delicate balance of force and thought shifted in the first part of the twentieth century. Intellectuals gave up on serving philosophical ideals and became masters of justifying the status quo.

Q: Still true?

A: Certainly still relevant. I would say that the problem today is less intellectuals abandoning the Enlightenment in favour of nationalism, though that still happens, and more the embrace of capitalism as the only framework of meaning. The most successful are the ones who parrot sociological evidence in smooth deployment of "ideas" that sound kind of neat, a little obvious, but are given catchy new labels, and so manage to challenge nothing and nobody even while creating the illusion of being "smart." Never mind if there are jaw-dropping errors here and there.

Q: Malcolm Gladwell.

A: Malcolm Gladwell.

Q: But this doesn't apply to most university-based intellectuals, does it? I mean, if anyone is working in the field of Benda's "non-material advantages," it's them.

A: Yes and no. In this country they are paid pretty well, and from the public purse at that. Still, we should always be prepared to argue for the value of the things they do, especially when those things seem to have no value as the market understands the notion. I'm more worried about something else, namely, self-delusion.

Q: Lost me again.

A: This is the trap in Benda's idea of "non-material advantages." Intellectual rewards may be non-material, but they're still advantages. Intellectuals mask their own privilege even as they claim to expose privilege elsewhere. That's their problem: their thought is limited precisely by the illusion of thought having no limits. Their representation of themselves is therefore askew, even more than such representations usually are, because they believe they are above such representations. And they're struck in these representations, usually based on "superior taste" or "excellent critical judgment" or some such, just as much as their egghead-mocking opponents are stuck in representations of the intellectual as a dork.

Q: I think I see that. Anti-intellectualism is a conceptual and political dead end, but so is this kind of pro-intellectualism. Pro-intellectualism leads to elitism, in particular to an outcome where there are entrenched rather than circulating elites, a privileged classification class in fact.

A: There you go.

Q: Again, though, where does it leave us?

A: Well, to avoid the endgame of fully entrenched intellectual elites, you have to be on guard all the time. You can't escape class position entirely, nobody is able to do that, but you can cultivate better awareness of its follies and limits. You need master self-investigators like Adorno and Žižek and Houellebecq and Ballard around. You have to be HiLo-brow rather than Highbrow.

Q: Hmm. Still not sure I totally get this. Anyway, what happened to the fourth type of the public intellectual.

A: It's all related. Here, look at Frye again, in *The Modern Century*. He's comparing the experience of critical awareness, what Martin Amis called "the war on cliché," to that of looking out the window of a railway carriage as the sun goes down. "Even the most genuinely concerned and critical mind finds itself becoming drowsy in the darkening carriage," Frye says. "The very ability to recognize the cliché works against one's sense of full participation. Self-awareness thus operates like a drug, stimulating one's sense of responsibility while weakening the will to express it."

Q: Right. You become your own worst enemy – though only just.

A: Yes, good. And there's no way out, no transcendence possible. But what you can do is hold on to an awareness of that fact. Frye once more, capturing that larger stakes of critical intellectual engagement: "Democracy is a mixture of majority rule and minority right, and the minority which most clearly has a right is the minority of those who try to resist a passive response, and thereby risk the resentment of those who regard them as trying to be undemocratically superior." Hence anti-intellectualism, which is really a resentment against assumed claims of elite status. Who do you think you are, being critical?

Q: Yeah, that sounds familiar.

A: But the real issue in the interior tension, not the external hostility. Frye nails it: "I am speaking however not so much of two groups of people as of two mental attitudes, both of which may exist in the same mind. The prison of illusion holds all of us; the first important step is to be aware of it as illusion and as a prison."

Q: I do like that, it sounds right. But if that's the first important step, what's the second?

A: Now we finally get to the fourth type. The second step is: make yourself indigestible.

Q: Uh ...

A: Make yourself indigestible. Refuse to be assimilated or domesticated, tamed or bought out. I called this the persistent xenocyst role, right? A xenocyst is just a lump of foreign matter, a speck of something that doesn't belong. Any organism, sensing the presence of a xenocyst, will work to solve the problem it poses. The commonest recourse is rejection: refuse the challenge, expel the alien matter via whatever mechanism or orifice will serve. Next in popularity comes assimilation: make what was foreign conform to the organism's dominant patterns. Rarely, if ever, does the host organism respond by rearranging its own patterns to accommodate the foreign particle, though if the xenocyst is large enough, sometimes that's the only option.

Q: Uh ...

A: You see it. My proposal here is modest – it is not entirely pessimistic, though it is misanthropic, hopeful without being optimistic. Optimism is about expectations, reasons to believe. Hope operates beyond reasons, it is a kind of openness without expectation.

Q: So?

A: So the best public intellectuals can hope for themselves is to be good citizens, and to engage the semi-conscious majority with as much self-awareness, wit, and eloquence as they can muster. But they cannot expect to be thanked for this, nor should they take refuge in the soft tyranny of "non-material advantages." Especially in an age when there is no such thing as real public discourse, they will always be in danger of being consumed by the system they inhabit. More insidiously, they may find themselves doing the consuming, calculating the costs and benefits of their buy-ins of the mind, their mental self-cannibalizing. At that point, the best strategy – the only alternative – is to be as indigestible as possible.

Q: Uh ... Modest proposal? Consumption? Has this whole discussion been an example of the militant irony you were talking about before? Do you really mean any of it?

A: Not for me to say.

Q: But come on, this is important! Don't you worry that we live in an age where irony is out of fashion, lost equally on militants who don't care about reason and on those autistic narcissists who spend all their time checking email on their phones?

A: Yes. Yes, I do. But you have to keep trying, and by any means necessary. Because if you give up, the system will eat you alive. It might do that anyway, but you can at least make it hurt a bit going down. Do you know Michael Foot? A British politician. He said this about intellectual engagement, in a campaign speech for an election his party went on to lose: "We are not here in this world to find elegant solutions, pregnant with initiative, or to serve the ways and modes of profitable progress. No, we are here to provide for all those who are weaker and hungrier, more battered and crippled than ourselves."

Q: Yes.

A: Yes. Never worry about those on top – they will always find a way to take care of themselves. And never try to be on top yourself – you won't like it there. No, worry about those stuck at the bottom, speak and provide for them as best you can. There's no other point to being here.

Q: Thanks.

A: As we say, you're welcome. And everybody should be welcome.

PART TWO

Who Are They?

5 Public Intellectuals in Twentieth-Century Canada

NELSON WISEMAN

The preceding chapters explored the nature and roles of public intellectuals. This chapter asks, "Who were Canada's most influential public intellectuals in the twentieth century?" It identifies some of the more noteworthy intellectuals and analytically locates their ideas through the ideological lenses of conservatism, liberalism, and socialism. The selection of individuals and groups who in some measure represented these competing philosophical creeds across the century's four quarters provides some context for the experiences recounted and the arguments advanced in the other chapters. Those identified reflect the diverse richness of Canadian political and social thought as Canada evolved from British colony to independent state and then redefined itself as a multinational and poly-ethnic federal society.

1

Canadian imperialists, continental nationalists, and preachers with an ecumenical Christian message offered alternative visions as the new century dawned, a century that, in Prime Minister Wilfrid Laurier's vacuous phrase, would "belong to Canada." The imperialists cheered their membership in a globally federated and heterogeneous British Empire that ostensibly strove to civilize backward races and nobly aimed to maintain world order. Continentalists, more attuned to French Canadian sensibilities, aspired to shape an independent national identity more oriented to North America. Social gospellers, as prophets of a new age driven by ideas of reform Darwinism and moral progress, condemned capitalism's competitive possessive individualism and the inequalities it gave rise to as inhibitions to democracy.

Many imperial federationists dwelled on the sentimental and emotional attachments of Anglo Canadians for their mother country. They wished for Canadian equality as a self-governing state, neither ward nor subaltern, within the British Empire. William L. Grant, the son of conservative scion and Queen's University principal G.M. Grant, believed that to conceive of the empire strictly in economic terms vulgarized the idea of imperial unity.[1] Imbued with an ingrained scepticism about social reform, such conservative intellectuals were conscious of their ambiguous position as an educated, enlightened elite in a Canadian society increasingly democratic and, in their estimation, lacking social discipline. For some such as George Wrong, founding editor of the *Canadian Historical Review* and a founding member of the Round Table movement in Canada, Canada's crude loathsome politics of spoils betrayed what they perceived as the principled and more democratic politics of Britain, Australia, and New Zealand.[2]

Stephen Leacock, an ardent imperialist like most of his generation, became the best-selling humorist in the English language between 1910 and 1925, but he never poked fun at Canada's British system of parliamentary government; his monuments and wars (like the Boer) were British. One of the country's best platform orators and a political scientist, he wrote seriously on education, culture, religion, morality, prohibition, and feminism (no sympathizer he), and harboured deep-seated racial prejudices. Over three dozen American universities and schools in other parts of the British Empire, Japan, and China adopted his politics textbook.[3] Leacock, a conservative, was critical of the materialism and hunger for wealth that pervaded Canadian society. Some of his works anticipated the nationalist Toryism of George P. Grant (the son of William L. and referred to earlier in this collection by Hugh Segal and Mark Kingwell) and the connections between technology and Canadian identity made by Harold Innis and Marshall McLuhan in later decades[4] (whose contributions are mentioned by Segal, Doug Saunders, Kingwell, and Pierre Fortin).

O.D. Skelton and Mackenzie King offered more liberal views of industrialization, but like the imperial patriots, they were averse to socialism. Skelton skewered it in his PhD thesis and in his two-volume study of Laurier, the Liberal leader could do no wrong.[5] An uncompromising ardent nationalist, Skelton dismissed the imperial view of Canada as doomed. Economic prosperity, in his estimation, dictated divergent national interests: the British link impeded Canada's independence and nourished disunity because French Canadians could not identify with it.[6] King, a zealous "uplifter" prone to axiomatic moralizing, plucked Skelton from his professorship at Queen's University to serve as his deputy minister of foreign affairs and trusted adviser on domestic issues.[7] From this position, Skelton guided Canada's aloofness from international commitments and helped shape its merit-based civil service, recruiting figures such as future Nobel Peace Prize–winner and prime minister Lester Pearson.

King's pedantic and largely indigestible book, *Industry and Humanity*, propounded the nebulous principle of "industrial democracy." Neither his nor Skelton's books were widely read, but their ideas regarding Canada's place in the world steadily steered Canada from beseeching colony to sovereign dominion. Their alertness to French Canada kept Quebec onside through a wrenching military conscription crisis of 1917 and a divisive referendum during the Second World War. King's obfuscations as Canada's longest-serving prime minister – he entered the office in 1921 and finally exited it only in 1948 – embodied the conflicting aspirations of many Canadians. His Machiavellian cunning and the incompetence of his rivals led the widely read journalist Bruce Hutchison to depict him as "The Incredible Canadian."[8]

Social gospellers such as Salem Bland and William Irvine offered broad surveys of social conditions and urged more radically prescriptive reforms than did King.[9] Bland's Wesley College churned out radical Methodist clergymen and his book *The New Christianity* – whose thesis was that workers' control of industry needed to supplant capitalism – garnered rave reviews in the western Canadian press and attracted front-page coverage in the Toronto *Daily Star*.[10] Instrumental in politicizing Alberta's farmers, his student Irvine served as an MP between the 1920s and 1940s while another protégé, William Ivens, founded Labour Churches across the prairies. Their pulpits served as vehicles from which to urge social salvation by way of philosophical idealism. For social gospellers, the betterment of man's material condition had a religious significance eclipsing any evangelical desire to save his soul. Their reform agenda ranged widely – from prohibition and women's suffrage to direct legislation, the single tax, civil service reform, co-operatives, and more state direction of the economy.[11]

With an optimistic view of human nature, the social gospellers sermonized that God's work required a new moral order based on social justice. J.S. Woodsworth, who as "A Prophet in Politics," went onto a parliamentary career of over two decades and leadership of the socialist Co-operative Commonwealth Federation (CCF), drew attention to urban ills and the conditions of immigrants in the century's first decade when Canada's urban population increased by over 60 per cent and half of western Canadians were foreign-born.[12] Woodsworth's All People's Mission – offering foreign-language religious services, lectures and science classes, women's clubs, libraries, and concerts – and his imprisonment during the 1919 Winnipeg general strike, which garnered international attention, solidified his popularity. Nellie McClung's many public interventions (see Sylvia Bashevkin's essay) complemented the social gospellers' efforts, as she placed women, their issues and participation, at the vital centre of the social reform agenda.

Quebec's muted Catholic version of the social gospel, the *École sociale populaire*, preached the gospel of confessional unionism in response to papal encyclicals concerned with the rise of a new urban labour class. At the same time, Henri Bourassa as the founding editor of *Le Devoir*, Quebec's intellectual newspaper of record, articulated a pan-Canadian nationalist creed. He warned of Americanization, something that in later decades alarmed English Canadians more than it did the French. As the first of a host of weighty twentieth-century French Canadian journalists who came to lead political parties – André Laurendeau, René Lévesque, Claude Ryan – Bourassa's status was unparalleled in English Canadian journalism. John W. Dafoe of the *Winnipeg Free Press* had the ear of cabinet ministers and prime ministers but no comparable gravitas in his public's mind.

2

A second burst of public intellectualism came after the relatively prosperous 1920s, when "the popular mind in Canada," in Tory historian W.L. Morton's assessment, thoughtlessly embraced "the doctrine of continual, automatic progress, moral as well as material."[13] Against this backdrop, a band of professors known as the League for Social Reconstruction (LSR) proposed a nationally centralized social and economic planning project.[14] Debunking ideas that improvidence and idleness produced want, the LSR's widely circulated publications provided the intellectual infrastructure for Woodsworth's CCF, which continues today as the New Democratic Party (NDP), a member party of the Socialist International. A difference between Canada and the United States was that Franklin Roosevelt's New Deal co-opted many American intellectuals, while the LSR remained outsiders.

The LSR's most influential thinker, Frank Underhill, wrote a first draft of the CCF's founding manifesto, whose concluding flourish famously read, "No CCF Government shall rest content until it has eradicated capitalism and put into operation the full programme of socialized planning."[15] As an editor of the *Canadian Forum* – the country's leading journal of arts and politics – Underhill wielded his iconoclastic, journalistic "O Canada" column to expose the fatuously sham pretensions of the British constitutionalist-imperialist view of Canada, which he felt underplayed economic forces and American political influences. Although the LSR was replete with them, Underhill contemptuously dismissed economists as capitalism's "intellectual garage mechanics."[16] The LSR faded, as did Underhill's socialism, but social-democratic ideas took root and gained popularity. *Make This Your Canada,* by original LSR member and future CCF chairman Frank Scott and future NDP leader David Lewis, became a Canadian best-seller. It sold a remarkable 25,000 copies in 1943 alone.[17]

Obsessively dedicated to pure scholarship and fearful of the demands of politics, the liberal economist Innis – Adam Smith figures more frequently in his writings than any other economist – thought badly of the LSR's prescriptive endeavours. He implored academics to stay aloof from politics lest it compromise their scholarly integrity.[18] One might question his credentials as a public intellectual, for although his scholarship was influential among academics, he shunned participation in daily public life and the general public did not read his books. The popularization and diffusion of his ideas by others, however, stirred a more widespread public consciousness of those ideas, so that there is lustre to Innis and his ideas that they did not enjoy in the past.

Graceless prose and ideas too confounding and complex for a general audience sadly marked Innis's magisterial but dense studies of Canada's natural resource industries and the lessons he drew from studying them. His mechanized, meticulous dissections of the country's natural, or staple, resources would have fossilized but for his brilliant overarching framework. Focused on the trade and cultural flows of North America's waterways and railways, it captured the imagination of others and embedded itself as a cliché of Canadian thought. His later studies, preoccupied with time and space and their relation to history came across to most readers as enigmatic, non-sequential, and untidy.[19] He proved "To Have Insight into Much and Power Over Nothing,"[20] but his analytical pivot triggered McLuhan's ruminations on the seminal power of airwaves. Innis had discerned by analogy how communications technologies such as newspapers and radio shaped cultures in the way that natural resource development did, and McLuhan picked up the theme.

The links between economic and cultural imperialism in Innis's *Empire and Communications*,[21] found a conservative expression in the imperial political story woven by Donald Creighton. His high intent and polemics, like those of Leacock, reflected Canada's more austere antirevolutionary Tory tradition. Like Edmund Burke, Creighton viewed society as a partnership between generations. Writing solemnly "to the living on behalf of the dead," he assailed both laissez-faire doctrines and the decentralization of the Canadian state.[22] Creighton recognized that Innis's chronicling of how foreign markets drove Canada's successively exploited staples industries – fish, furs, farms, forests, and minerals – could be related to a theory of communications, and his biography of Innis showed him as the brilliant master he was.[23] But where Innis thought analogically and comparatively, Creighton thought and wrote serially, his distinctive scholarly narrative style a form of idiosyncratic literary art. "History's closest affiliation," he opined, "is with literature: it is not a science … and differs from political science, economic theory and sociology." His epoch-making *Commercial Empire of the St Lawrence* evidenced this affiliation.[24] Although Britain's moral and political authority grew fainter, Creighton countered a liberal Whig interpretation of Canadian history associated with Skelton, Mackenzie King, Underhill, and historian A.R.M. Lower; he championed the Conservative party's economic nationalism to counter American commercialism and he decried the undermining of Canada's traditional and British institutions.

At the same time, Quebec's foremost nationalist historian, the conservative priest Lionel Groulx, levered the British conquest of New France in 1760 to synthesize Catholic ideology with values he claimed to uncover in French Canada's quasi-feudal past. Portraying French Canadians to themselves as a conquered but spiritually undefeated people who persevered through their relative goodness, the superiority of their religion, and their rural lifestyle, Groulx's trope – articulated in books such as *Notre maître le passé* – presented French Canada as mauled by the cumulative, catastrophic impact of subordination and subjugation.[25] This storyline underpinned Quebec's passive defensiveness until its liberal Quiet Revolution and its opening to the wider world in the 1960s.

3

Tories, liberals, and socialists articulated competing nationalist narratives in the century's third quarter as the Canadian state marked its first century and Canada's culture and economy increasingly revolved in American orbits. In the 1960s, new "isms" – feminism, environmentalism, globalism, and identity politics – jostled the classical conservative, liberal, and socialist "isms." As well, new technologies stimulated novel perceptions of social organization. McLuhan's idea "the medium is the message" transcended national boundaries and burst him onto the international stage as a global public intellectual, a communications guru, who revised people's thinking about their environment. He admired Innis's focal shift from the world's trade routes to the trade routes of the mind, but where the astringent Innis was shy of publicity, the cleverly complex McLuhan was very public, highlighted in his cameo in Woody Allen's Oscar-winning film *Annie Hall*. Innis and McLuhan – lauded abroad as being "alone among students of human society, [to] make the history of the mass media central to the history of civilization itself" – distinguished structure from content, but McLuhan did so consciously.[26] Where Innis had communications structuring economics, McLuhan had them structuring perceptions.

A poet of technology, McLuhan used typography brilliantly and paradoxically to derail his readers from the orderly smoothness of linear, sequential reading. His intuitive vision and provocative metaphors – simultaneously confusing, oblique, and ambiguous – appeared as attractive as they were alienating, bewildering, and exasperating. They mesmerized readers with their radical radiance. Often freely associating, he related social structures to art forms and physics models to demonstrate how propagandists and advertisers shape popular attitudes with images and symbols.[27] He deemed communications technology as the extension of man's consciousness and presented technology as an extension of man as the wheel is an extension of the foot. Where Innis had illuminated the impact of print technology on social organization, McLuhan cast light on the effects of technology on sensory organization. His revolutionary secular prayer to technology coincided with Canada's television revolution in the 1950s.

Against the backdrop of a booming economy and unprecedented expanded state capacity, new counter-cultural currents flowed. The intellectually lethargic Cold War politics of the 1950s had ended. As Canada's centennial in 1967 approached, issues of national and more limited regional and ethnic identities arose. Sociologist John Porter probed behind formal institutions to identify where power actually resided in *The Vertical Mosaic*, which won the American Sociological Society's best book award in 1966. He documented and challenged masterfully the country's vertical mosaic in which those of British ethnic origins sat atop the political, economic, and social pecking orders.[28] The dispositional prerequisites of British Canadians' Britishness evaporated as Britain's power internationally ebbed further. At the same time, the children and grandchildren of Woodsworth's early-twentieth-century immigrants unwound their lingering Old World identities as they acculturated, intermarried, and assimilated in a post-Holocaust world taken with individual rights. This fed the populist revolt that catapulted John Diefenbaker and his ethnically recast federal Conservative party, no longer an exclusive Anglo fraternity, to power and saw the debut of Canada's first female and first Slavic cabinet ministers in 1957. No longer thinking of themselves as British subjects, however, English-speaking Canadians lacked a common sense of identity as a coherent national community.

Porter diagnosed the malaise in the body politic as an absence of creative politics, of retarded institutional innovation. Porter's thesis, as in the case of Innis's, embedded itself in a broader public consciousness by proxy, by others popularizing his ideas. The 1965 federal election demonstrated his influence in the real world of politics as NDP leader Tommy Douglas – considered the father of Canada's Medicare program and voted the "greatest Canadian" in a nation-wide CBC poll in 2004 – repeatedly referenced Porter's *Vertical Mosaic* to buttress his contention that an "an economic oligarchy" governed Canada.[29] Roused from their slumbers in good measure by Porter, English Canadian intellectuals ignited popular imaginations and contributed to launching Canada's modern and expansive welfare system after more than two decades of dull, grey, bureaucratically stultifying one-party Liberal rule in Ottawa.

The political class, compelled to take notice of a redefined Canadian nationalism, attached themselves to it. The Liberals proposed a new national flag, but not without Conservative opposition. George Grant dropped a depth charge under the liberal foundations of nationalist thinking in his best-selling invective *Lament for a Nation*. He hailed Creighton as the leading contemporary conservative theorist of Canadian history and enunciated a classical conservative nationalist *cri de coeur*, but its time had passed.[30] Where McLuhan, a conservative in his private life, welcomed technology as a harbinger that signalled the undermining of autonomous nation-states with his "global village" metaphor – the soon-to-become hackneyed cliché that predated "globalization" by more than a generation – Grant decried technology's seductive charms, capitalist cybernetics, and America's cultural Coca-Colonization. They subverted, in his view, national identities. Bewailing Canada's apparent embrace of America's version of liberal individualism, its market-driven psychology, and cultural homogenization, Grant deemed the defeat of Diefenbaker's anti-American Conservative government as the death of Canada's distinct identity and value system. His diatribe marked him as a "red Tory," a term that entered the lexicon of Canadian politics in the 1960s to denote those prepared to limit private corporate freedoms in the name of the public good.[31]

A radically different iteration of the new nationalism, on the port side of the ideological divide and detached from Canada's British imperial moorings, came from academic socialists such as Mel Watkins and James Laxer, leaders of a group with the unlikely name Waffle that challenged the NDP to be less timid. Their manifesto depicted the United States as a bully abroad and racist at home and reflected repulsion from the American behemoth as virulent as Grant's conservatism.[32] His foreword to James and Robert Laxer's *The Liberal Idea of Canada: Pierre Trudeau and the Question of Canada's Survival* voiced the anti-American, anti-liberal affinities of Tories and socialists; he railed against "American imperial capitalism" and cast the Liberals as "the chief political instrument of continental integration."[33] Meanwhile, Canada's academic Marxists embraced Innis as they shared his thesis that economic forces drive culture.[34]

Pierre Trudeau – enigmatic, paradoxical, at turns liberal and socialist – debunked Quebec's aggressively assertive nationalism in the 1960s as the "New Treason of the Intellectuals." His *Cité Libre* journal had earlier voiced what others had only dared whisper in taking on the clerics and educators of Quebec's corrupt and discredited conservative regime. Contemptuous of nationalism as breeding intolerance, totalitarianism, and discrimination, Trudeau castigated the separatist quest of Québécois nationalists as a self-deluding passion, dismissing them as intellectually indulgent sorcerers and spiritual escapists. He prodded French Canadians to break away from their ethnically nationalist wigwam complex to spur Canada's redefinition as a multi-national, poly-ethnic, federal state.[35]

4

In the century's last quarter, as the faces and constitutional identities of Canadians changed, identity politics came to the fore, neoconservatism displaced Toryism, and welfare-liberal and social-democratic thinking converged. Canada's countenance perceptibly changed during Trudeau's prime ministership, with most new Canadians hailing from non-traditional sources. New accents and surnames – Michael Ondaatje, M.J. Vassanji, Rohinton Mistry, Josef Škvorecký (born in Sri Lanka, Kenya, India, and Czechoslovakia, respectively) among others – found voice in the arts and letters, although Margaret Atwood, calling herself a red Tory, continued as English Canada's foremost writer.[36] *Survival*, a thematic guide to Canadian literature, and her novel *Surfacing* coincided with and impelled nationalist, feminist, and counter-cultural movements. The language of diversity and post-materialism eclipsed that of economic class and shifted public-policy discourse. Pacifist and feminist Ursula Franklin wrote and spoke widely on the political and social effects of technology, while a Canadian school of multiculturalism articulated by philosophers such as the liberal Will Kymlicka and the socialist Charles Taylor – who served as foot soldiers in a global network engaged in liberal multicultural discourse – proposed that the recognition and accommodation of ethnic diversity expands human rights and freedoms to strengthen democracy by diminishing ethnic hierarchies.[37]

Trudeau's government extended the bilingualism but jettisoned the biculturalism of the Royal Commission on Bilingualism and Biculturalism, appointed by his Liberal predecessor Lester Pearson, in favour of multiculturalism, an umbrella term referencing non-dominant ethnocultural groups. In a global first, Canada gave its imprimatur in 1971 to a multicultural policy framed in the language and ciphers of inclusion, participation, individual rights, and equity. Trumpeting the "just society" – a phrase deployed decades earlier by liberal historian A.R.M. Lower,[38] who had influenced popular and academic interpretations of Canadian development – Trudeau liberalized divorce and abortion regimes and instituted employment-equity laws. Poet and constitutional law professor Frank Scott, an adviser to Tommy Douglas's CCF government, served as an intellectual father figure to Trudeau and key inspiration for Trudeau's Charter of Rights and Freedoms. Like Trudeau, Scott linked Canada's liberal and social-democratic traditions. Courts, empowered by a constitutionally entrenched Charter, advanced the status of vulnerable and disadvantaged groups – visible minorities, women, Aboriginals, gays, lesbians, and the disabled.

By the 1970s, less than a third of Canadians were of French ethnic origins, a quarter had French as a mother tongue, and less than one fifth were unilingual French. French West Africa's decolonization in the 1960s had offered an impetus and ideological model for a redefined, assertive Québécois nationalism. Quebec's separatist turn in the 1976 election of René Lévesque's social-democratic Parti Québécois made for a clash of titans engaged in an ideological civil war. More passionate than the relatively aloof Trudeau, Lévesque saw Quebec as a country that must be made and he diagnosed Canada's condition as one of two paralysed majorities. He urged the Québécois to make history rather than submit to it and urged them to extricate themselves from Canada's federal system and a false pan-Canadian identity in favour of a new union of two sovereign but economically associated nations.[39] Various permutations of the idea – "special status," "*statut particulier*," and "distinct society" – proliferated and fed five rounds of mega-constitutional negotiations between the 1960s and 1990s. Some Québécois went further: posing as a revolutionary in the tradition of Che Guevara and with more than a tincture of militant rage, Pierre Vallières's penned-in-prison best-seller depicted the Québécois as "The White Niggers of America."[40]

To Quebec's nationalist intellectuals, Ottawa's provision of French-language services in places such as British Columbia, where few francophones lived, was "a cruel farce."[41] Having gained political power like Trudeau without surrendering his moral courage, Lévesque dismissed the francophone minorities outside Quebec as cultural "dead ducks" who would inevitably be assimilated into the larger anglophone community. His vision gained such wide currency that much academic writing about nationalism in Quebec read as little more than a rationalization for it.[42] His provincial government regulated language so successfully through its Charter of the French Language – a more detailed, comprehensive, and controversial linguistic regime than in any other Western democracy – that by the end of the century, a higher percentage of public discourse in Quebec's shops and streets was in French than the percentage of Quebecers speaking French in their homes.[43] Wielding state power in the economy, the PQ government styled itself as social democratic. Former French prime minister Pierre Mauroy, the president of the Socialist International, attended Lévesque's funeral in 1987.

Trudeau's response to Lévesque's challenge no less challenged an understanding of Canada as a federal state. Trudeau was intent on wooing his compatriots away from a Quebec conception of their national identity. His Charter of Rights elevated individual Canadian citizens as the bearers of the most fundamental constitutional rights by limiting the prerogatives of Canada's governments. Trudeau's political mandate came from his winning seventy-four of Quebec's seventy-five parliamentary seats, while he fared relatively poorly in English Canada. Ironically, as he reaped vilification in his native Quebec, where his victory over Lévesque in constitutional negotiations turned sour, English Canada came to embrace Trudeau's Charter as scripture and him as its infallible exegete. His intervention against proposals in the 1980s and 1990s for further constitutional reform to accommodate Quebec helped turn English Canada against those proposals in a referendum.[44]

At the same time, much intellectual energy in English Canada shifted ideologically from left to right with the rise of think tanks such as the Fraser Institute and the Atlantic Institute for Market Studies. They sought to counter the influence of welfare-liberal academics. Perceptions of a fiscally overextended and overly intrusive state that fostered identity politics elicited a backlash. The upstart populist Reform Party, drawing on ideas centred in Calgary's boardrooms and university re-imagined Canada through an American lens. Tom Flanagan, an American-born political scientist served as the party's director of policy, strategy, and communication. Like George Grant, Reform cried out over the collapse of a cherished imagined older Canada, but, unlike Grant, Reform's orientation was neither apocalyptic nor Tory. Reform represented a neoconservative turn in political life It embraced "universal citizenship" to counter the "politics of recognition"; it decried special status for Quebec or Aboriginals and denounced bilingualism, increased immigration, and multiculturalism. A product of the old left, English Canada's new right assaulted the welfare state and revealed how deeply the left's influence had ingrained itself in national life.

Public intellectuals in the media, think tanks, policy institutes, and social movements live *off* as well as *for* ideas. Writing for the educated public, their audience had grown as the percentage of Canadians with post-secondary education had grown; it exceeds levels in any of the other thirty OECD states.[45] Think tanks and policy institutes in the last quarter of the century represented a distinct development in public inquiry and public intellectualism.[46] The media regularly regurgitated their press releases, while Ottawa turned to five policy institutes to organize a series of public conferences on its constitutional reform proposals in the 1990s. Serving a public education function in articulating alternative visions of the world, think tanks evoke images of scientific expertise and deflect perceptions of them as political partisans. In challenging governmental and traditional academic research, they contributed to displacing them as the main drivers of policy inquiry.[47] Older organizations like the Canadian Council on Social Development became more policy-oriented while some left-wing think tanks like the Caledon Institute on Social Policy and the Canadian Centre for Policy Alternatives arose to counter neoconservative ones. More than mental technicians, some think tanks appeared as advocates shut out from power, while others appeared as sell-outs to it.

Organically linked to their society, Canada's twentieth-century public intellectuals – conservative, liberal, and socialist – exhibited the creative tension between affirming and protesting their society's values. Social gospellers, the LSR, and movements like the Waffle remonstrated against Canada's soulless materialism and the ugly exploitation of capitalism, while conservatives such as Stephen Leacock, Donald Creighton, and George Grant sought to uphold older traditions and institutions. Liberals O.D. Skelton and Mackenzie King, as mugwumps determined not to commit to very much ideologically, pursued a path of political neutrality, while the radical liberal Pierre Trudeau refashioned constitutional identities. Quebec's liberals and socialists shared a critique of Quebec's older order, but they preached alternative paths for its future. Theorists such as Charles Taylor tried to reconcile divergent views of Canada as seen through the prisms of biculturalism, multiculturalism, and distinct Aboriginal cultures and implored that Canadians' multiple identities and allegiances be given space to exist and flourish. As Canada developed in the twentieth century, it produced individuals and ideas that were distinctly Canadian.

NOTES

1 Carl Berger, *The Writing of Canadian History: Aspects of English-Canadian Historical Writing, 1900–1970* (Toronto: Oxford University Press, 1976), 25.

2 George M. Wrong, "Democracy in Canada," *Canadian Historical Review* 2, no. 4 (1921), 325–6.

3 Stephen Leacock, *Elements of Political Science* (Boston: Houghton Mifflin, 1906).

4 Stephen Leacock, *The Social Criticism of Stephen Leacock*, intro. by Alan Bowker (Toronto: University of Toronto Press, 1973), xxxix.

5 O.D. Skelton, *Socialism: A Critical Analysis* (New York: Houghton Mifflin, 1911), and *Life and Letters of Sir Wilfrid Laurier* (Toronto: S.B. Gundy, 1921).

6 O.D. Skelton, "General Economic History, 1867–1912," in Arthur G. Doughty and Adam Shortt, eds, *Canada and Its Provinces*, vol. 9 (Toronto: Glasgow Brook, 1914–17), 205–15 and 238–42; and Barry Ferguson, *Remaking Liberalism: The Intellectual Legacy of Adam Shortt, O.D. Skelton, W.C. Clark, and W.A. Mackintosh, 1890–1925* (Montreal and Kingston: McGill-Queen's University Press, 1993), chap. 3.

7 R. MacGregor Dawson, *William Lyon Mackenzie King: A Political Biography* (Toronto: University of Toronto Press, 1958), 249.

8 Bruce Hutchison, *The Incredible Canadian. A Candid Portrait of Mackenzie King: His Works, His Times, and His Nation* (Toronto: Longmans Green, 1952).

9 Salem Bland, *The New Christianity* (Toronto: McClelland and Stewart, 1920); and William Irvine, *The Farmers in Politics* (Toronto: McClelland and Stewart, 1920).

10 "New Christianity will supersede religions," *Toronto Daily Star*, 1 June 1920.

11 Richard Allen, *The Social Passion: Religion and Social Reform in Canada, 1914–28* (Toronto: University of Toronto Press, 1973).

12 Kenneth W. McNaught, *A Prophet in Politics: A Biography of J.S. Woodsworth* (Toronto: University of Toronto Press, 1959); J.S. Woodsworth, *My Neighbor: A Study of City Conditions, a Plea for Social Service* (Toronto: Missionary Society of the Methodist Church, 1911); Woodsworth, *Strangers within Our Gates: or, Coming Canadians* (Toronto: Missionary Society of the Methodist Church, 1909); and *Canada Year Book, 1913* (Ottawa, 1914), chap. 3, table 21, p. 79.

13 W.L. Morton, "The 1920s," in J.M.S. Careless and R. Craig Brown, eds, *The Canadians, 1867–1967* (Toronto: Macmillan, 1967), 229.

14 Research Committee of the League for Social Reconstruction, *Social Planning for Canada* (Toronto: Nelson, 1935).

15 Frank H. Underhill, *In Search of Canadian Liberalism* (Toronto: Macmillan, 1960), xii.

16 F.H. Underhill, "The Conception of National Interest," *Canadian Journal of Economics and Political Science* 1 (August 1935), 404.

17 David Lewis, *The Good Fight: Political Memoirs, 1908–1958* (Toronto: Macmillan, 1981), 198.

18 W.T. Easterbrook, "Innis and Economics," *Canadian Journal of Economics and Political Science* 19 (1953), 291; and Alexander John Watson, *Marginal Man: The Dark Vision of Harold Innis* (Toronto: University of Toronto Press, 2006), 4.

19 Graeme Patterson, *History and Communications: Harold Innis, Marshall McLuhan, the Interpretation of History* (Toronto: University of Toronto Press, 1990), 71.

20 Reginald Whitaker, "'To Have Insight into Much and Power Over Nothing': The Political Ideas of Harold Innis," *Queen's Quarterly* 30, no. 3 (1983), 818–31.

21 H.A. Innis, *Empire and Communications* (Oxford: Clarendon Press, 1950).

22 Berger, *The Writing of Canadian History*, 233; and Donald G. Creighton, *Dominion of the North* (Toronto: Macmillan, 1944), 378–80 and 466–7.

23 Donald Creighton, *Harold Adams Innis: Portrait of a Scholar* (Toronto: University of Toronto Press, 1957).

24 Donald G. Creighton, "History and Literature," in *Towards the Discovery of Canada: Selected Essays* (Toronto: Macmillan, 1972), and *The Commercial Empire of the St. Lawrence, 1760–1850* (Toronto: Ryerson Press, 1937).

25 Lionel Groulx, *Notre maître le passé* (Montreal: Granger, 1937).

26 Marshall McLuhan, "The Later Innis," *Queen's Quarterly* 60 (1953), 385; and James W. Carey, "Harold Adams Innis and Marshall McLuhan," *Antioch Review* 21, no. 1 (1967), 5.

27 Marshall McLuhan, *The Mechanical Bride: Folklore of Industrial Man* (New York: Vanguard Press, 1951).

28 John Porter, *The Vertical Mosaic: An Analysis of Social Class and Power in Canada* (Toronto: University of Toronto Press, 1965).

29 Wilfred List, "Only selves to blame, NDP chief tells voters," *Globe and Mail*, 30 Sept. 1965.

30 George Grant, *Lament for a Nation: The Defeat of Canadian Nationalism* (Toronto: McClelland & Stewart, 1965), 24.

31 Gad Horowitz, "Conservatism, Liberalism, and Socialism in Canada: An Interpretation," *Canadian Journal of Economic and Political Science* 32, no. 1 (1961), 143–71.

32 "For an Independent Socialist Canada" (1969), at http://www.socialist history.ca/Docs/Waffle/WaffleManifesto.htm.

33 George Grant, "Foreword," in James Laxer and Robert Laxer, *The Liberal Idea of Canada: Pierre Trudeau and the Question of Canada's Survival* (Toronto: James Lorimer, 1977), 9 and 11.

34 Ian Parker, "Harold Innis, Karl Marx and Canadian Political Economy," *Queen's Quarterly* 84, no. 4 (Winter 1977), 545–63.

35 Pierre Elliott Trudeau, "New Treason of the Intellectuals" and "Separatist Counter-Revolutionaries," in *Federalism and the French Canadians* (Toronto: Macmillan, 1968). Originally published in *Cité Libre*, April 1962 and May 1964.

36 Allan Gould interview with Margaret Atwood, at http://www.allangould.com/magazines/interviews/margaretatwood/magazines_interviews_margaretatwood.html; Margaret Atwood, *Survival: A Thematic Guide to Canadian Literature* (Toronto: Anansi, 1972); Atwood, *Surfacing* (Toronto: McClelland & Stewart, 1972); and Judith McCombs, "Introduction," in *Critical Essays on Margaret Atwood* (Boston: G.K. Hall, 1993), 8.

37 Will Kymlicka, *Finding Our Way: Rethinking Ethnocultural Relations in Canada* (Toronto: Oxford University Press, 1998), and Charles Taylor, *Reconciling the Solitudes: Essays on Canadian Federalism and Nationalism* (Montreal and Kingston: McGill-Queen's University Press, 1992).

38 A.R.M. Lower, "Two Ways of Life: The Spirit of Our Institutions," paper presented at the Annual Meeting of the Canadian Historical Association, May 1947.

39 René Lévesque, *My Quebec* (Toronto: Totem, 1979), 132.

40 Pierre Vallières, *The White Niggers of America: The Precocious Autobiography of a Quebec "Terrorist"* (New York: Monthly Review Press, 1971).

41 Pierre Fournier, "The Future of Quebec Nationalism," in Keith Banting and Richard Simeon, eds, *And No One Cheered: Federalism, Democracy, and the Constitution Act* (Toronto: Methuen, 1983), 156.

42 Richard Handler, *Nationalism and the Politics of Culture in Quebec* (Madison: University of Wisconsin Press, 1988).

43 Ingrid Peritz, "Sign rules struck down in Quebec: English-rights groups plan further attacks on Bill 101," *Globe and Mail*, 21 Oct. 1999, A1.

44 Pierre Elliott Trudeau, *A Mess That Deserves a Big NO!* (Toronto: Robert Davies, 1992).

45 Table A3.4a "Trends in Educational Attainment of the 25- to 64-year-old Population (1991–2002)," at http://www.oecd.org/dataoecd/32/26/33710913.xls.

46 Evert A. Lindquist, "Think Tanks or Clubs? Assessing the Influence and Roles of Canadian Policy Institutes," *Canadian Public Administration* 36, no. 4 (Winter, 1993).

47 G. Bruce Doern and Richard W. Phidd, *Canadian Public Policy: Ideas, Structures, Process* (Toronto: Methuen, 1983), 542–3.

6 *Le Devoir*, Forum for the Exchange of Ideas

GREGORY BAUM

The American scholar Richard Posner gave his book *Public Intellectuals* the subtitle *A Study of Decline.*[1] He opens his introduction with this quotation: "The correspondence between the decline of the great public intellectuals and the resurrection of the professors is ... no mere coincidence."[2] His book offers several reasons for the present decline: the increasing specialization within the disciplines, the waning of reformist and revolutionary ideas, the positivistic ideal of value-neutrality in social and political science, and the government's financial support of research in accordance with military purposes and neoliberal economic interests.

When Professor Nelson Wiseman invited me to write an article for a volume on public intellectuals in Canada, I wanted to paint a more positive picture, describing the discovery I made in 1990 when I became a daily reader of *Le Devoir* and encountered in its pages a vigorous debate among intellectuals over issues of the public good. Here academic and non-academic researchers and thinkers were engaged in an ongoing debate about the purposes and the problems of their society. Because thinking people in Quebec who take politics seriously are readers of *Le Devoir*, this relatively small independent newspaper plays a significant role in society, provoking critical thinking and drawing intellectuals into conversation.

In *Le Devoir, reflet du Québec au 20e siècle,*[3] several academics express their appreciation of this newspaper for opening its pages to the debate among intellectuals. The sociologist Guy Rocher, one of the most prominent public intellectuals of Quebec, writes that *Le Devoir* has belonged to his social and cultural space for at least half a century and has become part of his personal and social identity. *Le Devoir*, he writes, stimulates thought, offers reflections, invites dialogue and debate, and influences the development of Quebec society.[4]

When *Le Devoir* celebrated its hundredth anniversary in January 2010, many of its readers – among them politicians, academics, artists, and labour and community leaders – made statements, published over several weeks in *Le Devoir*, expressing their appreciation of this altogether unique newspaper.[5] All recognized that *Le Devoir* exercises an important function in the evolution of Quebec society.

The Role of Intellectuals

The place of intellectuals in Quebec is somewhat different from their place in English-speaking Canada and the United States. Prior to the 1960s critical intellectuals had little credibility in Quebec, yet this changed during and after the Quiet Revolution. According to Posner, small societies with a homogeneous elite – political leaders, business executives, academics, artists, and communicators – assign a prominent role to public intellectuals. He writes: "The public intellectuals in these countries, ... having attended the same schools and travelled in the same social circles, and sharing the same manner and mores and general outlook with the other members of their class, will, even if their stance is oppositional, tend to have more credibility with, indeed be part of, the nation's establishment."[6] The author certainly did not have Quebec in mind, yet his remark sheds light on the role of public intellectuals in this small francophone society. The intellectuals in Quebec have connections through their schooling, are acquainted with one another, know one another's family backgrounds, speak the same cultural language, and share a certain pride, representing as they do the intellectual creativity of their small nation. They all read *Le Devoir*. Their voices are heard by political leaders, decision makers, and social actors.

There is an additional reason why so many Quebec intellectuals have involved themselves in public debates. Quebec's status as a society remains uncertain. In the Quiet Revolution of the early sixties, "les Canadiens-Français" living in Quebec became "les Québécois": they moved from an ethnic identity inherited from their ancestors to a national identity defined by citizenship. They rejected the authoritarian regime of Maurice Duplessis, elected Liberal Jean Lesage as premier, supported social democracy, and wanted to become a modern industrial society. Lesage's political slogan "maîtres chez nous" revealed that the new Quebec was unwilling to accept its assigned place in the Canadian federation. Quebeckers eventually became divided between federalists and sovereignists: federalists wanting constitutional changes that recognize Quebec as a nation within Canada and sovereignists wanting a sovereign Quebec allied to Canada in some way. The Canadian Constitution Act of 1982 was rejected by Quebec's national assembly: even federalists were unable to accept it.

Quebec's status as a society remains uncertain. Since Quebeckers have the feeling that their society is still in the making, they continue to discuss who they are and who they want to be; and their intellectuals engage in public debates over what is good for their society.

My Relation to the Public Debate

I wish to say a few words about my own relation to this public debate. Moving to Quebec in 1986 started an adventure that I did not anticipate. I had been a professor of theology and religious studies at St Michael's College in the University of Toronto for twenty-eight years when I accepted an invitation to become a professor at the faculty of religious studies of McGill University in Montreal. Since McGill is an anglophone university, and since it is possible to live in the west of Montreal in English, professors at McGill do not easily become integrated into the francophone society. Yet I was fortunate. The Jesuit-sponsored Centre justice et foi, acquainted with some of my theological writings, invited me to become a member of the editorial committee of its monthly review *Relations* dealing with social, political, and religious issues. *Relations* had become a left-wing Catholic review in the 1970s, especially after 1975, when the entire Jesuit Order committed itself to faith and social justice in solidarity with the poor and oppressed.[7] Since the Centre is engaged in critical social analysis, I became acquainted with the problems and aspirations of Quebec and followed the debates on public issues, including the contribution of academics. Like all members of the Centre and the great majority of intellectuals, I read *Le Devoir* every morning.

It is often said that French Canadian Quebeckers are clannish and do not welcome people of foreign origins. It is true that the small francophone society defends itself against the cultural power of the English language in North America. Without a firm resistance against the otherness that impinges upon them, Quebeckers would gradually disappear. At the same time, when persons of whatever origin are interested in issues that concern Quebeckers and are willing to wrestle with the problems of Quebec and its place in the world, these persons are welcomed to join the debate and make their contribution to society. That is why Quebeckers can elect as members of the national assembly an immigrant from Iran, Amir Khadir, co-founder of le Parti Québec solidaire, and Maka Kotto, an immigrant from Cameroun, representing le Parti Québécois. I feel that I too have been adopted by the francophone society.

A Brief History of *Le Devoir*

Le Devoir was founded in January 1910 by Henri Bourassa, who had become at odds with the two federal political parties. He had opposed the Liberal prime minister Wilfrid Laurier when the latter committed Canada to join Great Britain in its second war against the Boers. Bourassa was an anti-imperialist: he wanted a Canada independent from Britain, a Canada in which the English and the French were equal partners, and in which the rights of the French minorities in the West were protected. He wanted *Le Devoir* to be an independent paper, committed to a Catholic ethic, offering support for honest causes and denouncing political intrigues, corruption, fraud, and personal greed. He realized that calling his paper *Le Devoir* (Duty) would displease many of his contemporaries, yet he justified his choice in terms of his moral philosophy. "To assure the triumph of ideas over selfish desires and of the public good over partisanship, there is only one way: to awaken in the people, especially in the leading classes, the sentiment of public duty under all its forms, religious, national and civic. Hence the name of this paper, which surprises some people and makes others smile."[8]

Le Devoir has changed over its long history. In the 1930s it became narrowly conservative and fearful of modernity, yet in the 1950s, under Gérard Filion, it became a critic of Maurice Duplessis, the premier of Quebec, and an ardent promoter of democracy. In the 1960s *Le Devoir* became a progressive paper supporting the Quiet Revolution. Claude Ryan, who became its editor in 1964, put great emphasis on political ideas and made the paper into a forum of the public debate in Quebec. In his book on *Le Devoir*, Pierre-Philippe Gingras writes: "While, twenty years ago, the paper understood itself as dedicated to provide information, it became with Ryan the intellectual host of ideas, events and people."[9] After Ryan left *Le Devoir* in 1980 to assume the leadership of Quebec's Liberal Party, the emphasis on ideas continued. Michel Roy, an influential team member of *Le Devoir*, urged the paper to welcome contributions from intellectuals, writers, artists, and cultural communicators. The editors of the paper between 1980 and 1990, Jean-Louis Roy and Benoît Lauzière, continued this policy and made an effort to listen also to Quebeckers of the ethnic communities. Lise Bissonnette became the editor of *Le Devoir* in 1990 – the year I became a daily reader.

It is interesting that in the 1980s, two major studies were published lamenting the increasing silence of intellectuals in Quebec.[10] They showed that in the sixties, during the Quiet Revolution, intellectuals had been very active in public debates. In the seventies, they had become more radical, inspired by Marxism variously interpreted, and continued to speak to public issues. Yet, according to these two studies, intellectuals had become quiet in the 1980s. The loss of the referendum of 1980 depressed the sovereignists, and the Canadian Constitution Act of 1982 depressed the federalists. Yet there were other reasons for this increased apathy. The two studies argued, even if in slightly different ways, that what occurred in Quebec in the 1980s happened also in other Western societies: the collapse of Western Marxism, the decline of social idealism, suspicion of ideology, the spread of neoliberalism as an economy and a culture, and government's turn to narrow pragmatism. Intellectuals, these studies argued, were serving this society with their research and teaching, instead of challenging it.

In the 1990s important political events prompted Quebec intellectuals to become engaged in public debates about social and political issues. In 1990 occurred the failure of the Meech Lake Accord and the founding of the Bloc Québécois party; in 1991 the report of the Bélanger-Campeau commission was published;[11] in 1992 the Charlottetown Accord collapsed, and the Parti Québécois, led by Jacques Parizeau, came to power; and in 1995 was held a second referendum on Quebec sovereignty that was rejected by a slight majority – 50.58 per cent of the population to be precise. In those years the whole of the francophone society was involved in an intense political conversation. Yet when the mood calmed down after 1995, intellectuals continued their public debate in *Le Devoir*.

Lise Bissonnette

In 1990, Lise Bissonnette became the editor of *Le Devoir*. To find out what her political philosophy was and how she understood the role of her newspaper, I have just reread many of her pertinent editorials. Like all the editors of *Le Devoir*, she wanted it to carry on the mission defined in 1910 by its founder, Henri Bourassa: to be an independent newspaper committed to the truth, based on ethical convictions, fostering just causes, and denouncing fraud, corruption, and social injustice. As society has greatly changed since 1910, she writes, so have the policies of *Le Devoir*. While Henri Bourassa was nervous about the aspirations of women and the arrival of immigrants, *Le Devoir* has become a supporter of equality between men and women and an advocate of mutual respect and equal rights for all Quebeckers, old and new. Even if many other policies have changed, *Le Devoir* continues its interest in ideas and critical reflection on the events of society. Bissonnette sees the paper as the place for the exchange of ideas and counts on intellectuals to join the public debate that, in her mind, belongs to the essence of democracy.

Since I am particularly interested in the ethical orientation of *Le Devoir*, I shall quote an entire paragraph from Lise Bissonnette's editorial of 24 September 1990:

> From its Catholic origins *Le Devoir* has moved on, just as the society of Quebec has, to become institutionally *laïque*. It no longer sees itself bound by the teachings of a church, and in regard to several moral issues, it even deviates from the path it followed in the past with confidence and deference. Yet the values of *Le Devoir* remain "profoundly Christian," an expression often used after the Quiet Revolution. Since I wish to include people of other traditions who are one with us, I prefer to say that *Le Devoir* follows an ethics of high demands. Taking part in the debate on social ethics, it looks for a balance between personal freedom and collective responsibility, rejecting both laissez-faire economics and cynicism. Too often in our daily routine, like others we forget our basic values. Yet when shocking events occur, *Le Devoir* maintains the good virtue of indignation that often leads to action.

Guy Rocher has suggested that the humanistic orientation of *Le Devoir*, derived from a Catholic tradition, resembles the ethical orientation of *Le Monde Diplomatique*, founded in 1954 by Hubert Beuve-Mery, who had been the editor of the Catholic paper *Le Temps* and an associate of Emmanuel Mounier and the *Esprit* circle.[12] The two publications have a progressive, non-ideological orientation based on an ethical commitment to social justice.

The difference between the two papers is, of course, considerable. *Le Devoir* is a daily newspaper that reports on significant national and international events. It has an editorial policy, yet it opens its pages to ideas on public issues, declarations made by thoughtful people and manifestos produced by groups of citizens, even if they run counter to its own editorial policy. *Le Devoir* respects a pluralism of ideas and sees itself as serving the public debate in society.

This is a paragraph taken from Bissonnette's editorial of 25 September 1990:

> Society wants a newspaper to have a clear editorial policy, yet the people who demand this also want to think for themselves. This is all to the good. For it is precisely this debate of ideas that *Le Devoir* is meant to serve with an unrelenting effort. We offer the large community of people interested in such debates a second look at events in society and an interpretation of their meaning. We do this on the editorial page, to be sure; yet we do this also on other pages ... with interviews, analyses and critical evaluation of current issues. *Le Devoir* does not hesitate to claim its place in the intellectual community, which is greatly enlarged today, including the universities as well as small and large enterprises, the unemployed as well as students; in fact, all citizens interested in public life and the issues of today.

It is worth mentioning that under Claude Ryan and his immediate successors *Le Devoir* favoured a renewed federalism. Ryan, as is well remembered, was a vocal defender of the *Non* choice in the referendum of 1980. Still, as a strong supporter of democratic pluralism, he readily accepted articles for publication that favoured the independence of Quebec. When Bissonnette became the editor of *Le Devoir* in 1990, soon after the collapse of the Meech Lake Accord, she adopted a more nationalistic editorial policy. Quebeckers remember well that after this event, Quebec's Liberal premier Robert Bourassa made a declaration before the national assembly on 22 June 1990, saying, "English Canada must understand quite clearly that, whatever it might say or do, Quebec is, today and always, a distinct society, free and capable of assuming its destiny and development." In this historical context, *Le Devoir* came to lean towards Quebec sovereignty, yet faithful to its commitment to pluralism, it continued to open its pages to articles defending federalism in one form or another.

From the very beginning, *Le Devoir* had to do its work with limited financial resources. Since it addressed the educated and not the crowds, its circulation has always been relatively small. Finding the paper again

in a financial crisis, Lise Bissonnette acted with competence and imagination. In the fall of 1990 she celebrated *Le Devoir*'s eightieth anniversary with a fund-raising banquet at the Queen Elizabeth Hotel, bringing
together 750 guests and raising $400,000. Present were the premier, the
prime minister, and leading personalities of Quebec in the fields of politics and industry, many of whom had been habitually criticized by the
paper. Yet even those who disagreed with the orientation of *Le Devoir*
were proud of it as a unique national institution.

In the years following Bissonnette created a sounder financial basis
for *Le Devoir*. She persuaded socially concerned financial institutions –
credit unions and labour funds – to make a major contribution to the
paper, without in any way giving up its independence. This allowed
her to make major changes in the paper itself, such as limiting paid advertising, dropping the stock-exchange reports, reducing the coverage
of sports, and providing more space for ideas and public debate.

In addition to the editorials and columns written by staff members offering reflections on contemporary issues, one finds today in each issue
of *Le Devoir* a page called "Idées" and, on the editorial page, the column
"Libre opinion," spaces open for public debate. The book reviews in
the weekend edition survey the literature produced in Quebec, including scholarly works in history and the social sciences. In recent years,
a philosopher has been invited once a month to choose a great thinker
of the past and show how he or she provided ideas that continue to be
relevant and shed light on the options before society in the present.

A Forum for the Exchange of Ideas

Although I have not found in the literature on *Le Devoir* a study on
the intellectuals who have been in conversation in that paper over the
years, I did find an article by Jean Robitaille[13] on the attention paid by
Le Devoir in the 1990s to what Quebeckers call "les projets sociaux," or
plans for social development. While in the 1960s and 1970s these plans
belonged to the platforms of political parties, in the 1990s they were
thought out and articulated by associations of civil society. In 1991 the
Estates General of the agricultural communities analysed the precari-
ous situation of rural life in Quebec and called for help. In 1992 a commission of the Federation of Quebec Women produced a social project
entitled "Un Québec féminin pluriel," expressing its solidarity with
women of immigrant origin. In 1993 a colloquium was held by Le Centre pastoral en milieu ouvrier, a labour-oriented Catholic organization

that proposed a social project inspired by justice and equality; and in 1998 a long consultation involving labour unions and community development groups produced a charter document, "Une Charte d'un Québec populaire,' outlining social planning in accordance with justice and equality. The 1995 referendum was followed by several commissions, appointed by the Parti Québécois government, to engage in social planning for various sectors of society.

The point of Jean Robitaille's article is that *Le Devoir* took a lively interest in these efforts of social planning, reacted positively to them in its editorials, published in its pages summaries of the statements produced by the various commissions, and thus made them known to the wider public. According to Robitaille, this stimulated the debate among activists and intellectuals on social and political issues in Quebec.

La laïcité

Many other social and political topics are debated in the pages of *Le Devoir*, involving academic and non-academic intellectuals as well as the wider public. To show more concretely (1) the passionate public concern of Quebec intellectuals and (2) the broad scope *Le Devoir* offers them for their ideas, I shall present a brief report on the contemporary debate, as yet unfinished, over "la laïcité de l'État." This debate is of particular interest to me, since my own field of research is the interaction of religion and society; at the same time, the debate seems rather strange to me since I do not share the cultural experience of the Quebec people. It is significant that the French word *laïcité* has no English equivalent: it refers to the separation of church and state.

To explain why *la laïcité* as a socio-political issue excites Quebeckers more than Canadians of other provinces, I wish to refer to a study by the British sociologist David Martin[14] showing that Protestant and Catholic societies have entered modernity in slightly different ways. Protestant societies recognize a variety of churches, tolerate the drift towards religious liberalism, and thus move into secular culture without great upheaval. Societies of Protestant origin find it easy to come to terms with modern pluralism. By contrast, Catholicism is a religion that defines the totality of human life, personal and social, and – at least in the past – left no room for dissidence. When Catholics came to disbelieve a particular doctrine, they had to reject the whole of Catholicism; and because they rejected the whole, they had to recreate the whole and elevate their non-belief to be the ultimate truth. Societies of Catholic origin tend to move into modernity through great upheaval: they find it difficult to be reconciled to modern pluralism and often generate a cultural schism between the defenders of secular truth and the defenders of inherited religion. In his study Martin refers especially to European societies of Catholic origin, yet his reflections also shed light on the difference between Quebec and English Canada.

Resentment against the Catholic Church is widespread among Quebeckers and finds ready expression in newspapers and programs on radio and television.[15] Prior to the Quiet Revolution, the Catholic Church was responsible for education, public health, and social services in Quebec: the church also exercised firm cultural control and, despite certain progressive clerics, resisted the intrusion of modernity and supported the authoritarian government of Duplessis. The Quiet Revolution, in which progressive Catholic believers played an important role, fostered the secularization of society, led to the loss of faith, and generated resentment against the church. That this resentment still exists after more than forty years is surprising, since the bishops of Quebec have become socially progressive pastors and are tolerant of divergent interpretations of church doctrine. Only Marc Ouellet, cardinal archbishop of Quebec City from 2002 to 2010 represented a narrow, intransigent Catholicism.

The widespread resentment against Catholicism makes many Quebeckers impatient with the religion of immigrants that is becoming increasingly visible in public life. Thinking that religion belongs to the past and has become a dead issue, these Quebeckers are troubled by the ardent faith of immigrants, especially Muslims, and their foreign religious symbols and practices. These Quebeckers criticize the concessions or accommodations made to religious believers, in the name of the Quebec Charter of Human Rights, exempting them from the requirements of certain general rules. To respond to what was regarded as a major social problem, the government appointed the Bouchard-Taylor commission[16] to investigate Quebec's legal tradition and the opinions of the public, and then produce a report with concrete policy proposals. Their final report, published in 2007, recommends (1) the neutrality of the state in regard to religion, (2) restricting state officials of authority from wearing visible religious symbols, (3) granting freedom to wear religious symbols to lower-level employees of the state, like teachers and nurses, and (4) the exemption from certain general rules (reasonable accommodations), allowing believers to keep their religious practices. The Bouchard-Taylor report referred to this approach as *la laïcité ouverte*.

This report has been praised in several European countries as a model for contemporary societies. Yet, in Quebec it has been severely criticized. Critics have argued that *la laïcité ouverte* opens the door to multiculturalism. The Quebec government, as is well remembered, has never accepted Ottawa's multicultural policy. Quebec's "intercultural" policy envisages interaction between the host culture and incoming cultures, fostering a certain convergence among them, while preserving their difference. The policy of Quebec stresses the integration of immigrants, without aiming at their assimilation. The federal government thinks that its multicultural policy helps to overcome racism because it calls for the respect of cultural pluralism, while the Quebec government thinks that its intercultural policy is a better shield against racism since it urges newcomers to become integrated into society. Special concessions or accommodations made to religious believers, certain Quebeckers argue, encourage multiculturalism.

The Bouchard-Taylor report has also been criticized because it does not sufficiently acknowledge the threatened condition of Quebec's francophone culture or the surprising creativity of its social and cultural evolution.

The Debate over *la laïcité*

Le Devoir records this endless debate. The exchange of ideas beginning in 2010 includes the following statements and articles. In an article of 12 January, Gérard Bouchard replies to the critics of *la laïcité ouverte* recommended by the report he had co-authored. He reminds his critics, especially those associated with Le Mouvement laïque québécois, that Quebec has now become a pluralistic society and that solidarity with newcomers and their introduction to the symbols of Quebec becomes possible only if all Quebeckers have a respect for diversity. He writes, "I am against a monolithic concept of national identity."

Le Devoir of 22 January published an article by Jacques Beauchemin, a well-respected sociologist at l'Université du Québec à Montréal, entitled "Welcoming without Giving Up on Oneself." Beauchemin argues that the discourse on pluralism in Quebec has become obsessed with "the other," with diversity and with harmonious social relations, and avoids with suspicion the history and memory of the people and culture of the great majority. Welcoming newcomers, he argues, demands a collective self-understanding grounded in history that is capable of offering them a share in a social project with common goals.

Provoked by what they regarded as opposition to pluralism, a group of professors of l'Université de Montréal and l'Université Laval produced "A Manifesto for a Pluralist Quebec," published in Le Devoir on 3 February 2010, that was subsequently signed by over a thousand academics and activists. It begins: "The debate about national identity has taken a dangerous turn. An open and pluralistic vision of la société québécoise is being attacked by two currents of thought that oppose the major orientations of modern Quebec." The manifesto accuses "conservative nationalism" for refusing to make concessions to cultural diversity and "a strict understanding of la laïcité" for refusing to allow visible religious symbols in the public sphere. The manifesto is a carefully argued document in the best tradition of democratic theory, yet it remains silent on the collective right of a small people to defend its political and cultural identity.[17]

On 9 February 2010 Le Devoir published an article by the philosopher Michel Seymour deploring conservative nationalism because of its opposition to cultural diversity, yet affirming the progressive nationalism widely held in Quebec that favours political sovereignty and welcomes ethnic, cultural, and religious diversity.

Le Devoir of 13 February carried an article by Jacques Beauchemin and Louise Beaudoin, a prominent Parti Québécois member of the national assembly, that disagrees with the Manifesto for a Pluralist Quebec. The two authors insist that they too welcome pluralism and that diversity is not at issue in the present debate. The real question is how to respond to and manage this pluralism. The manifesto falsely believes that its own ideal is the only response, yet – the two authors argue – in its particular historical situation, Quebec must deal with diversity differently, extending its symbolic identity to embrace immigrants and offering them integration into their new society, while respecting their difference. The multicultural policy of the federal government, they argue, allows immigrant communities to remain apart, while Quebec's interculturalism and la laïcité strictly understood helps them to become participants in society as citizens on an equal footing.

On 6 March, Le Devoir published an article by three academics – Dimitri Karmis, Jocelyn Maclure, and Geneviève Nootens – that accuses Beauchemin and Beaudoin of having attacked a straw man: the manifesto actually praises Quebec's intercultural policy and recommends the social integration of immigrants. Beauchemin and Beaudoin are wrong, moreover, when they make a distinction between the great majority and the many minorities. In actual fact, the evolution of society inevitably produces an internal differentiation of the great majority. For example, Quebec, formerly a closely knit Catholic society, has become strongly secular, leaving believing Catholics as a minority. The majority is in fact internally divided. Thus, the new pluralism is not at odds, but fully in line, with the history of Quebec.

The critics of *la laïcité ouverte* continued the debate. On 16 March 2010, *Le Devoir* published the "Declaration of Intellectuals for *la laïcité*," "pour un Québec laïque et pluraliste." The declaration was eventually signed by over one hundred academics and activists. It claims that authentic pluralism in society is possible only if the state and its institutions are perfectly lay, that is, free of any association with religion. "*La laïcité* makes the administration of social pluralism possible without obliging the majority ... to give up on legitimate choices and without infringing upon the religious liberty of any one person. *La laïcité ouverte*, by contrast, leads in practice to the negation of the state's neutrality because it allows the accommodation of public institutions to one or other religion." What *la laïcité* in the full sense demands is that all men and women working for the state, including nurses and teachers, abstain from wearing visible symbols identifying them with a particular religion. Still, since religion is strictly speaking a private matter, restricting its place in the public realm is in no way an attack on religious liberty.

On 22 May 2010 *Le Devoir* reported that Premier Jean Charest had proposed a bill that would adopt as Quebec's official policy "la laïcité ouverte" as recommended by the Bouchard-Taylor commission. One implication of this policy has attracted the attention of the press: a person seeking services of the state or working for the state must uncover her face: this means that the niqab or burqa may not be worn in government offices, hospitals, and schools, while other religious vestments may be worn in these institutions, including government offices and police facilities. But the debate continues.

It is not easy to interpret this controversy. It is not an argument between federalists and independentists or between the Left and the Right in economic or cultural terms, for representatives of these different circles are found on both sides. The reason I have reported this debate in some detail is to illustrate the passionate involvement of Quebec intellectuals in issues of the public good and the willingness of *Le Devoir* to become the forum for the exchange of ideas.

It is worth mentioning that at the Centre justice et foi, with which I am associated, we are not happy with the present debate. To discuss issues of identity and the place of religion in society without attention to social injustices and economic exclusion disguises what actually goes on in society – the suffering of the people at the bottom and on the margins. The high percentage of unemployment among immigrants of Muslim origin forbids, from our point of view, the discussion of Muslim religious practices in an abstract way. We argue that the discourse about others affects the public attitude towards these others and will thus have social and economic consequences. We join the public debate in Quebec by emphasizing the creativity and the as-yet-unrealized potentiality of the people of Quebec to extend their solidarity to newcomers, welcome them as citizens of this francophone society, and struggle with them for a more just distribution of wealth and power.[18]

NOTES

1 Richard Posner, *Public Intellectuals: A Study of Decline* (Cambridge, MA: Harvard University Press, 2001, 2003).
2 Tony Judt, *Past Imperfect: French Intellectuals 1944–1956* (Berkeley: University of California Press, 1992), 297.
3 Robert Lahaire et al., eds, *Le Devoir, reflet du Québec au 20e siècle* (Montreal: Hurtubise, 1994). The translations of French texts in this article are my own.
4 Ibid., 465.
5 *Le Devoir*, 18 Nov. 2009, 11 and 12 Jan. 2010, 2 Feb. 2010.
6 Posner, *Public Intellectuals*, 12.
7 The 32nd General Congregation of the Jesuit Order, held in 1975, passed a decree entitled "Our Mission Today: Serving the Faith and Promoting Justice."
8 Henri Bourassa, *Le Devoir*, 10 Jan. 1910
9 Pierre-Philippe Gingras, *Le Devoir* (Montreal: Libre Expression, 1985), 261.
10 Marc-Henry Soulet, *Le silence des intellectuels* (Anjou, QC: Éditions Saint-Martin, 1987); Diane Lamoureux, "Le rôle des intellectuels en sciences politiques dans le débat politique actuel," in Louis Balthazar el al., eds, *Le Québec et la restructuration du Canada* (Montreal: Septentrion, 1991), 199–215.
11 The Bélanger-Campeau commission on the political and constitutional future of Quebec was created by Quebec's national assembly, responding to an initiative of Premier Robert Bourassa after the rejection of the Meech Lake Accord. The commission was chaired by Michel Bélanger et Jean

Campeau. Since the majority of the briefs submitted favoured Quebec's independence, the commission's report recommended holding a referendum on sovereignty-association in 1992.

12 Lahaire et al., *Le Devoir*, 471.

13 Jean Robitaille, "Le projet social québécois et *Le Devoir*," in Robert Comeau et al., eds, *Le Devoir, un journal indépendant (1910–1995)*, 345–8.

14 David Martin, *A General Theory of Secularisation* (Oxford: Blackwell, 1978).

15 Gregory Baum, *The Church in Quebec* (Ottawa: Novalis, 1991), 15–47.

16 The commission is named after its two presidents, Gérard Bouchard, sociologist at the University of Quebec at Chicoutimi, and Charles Taylor, philosopher at McGill University, both well known public intellectuals in Quebec.

17 Quebeckers attach great importance to the United Nations covenants of the 1960s on the collective rights of peoples to cultural and political self-determination. See Walter Laqueur, ed., *The Human Rights Reader* (New York: New American Library, 1990), 215–24.

18 In addition to the review *Relations*, the Centre justice et foi publishes the newsletter *Vivre ensemble*, which deals with refugees and recent immigrants in Quebec, denounces the discrimination experienced by them, often on account of their religious practices, and supports campaigns for greater justice and comprehension.

7 Quebec Public Intellectuals in Times of Crisis

ALAIN-G. GAGNON

Quebec intellectuals have taken the high road by stressing the political influence of ideas. This is in contrast to intellectuals in English-speaking Canada (ESC), who have tended to advance public policies incrementally and make adjustments as necessary. As a result, they have taken a more grounded approach to politics.[1] This is due largely to the fact that, in Quebec, the nation's place in the Canadian federation has been seriously debated over the years, whereas, in ESC, intellectuals have played dominant roles in the nation-building process. Quebec intellectuals have found themselves acting more as critics than as experts. However, of late, the roles of intellectuals in Quebec and ESC have been converging, as intellectuals have been contributing more and more to the development of state policies.[2]

This text has three parts. In part 1 ("Entering the Fray"), I will explore a significant shift among intellectuals in Quebec away from working mainly with ideas and ideologies, and towards occupying positions as social scientists. In part 2 ("Concurrent National Projects"), special attention will be given to the role of social science specialists in the emergence of Quebec's own national project. Here I will examine tensions between universalism and specificity (a form of particularism) and illustrate the extent to which Quebec intellectuals have not hesitated to embrace both specificity and universalism in their quest for a better future. Such public intellectuals are best exemplified by Pierre Trudeau, René Lévesque, Claude Ryan, Lucien Bouchard, and their followers. They have all sought to build a better, fairer society. However, in the end, everyone was talking and no one was listening, as the long political and constitutional crisis has shown. In the aftermath of three failed referenda, several constitutional rounds, and changing of the guard in Ottawa and Quebec, public intellectuals have lost a lot of lustre in the eyes of the general public, which is now showing signs of indifference towards promises of a better future. In Part 3 ("Building from Within"), I will focus on intellectuals' weakened roles in the public realm. It is not that they are no longer present or that they have become irrelevant, but that they are invited to contribute to their society more as public servants than as "men of ideas." A case in point is provided by the Bouchard-Taylor commission, during which Gérard Bouchard and Charles Taylor, two of Canada's top intellectuals, with the help of numerous social scientists, suggested ways out of current identity/citizenship crises. As a result, "public intellectuals [are] becoming an endangered species as academic professionalism, corporate- and government-sponsored think tanks, and a culture saturated by mass media rendered the independent social critic a thing of the past."[3] Elsewhere and in Quebec, public intellectuals are now under threat, confirming the dark image that Russell Jacoby had painted two decades ago in *The Last Intellectuals*.[4]

Part 1: Entering the Fray

The Second World War helped to give a central place to public intellectuals in Quebec. Indeed, there was major mobilization of political forces in Quebec that rallied in opposition to Canada's involvement in the conflict. The movement took different forms. For example, one group of intellectuals and political leaders gathered around the League for the Defence of Canada. They argued that Canada should act free from outside pressures, which at that time came from the new motherland, England. An important study by Pierre Hébert and Marie-Pier Luneau reveals that during the Second World War pressure was coming especially from the central government and the church in Quebec. Even Lionel Groulx was kept at bay by the church, and was forced to limit his intrusions into the debate to texts published under pseudonyms.[5] Nevertheless, such pressures did not stop social leaders from entering the political fray, as evidenced by the establishment of the League for the Defence of Canada.

The Second World War had a number of repercussions on political life in Quebec. Quebeckers, like other in the Western world, were exposed to scenes of unprecedented cruelty, due to Nazism, as well as to new narratives of freedom. Notions of decency and justice were taking hold in the province; Quebec was entering the modern era. Ideas circulating in the Western world were less and less a threat to French Canada, as it was entering a phase of significant catching-up in culture, society, economics, and politics. In the cultural sphere, artists and intellectuals were going into action with a vengeance. A good illustration of this is the publication of *Refus global* in 1948 by a group of young intellectuals and artists who had been gathering around Paul-Émile Borduas. The manifesto focused on the fight against conservative forces and, especially, the counterproductive role of the Catholic clergy, which had dominated Quebec institutions for so long, as illustrated by this excerpt: "We reached beyond Christianity to touch the burning brotherhood of humanity, on which the Church had become a closed door."[6]

Refus global is now considered a turning point in Quebec's history, since it is equated with a time of significant cultural, ideological, and political transformations characterized by an opening up to world influences.[7] Modernity had really taken hold and displaced conservatism as the main frame of reference.

The Asbestos strike was another high point in the fight against conservatism in Quebec and confirmed the central role played by Quebec intellectuals and union leaders in the years that followed.[8] At the same time, labour unions in Quebec had started to distance themselves from their Canadian partners. The Confédération des travailleurs catholiques du Canada (the CTCC) was mounting strong opposition to the Duplessis regime and promoting workers' rights to decent, fair working conditions. This subsequently led to secularization of the union and its change of name to the Centrale des syndicats nationaux (CSN).

Social scientists based at Laval University played a key role in the mobilization, not only by confronting the Duplessis regime and its retrograde policies, but by opposing the social doctrine of the church.

The 1949 Asbestos strike has justly been considered both a "litmus test" of these social changes in Quebec and a catalyst in the emergence of a vast social movement against the old ideology and practice embodied in the Duplessis regime. Social science intellectuals, especially those at Laval University, constituted the ideological vanguard of this social movement. Their development of a counter-ideology was not only a result of a greater positive knowledge of society, but also a part of the struggle for the institutionalization of social sciences in Quebec: both a product and an expression of the transformation of Quebec society.[9]

Challenges to the regime were coming from different sectors of society and took concrete form in various magazines and journals. *Maintenant* and *Liberté* are among the best-known journals that proposed counter-narratives, though *Cité Libre* is the one that is the most famous owing to the later political successes of Pierre Elliott Trudeau, its co-founder, at the federal level. In line with *Refus global*, which turned its back on Quebec's past traditions, *Cité Libre* wanted, according to Georges Vincenthier, "to clean the slate of everything that had been said, of everything that had been done"[10] until then. The *Citélibristes* mainly insisted on universalism as a new modus operandi and challenged any expression of particularism, which they accused of being retrograde and reactionary. Vincenthier argues that while the new world that was envisioned "has the advantage of relegating to oblivion objectives that are too petty, it also has the defect of making individuals abstract by forcing them to reject any specific features that tie them to the corner of the Earth where they were born and away from which they cannot tear themselves without destroying their emotional and even their cultural balance."[11]

The long road travelled by Quebec intellectuals helped give them a feeling of membership in their social group. They gradually acquired legitimacy and their community began looking to them for leadership as they gave their support to a modernist ideology. Intellectuals replaced the clergy in most domains. However, as intellectuals became more and more socially relevant and took the lead in the social sciences revolution in Quebec, they institutionalized various fields of study, including economics, industrial relations, political science, sociology, and management. They became essential to the launch of the Quiet Revolution[12] and to elaboration of public policies in tune with the modern world. The next section will focus on their role as political and social agents in the construction of a national program that rapidly gained legitimacy in Quebec while challenging the authority and political leadership of the central government.

Part 2: Concurrent National Programs

In the 1960s, Quebec gained newfound confidence. This led to implementation of a series of measures that amounted to nothing less than a national program rallying the support of a large number of political, social, and economic stakeholders. There were two general trends prevailing at the time. The first rallied intellectuals around the idea that the best way to secure Quebec's place in Canada was for Quebec City to recover as many powers as possible from Ottawa. This would improve accountability, economic performance, and efficiency. Competing with this trend was the idea promoted by federalists that in order to improve Quebec's situation in the Canadian federation, Quebeckers ought to play a more significant role in Ottawa. The latter group promoted a mononational vision of the country. Two Quebec intellectuals galvanized Quebeckers' sentiments around those two trends: Pierre Trudeau and René Lévesque.[13] These two political leaders were both humanists and nationalists; the key difference between the two men had to do with whether the main playing field should be Quebec or Canada.

In the previous section, we saw the extent to which Quebec social scientists dominated their society and challenged traditions to provide their community with new horizons. The 1960s brought some important changes as social scientists saw significant benefits to be gained by playing major roles in the province itself. Also, "in order to consolidate the gains in professional and social status they had made, and to support their claims on public resources, Quebec social scientists had to establish alliances with other social groups which sought an increase in statist activities within Quebec society."[14] This strategy proved very successful and led to the creation of a significant number of positions in universities, research institutes, labour organizations, the public service, as well as private firms. As their visibility grew, so did their social and political relevance and their prestige.[15] To quote Mildred Schwartz, who has explored the field of Canadian politics at length:

> The events in Quebec led to closer ties between researchers and intellectuals than in English-speaking Canada. The reason for this is, at least partly, because French-speakers define themselves by their language and culture. In other words, no matter what his or her role is in society, the general identity features of French-speakers remain the same ... In Quebec, the strength of a single theme that goes beyond all others not only ensures that it will be easier to establish relations between the roles of researchers and intellectuals, but also that respect for intellectuals will increase. In contrast, English-speaking intellectuals are considered to be outside of any form of scholarly research, and rarely have clearly defined political roles. This results partly from the lack of a theme that encompasses all the others, and that can capture the attention of researchers, politicians and the public concerned.[16]

Quebec's public intellectuals have been leaders in many areas, but since the 1960s they have played major structuring roles at the state level and have contributed to making Quebec's claims both audible and credible in the Canadian federation. This has mainly been through depiction of Quebec as a global society, through use of state institutions to provide French speakers with jobs that had been until then generally closed to them, and gradually, as we will see in part 3, through the notion of *interculturalism* (in contrast with multiculturalism) as an ideal to be reached by all residents of Quebec.

Discussing this period, Georges Vincenthier makes the point that "we know that cultural freedom can be acquired only through the economic freedom that is the source of political freedom. This is why political commitment and action are not accidents but the logical, carefully thought-out consequences of a desire to experience one's cultural belonging with dignity and pride. Politics thus becomes the art of making our dreams into reality."[17] Rather than merely defending past or earlier traditions, as did conservative spokespersons at the time, most upcoming public intellectuals were inclined to open new vistas and to consider new strategies to improve the living conditions of members of their society. Public intellectuals became agents for social change and collective political emancipation. "By carving out for themselves a particular and exclusive object-domain to study, Quebec's social scientists were able to achieve a degree of professional and intellectual independence from both the international and Canadian scientific communities."[18] This helped to give Quebec's public intellectuals a stronger base in society and, concomitantly, greater social prestige.

With government departments and agencies developing in Quebec at an unprecedented rate, social scientists had no problem whatsoever getting jobs during the Quiet Revolution and the ensuing years. This created a large contingent of public servants that, in turn, helped to raise the level of confidence among citizens in their community and their "own" state. In many ways, Quebec was finally catching up with English-speaking Canada, which had succeeded in putting in place its own "government generation in earlier decades."[19]

From the early 1960s to the late 1970s, public intellectuals in Quebec gained significant momentum since a lot had to be achieved. They were involved in government deployment, constitutional discussions, party politics, labour organizations, social movements of various types, business organizations, universities, and so on. Everything had to be done. Following the defeat of the 1980 referendum, intellectuals tended to keep their distance from public life, and were increasingly satisfied with the idea of specializing in specific areas, such as teaching, publishing, communications, advising, and the like. They were intervening in specific domains as specialists and less and less as "political actors."[20] With this social withdrawal, what roles can we imagine public intellectuals playing today? This will be the focus of the last section.

Part 3: Building from Within

Sociologist Andrée Fortin reminds us that "one of the (logically and chronologically) first tasks of intellectuals is to ensure that there is a shared culture. They cannot exist without it, but they help to shape it."[21] Public intellectuals have done a lot towards constructing Quebec's shared global culture though political mobilization, songs, novels, social events, general opposition to military interventions abroad, defence of freedoms of speech and association, support for social rehabilitation rather than coercion, and so on. Public intellectuals and the general citizenry have come together on these fronts, thus reducing the long-standing distance between "highbrows" and citizens per se.

However, the functions of public intellectuals have changed greatly over the last decades in Quebec. Today, it is difficult to find intellectuals whose roles as social critics dominate their lives. Commitment has taken different forms. It seems that, over the years, public intellectuals have traded their roles as critics for those of experts. This transformation is somewhat troubling when we consider Quebec's uncertain future as a nation in the Canadian federation. While Quebeckers may have shared a common culture over the last decades, it remains that their culture is now frequently challenged in a world characterized by higher levels of international migration, faster circulation of ideas, and fractioning of the public sphere.

Mona-Josée Gagnon complains that "intellectuals have been instrumentalized, very often reduced to performing scholarly work."[22] Their roles have evolved from essentially making ideological contributions to providing support as experts.[23] She points out that "universities have 'swallowed' protest, and Marxism has become a 'field of study' that can lead to an international career."[24] In short, public intellectuals are less involved in defining their society and more and more active in concretizing pre-assigned roles.

There are exceptions to this general trend. Our colleague Guy Laforest from Laval University frequently alludes to a Meech Lake generation[25] of Quebec intellectuals. Those public intellectuals, like their predecessors, have been commenting on constitutional politics, assessing tensions between Quebec and Ottawa, debating the future of Quebec as a nation, discussing the social question, and so on. Members of that generation have tended to stay away from electoral politics, feeling that they should concentrate on nourishing public debate and evaluating the repercussions of public policies on building a sense of community among all residents of Quebec.

Some years back, Fernand Dumont aptly remarked that we are now faced with a concrete knowledge industry that is structured around a series of institutions. The problem, according to Dumont, lies in institutionalization of knowledge: "Institutionalization, in other words, widespread management, sews back together the scattered patches of knowledge. Fields and experts have diversified; a division of labour and a hierarchy of powers have developed."[26] As a result, public intellectuals are less and less interested in getting involved in defining (and mobilizing) their society and more and more concerned with managing social tensions. This has contributed to a certain disaffection that can be measured by the decline in political participation and a weaker sense of belonging to the broader community. Dumont stresses that "the political community is thus less a given, like state apparatus, than a foundation that must always be rebuilt based on a human legacy and with a view to pursuing collective ideals."[27]

The Consultation Commission on Accommodation Practices Related to Cultural Differences (CCAPRCD), also known as the Bouchard-Taylor commission, held hearings in 2007 and 2008, and is a valuable illustration of this point. The commission was led by two highly respected intellectuals: Charles Taylor, whose contributions in philosophy are world-renowned, and Gérard Bouchard, whose reputation in the history of genealogy and sociology is solidly established. While, in the past, intellectuals felt compelled to intervene and got involved directly in the political process, what happened with the CCAPRCD suggests that intellectuals' roles have undergone a significant transformation. Rather than being at the heart of a process of redefining society as social critics, intellectuals have become social engineers and are subordinate to state power. When there is a crisis, intellectuals are invited to help the state manage political and social tensions more efficiently.

Is this simply an indication of a tendency or, more profoundly, a revelation of the emergence of a trend? It would be misleading to argue that all of Quebec's public intellectuals have simply renounced their roles as "critics." The case of Gérard Bouchard remains highly relevant here since, a year after the commission had completed its work, he gave an interview in which he openly criticized the Charest government for its inaction.[28] Bouchard went on to accuse the government of having contributed to a "radicalization of public opinion" with respect to immigration policy in Quebec.

Conclusion

It is difficult to determine whether the role of public intellectuals as critics in Quebec has diminished and whether they are keeping more to themselves. Intense competition is taking place in the circulation of ideas, and intellectuals, like other social stakeholders, need to have public roles if they want their ideas to be heard by citizens. There are many reasons for disinterest in the work of public intellectuals: repeated failures of the nationalist leitmotiv, absence of significant alternative political projects that would lift people's spirits, commandeering of their work by politicians (e.g., the Bouchard-Taylor commission), as well as the "comfort and indifference" in which they find themselves.

Although the role of public intellectuals appears to have diminished since the failure of the first referendum in 1980, "highbrows" are still taking action in various domains, albeit not with the same fervour. This can be explained in part by the fact that, contrary to the time of the Quiet Revolution, the projects under consideration do not have the same magnitude. Public intellectuals in Quebec had their glory days during construction of the Quebec state, but with the advent of a stronger private sector, their roles have shrunk.

Nevertheless, what can explain the fact that Quebec's public intellectuals remain influential in their own society, more so than is the case for intellectuals in most other Western democracies? The changing position that Quebec occupies within the Canadian federation puts its public intellectuals at the centre of the equation. Their main role has shifted from acting as critics to acting as experts, but they still play active roles as definers of their own society. As a result, they tend to get involved at a level of "high politics." In contrast, English-speaking intellectuals in Canada tend to lean towards "low politics," since they focus their attention on maintenance of the status quo.[29] In short, public intellectuals in Quebec enlightened debates about Quebec's future in Canada and contributed to augment and deepen public space.

NOTES

1 I wish to thank Mary Baker, who has proofread this text and translated all quotations from French into English. The research assistance of Xavier Dionne, graduate student in the Department of Political Science at the Université du Québec à Montréal is also acknowledged.

2 See Stephen Brooks and Alain-G. Gagnon, eds, *The Political Influence of Ideas, Policy Communities and the Social Sciences* (Westport, CT: Praeger, 1994) for a development of this theme.

3 Neil McLaughlin, "Global Public Intellectuals, Autonomy and Culture: Reflections Inspired by the Death of Edward Said," in Petra Rethmann, Imre Szeman, and William D. Coleman, eds, *Cultural Autonomy: Frictions and Connections* (Montreal: McGill-Queen's University Press, 2010), 113.

4 Russell Jacoby, *The Last Intellectuals: American Culture in the Age of Academe* (New York: Basic Books, 1987).

5 Pierre Hébert and Marie-Pier Luneau, "L'écrivain circonscrit: La Seconde Guerre mondiale, la censure et les positions de trois écrivains québécois," in Manon Brunet and Pierre Lanthier, eds, *L'inscription sociale de l'intellectuel* (Quebec: Les Presses de l'Université Laval, 2000), 234–40.

6 An English version of *Refus global* can be found online at http://www.dantaylor.com/pages/refusglobal.html.

7 See the excellent work of Claude Gauvreau, *The Catholic Origins of Quebec's Quiet Revolution, 1931–1970* (Montreal: McGill-Queen's University Press, 2005). In addition, one might refer to Léon Dion, *Québec 1945–2000: Les intellectuels et le temps de Duplessis* (Quebec: Les Presses de l'Université Laval, 1993).

8 Pierre Elliott Trudeau, ed., *The Asbestos Strike*, trans. James Boake (Toronto: James Lewis & Samuel, 1974); Mona-Josée Gagnon, "Les intellectuels critiques et le mouvement ouvrier au Québec: Fractures et destin parallèle," *Cahiers de recherche sociologique* 34 (2000), 15–16.

9 Stephen Brooks and Alain-G. Gagnon, *Social Scientists and Politics in Canada: Between Clerisy and Vanguard* (Montreal: McGill-Queen's University Press, 1988), 24.

10 Georges Vincenthier, *Une idéologie québécoise: De Louis-Joseph Papineau à Pierre Vallières* (La Salle, QC: Éditions Hurtubise, 1979), 87; our translation.

11 Ibid., 93; our translation.

12 For an in-depth account of the Quiet Revolution, see Alain-G. Gagnon and Mary Beth Montcalm, *Quebec: Beyond the Quiet Revolution* (Scarborough, ON: Nelson Canada, 1990).

13 For a penetrating account on these two political leaders, see Gérard Bergeron, *Notre miroir à deux faces: Trudeau-Lévesque* (Montreal, Quebec: Amérique, 1985).

14 Brooks and Gagnon, *Social Scientists and Politics in Canada*, 50.

15 Alain-G. Gagnon, "The Influence of Social Scientists on Public Policy," in Stephen Brooks and Alain-G. Gagnon, *Social Scientists, Policy and the State* (Westport, CT: Praeger, 1990), 1–18.

16 Mildred A. Schwartz, "Scientifiques et intellectuels au Canada francophone et au Canada anglophone," in Raymond Hudon and Réjean Pelletier, eds, *L'engagement intellectuel: Mélanges en l'honneur de Léon Dion* (Sainte-Foy: Les Presses de l'Université Laval, 1991), 408; our translation.

17 Vincenthier, *Une idéologie québécoise*, 95; our translation.

18 Brooks and Gagnon, *Social Scientists and Politics in Canada*, 52.

19 Doug Owram, *The Government Generation: Canadian Intellectuals and the State 1900–1945* (Toronto: University of Toronto Press, 1986).

20 For a good discussion of this trend, see Marc Henry Soulet, *Le silence des intellectuels: Radioscopie de l'intellectuel québécois* (Montreal: Éditions Saint-Martin, 1987).

21 Andrée Fortin, "Lieux communs, espace public et postmodernité," in Manon Brunet and Pierre Lanthier, eds, *L'inscription sociale de l'intellectuel* (Quebec: Les Presses de l'Université Laval, 2000), 248; our translation.

22 Mona-Josée Gagnon, "Les intellectuels critiques et le mouvement ouvrier: Fractures et destin parallèle," *Cahiers de recherche sociologique* 34 (2000), 19; our translation.

23 Ibid., 20.

24 Ibid., 34; our translation.

25 Guy Laforest, "Dix ans après l'échec de l'accord du lac Meech: Des lumières catalanes pour le Québec," in *Pour la liberté d'une société distincte: Parcours d'un intellectuel engagé* (Quebec: Les Presses de l'Université Laval, 2004), 246–7.

26 Fernand Dumont, "L'intellectuel et le citoyen," in *Raisons communes* (Montreal: Boréal, 1997 [1995]), 242.

27 Ibid., 247.

28 See Agnès Gruda, "Le Québec sur une pente dangereuse," *La Presse*, 31 Oct. 2009.

29 My colleague Dominique Leydet made a similar point in a paper entitled "Réformer la constitution d'une fédération multinationale," which she delivered at a colloquium organized by the Centre de recherche interdisciplinaire sur la diversité et la démocratie (CRIDAQ) on 29 September 2009 at l'Université du Québec à Montréal.

8 Navigating Gendered Spaces: Women as Public Intellectuals

SYLVIA BASHEVKIN*

During recent decades, political theorists have highlighted a powerful dichotomy dating from classical Greek times between men's long-standing dominance of the public, political realm and women's traditional assignment to the private, apolitical one. While scholars have carefully probed the historical and normative sources of this public/private split, few have examined the impact of separate spheres thinking – and, in particular, the consequences such a division held for women as public intellectuals.[1] Nor has much attention been paid to the effects of changes dating from the late 1960s and following that directly challenged this construction, including "the personal is political" claims advanced by second-wave feminism as well as the breakdown of individual privacy boundaries for both men and women, resulting from around-the-clock electronic communications.

The relationship between older public/private dichotomies and women's ability to claim space as public intellectuals is intriguing on a number of levels. First, intellectuals are defined in formal terms as individuals who possess superior rational, analytic, and other cerebral attributes that distinguish them from, for example, people whose talents rest in physical strength or charismatic personality. What stands out for our purposes is the following: the ability to excel at mental reasoning has been conventionally viewed as a male attribute, contrasting with what are often portrayed as relative female advantages in the emotive and, to some degree, fine-motor-skill domains. The fact that only men could hold the status of full citizens in the ancient polis, while women were assigned the rank of

---

*I am grateful to Lama Mourad for her research assistance, and to Lama Mourad and Veronica Strong-Boag for their comments on an earlier version.

partial, impaired, or incomplete citizens through the Enlightenment era, reveals the extent to which both the adjective *public* and noun *intellectual* remained identifiably masculine categories for much of Western history.[2]

Second, and related directly to this first point, is the question of when women, whether individually or collectively, managed to make their voices heard as public intellectuals. Did their interventions build on presumed female talents in the domains of feeling and human sensitivity? How effectively could early feminist intellectuals engage in civic debate, given that binary male/female, public/private distinctions conflicted with women's rights to a full and meaningful democratic citizenship?

The relationship between second-wave feminist mobilization and women's ability to operate as public intellectuals is equally fascinating. Movement arguments that power structures in families were as political as, for example, the redistributive dimension of government tax policy directly challenged prevailing public/private conceptions. By placing such issues as child care, abortion, violence against women, and family law reform on the public agenda, activists expanded the scope of policy debates, but did not necessarily overturn assumptions that men would remain the legitimate, credible experts of record on older, seemingly more significant issues. Moreover, just as women began to obtain a greater proportion of faculty and academic leadership positions in Canadian universities, those same institutions confronted crucial challenges (detailed by other authors in this book) that undermined both their critical, thinking-based edge and the virtual monopoly they had long exercised over the creation and dissemination of knowledge.

This chapter explores the intellectual contributions of Canadian women. Following from Barbara Misztal's (2007) work, it argues that the creativity and personal courage of women who insisted they too could be purveyors of public wisdom strengthened the fabric of Canadian democracy.[3] We show how early feminist intellectuals, facing stereotypic views that confined women's expertise to a bounded private realm, often employed those same stereotypes as the basis for claiming greater rights in the public domain.

Over time, the shadow cast by a public/private split not only constrained the discursive space in which a small number of female public intellectuals could operate, since that terrain was narrower than the turf available to males, but also obscured women's contributions. When women were accepted or acknowledged as intellectuals, it was often with respect to such matters as spirituality, peace, ethics, and women's rights, leaving a far larger group of male intellectuals to dominate most everything else – including pivotal areas of politics and the economy. Women's visibility as public intellectuals, as a result, tended to ebb and flow with the fortunes of feminist movements, such that quiescent times (including the present) tend not to be promising in terms of breaking out of this pattern.

Whether the explosion of websites, blogs, Twitter, and Facebook will ultimately advance women as public intellectuals remains an open question. Given that burdens of family and household responsibility typically create time pressures which limit women's ability to engage in leisure activities – including social media – it is difficult to argue that shifts in the means by which citizens share ideas and information with each other will necessarily overturn older gender-segregating patterns. Moreover, the visual dimension of Facebook-type communication arguably commodifies physical appearance beyond the levels already reached via television and Internet news, meaning women who seek to raise their profiles via that medium risk being trivialized and dissected along the lines of body image, hair, clothing, and so on – which in turn overshadows whatever substantive content they may bring to civic discussion.

One important caveat to bear in mind: the discussion that follows of specific cases, both Canadian and international, is necessarily brief and selective, consciously designed to provoke public debate, inspire private reflection, and stimulate future research. It makes no pretence to offer an exhaustive account of all women intellectuals, either on the world or Canadian stages, whether in historical or contemporary terms.

Locating Our Subject

Were women central to Canada's intellectual development? A.B. McKillop's entry under "intellectual history" in the second edition of the *Canadian Encyclopedia*, which comprises roughly five full columns of type spread over nearly two full pages, points towards a negative response to this question. Two names he mentions lack *Encyclopedia* entries of their own: Nadia Eid, cited with reference to Quebec liberalism and ultramontanism of the 1970s and 1980s; and Agnes Maule Machar, an English Canadian social critic of the late nineteenth century.[4] A third name in McKillop's article, University of Saskatchewan history professor Hilda Neatby, earned a brief biographical entry of her own summarizing her membership in the Massey commission as well as controversial arguments she proposed in favour of back-to-basics education at both the primary and secondary levels.[5]

The very minimal presence of women intellectuals in a Canadian reference text dating from the late 1980s is more than simply a historic artefact. Viewers of contemporary public affairs programing can be expected to reach conclusions parallel to those of readers who peruse McKillop's article, since they commonly witness one woman (sometimes this author) participating in a television panel in which every other expert as well as the moderator is a man. In the United States, the School of Public Affairs at American University launched a research project designed to document women's representation or, more accurately, underrepresentation in the domain of public affairs commentary. Known as the Sunday Morning Monitor, this study systematically tracked the round table participants who play an "important and influential role ... in establishing political discourse."[6] Longitudinal data gathered every week from top-rated NBC, CBS, ABC, CNN, and Fox news programs show very few cases in which women and men guests were equal in number, alongside a dominant pattern whereby one or zero women analysts appeared on major shows.

Do women lack the necessary knowledge, insight, and training to participate more extensively as public intellectuals? It is worth juxtaposing the paucity of both female names in McKillop's encyclopedia entry, and of women's voices in media discussions of current affairs, with enrolment patterns in post-secondary institutions. From holding a minority of places in first-degree programs as recently as 1987, women at present constitute about 60 per cent of undergraduate students in most Canadian universities.[7] They are also at or, in some instances, above numerical parity in medicine, law, business, and other second-entry professional degree programs, and growing towards that level in fields such as engineering. Yet the logical flow-through one might expect from educational attainment towards intellectual leadership has hardly happened. Rather than considering ways to redress this phenomenon, however, recent public policy debates have fixated on the reverse, namely, understanding how and redressing why young men are "falling behind" their more educated women peers.[8]

Suffrage-Era Notables

Given that women intellectuals in Canada obtained little recognition in a standard reference text, it is worth imagining the broad lines of an alternative account that would acknowledge and contextualize their contributions. Writing in 2007, British sociologist Barbara Misztal concluded that Nobel Peace Prize laureates drew much of their authority as public intellectuals from two main characteristics: creativity and civil courage. According to her account, these personal attributes not only raised the profile of individuals who went on to win the prize, but also directly enriched the democratic societies in which laureates lived.[9] Misztal thus offered a useful strategy for understanding the subject of this chapter, by encouraging us to ask which women thinkers evidenced the attributes of creativity and courage, with respect to what issues and when – regardless of whether their contributions were interpreted as the interventions of public intellectuals.

Arguably the first collective appearance of Canadian women as public policy advocates, experts, and activists occurred in the late nineteenth and early twentieth centuries with the rise of Progressivism and, in particular, suffragism. Among the core ideas that informed early feminist mobilization of this period was the view that access to the professions, notably medicine, and to basic political rights, notably the franchise, should be extended to women. It is worth noting that creative imagination played an important role in the founding of Canada's first suffrage organization, established in 1877 and known as the Toronto Women's Literary Society. Clearly, that name distracted critics from the main purpose of the group; in addition, it reminds those trying to recover the history of public intellectuals that women's book clubs of the late nineteenth century served as fertile breeding grounds for civic engagement, even though they were generally viewed as part of a private, apolitical realm.[10]

In Canada, suffragist demands generally emerged from two sets of arguments, one grounded in forthright political justice claims and one in a more moderate, reformist perspective known as maternal or social feminism.[11] A vocal proponent of the former view, Flora MacDonald Denison, endorsed across-the-board equality in her columns that appeared between 1909 and 1913 in the Toronto *Sunday World*. Denison's writings also promoted radical ideas concerning birth control, divorce, and a stream of mystical spiritualism that drew inspiration from the poetry of Walt Whitman. Her legacy includes a book detailing the psychic powers of her sister Mary Melville, as well as a Whitmanesque literary magazine she edited, titled *The Sunset of Bon Echo*.[12]

By way of contrast, the more influential stream of early feminism, championed by activists including Nellie McClung, justified its relatively moderate claims using the same separate spheres perspective that retained a powerful hold on Canadian understandings of gender relations. Social feminism advanced a maternalist argument for the right to vote and contest public office. McClung's many speeches, essays, novels, and theatrical scripts thus portrayed women as pivotal to the larger process of social reform; extending the suffrage was integral to urban improvement, temperance, and civic education activities (all linked to Protestant social gospel efforts of that period) because women would clean up the polity in the same no-nonsense way they cleaned up their homes and cared for their families. In fact, McClung merged maternal feminism with a direct critique of what she portrayed as the sordid, grubby world of party politics:

> If politics are corrupt, it is all the more reason that a new element should be introduced. Women will I believe supply that new element, that purifying influence. Men and women were intended to work together, and will work more ideally together, than apart, and just as the mother's influence as well as the father's is needed in the bringing up of children and in the affairs of the home, – so are they needed in the larger home, – the state.[13]

Among McClung's most courageous acts was the writing and performance in 1914 of a satire entitled "The Women's Parliament," in which she played a woman premier who, after hearing men's pleas for the franchise, denies them the right to vote. The script indirectly chastised Manitoba premier Rodmond Roblin for his anti-suffrage views. In the next provincial elections, Roblin's party lost power and, in early 1916, Manitoba became the first jurisdiction in Canada to grant women the rights to vote and hold public office.

War, Peace, and Women's Voices

Opposition to war figured prominently in early feminist activism in both Quebec and English Canada, and served as a crucial bridge between suffragism and second-wave mobilization. Starting in many cases from an essentialist assertion that females were by nature more peace-loving and less conflictual than males, proponents of this outlook believed a core maternal instinct to protect children meant women had both a responsibility and an innate ability to stop war. During the period of the First World War, for instance, when her own son served in the military, Flora Denison wrote in a newspaper article that "the male through centuries and centuries has been combative, whereas women's thoughts and actions have always been constructive."[14]

The belief that women and peace were innately linked is contestable on multiple levels. As sociologist Lynn McDonald points out in her social theory anthology, not all women are mothers, not all females (or, for that matter, mothers) in human history have pursued peaceful means towards conflict resolution, and not all Canadian feminists continued to defend their pacifist beliefs once public pressure to support wars intensified.[15] Yet a strong current of peace-oriented ideas directly underpinned public interventions by female intellectuals in Canada for much of the past century. Echoing Nobel Peace Prize–winner Alva Myrdal's emphasis on foundational ties among human and especially women's rights, international cooperation, and nuclear disarmament, many feminist leaders in Canada championed the establishment of the League of Nations and its successor organization, the United Nations, and remained committed to a view that international peace and justice offered the best hope for improving women's lives around the world.[16]

Reflecting this outlook, Nellie McClung travelled to Geneva in 1938 as the only woman member of Canada's League of Nations delegation. Prominent Quebec suffragist and journalist Thérèse Casgrain founded that province's branch of Voice of Women (VOW), a peace group established in 1960 with the aim of promoting nuclear disarmament and world peace. In English Canada, Muriel Duckworth and Ursula Franklin, both Quakers, presented compelling VOW statements to the House of Commons and Senate during the Vietnam War years; they urged greater Canadian independence from US foreign policy as well as Canadian withdrawal from NATO.[17] VOW went on to become a founding group within the National Action Committee on the Status of Women, Canada's second-wave feminist umbrella organization established in 1972.

Franklin, a retired metallurgist and philosopher of technology based at the University of Toronto, explained her understanding of Voice of Women's approach as follows: "To me, the struggle for women's rights and the opposition to militarism in all its forms are two sides of the same coin."[18] She contributed pioneering scientific research during the 1960s that showed how atmospheric testing of nuclear weapons led to an accumulation of radioactive substances in children's teeth, and consistently defended the view that women and children paid a heavy price for war – particularly when technological advances meant high-cost planning for the next conflict became a constant budget burden for governments. In her public commentaries, Franklin juxtaposed the bright promise of peace and social justice with the dark, looming presence of war, violence, and human fear.

Intellectuals, Activism, and the Contemporary Academy

In many respects, Franklin's ideas directly mirrored those of early Canadian feminism. Much like suffragists who drew inspiration from the social gospel message, Franklin viewed poor housing, lack of economic opportunity, and other forms of social disadvantage as matters requiring public policy attention not only because they impoverished the lives of individuals, but also because they diminished Canadian society generally. Franklin extended her critique further with a contemporary twist, arguing that the character of technological change in advanced capitalism assigned a commercial value to all transactions, including those in which people took care of each other. She argued that private sector models that maximized profit from each step of an increasingly hierarchical, fragmented, and compliance-based work process had spread far beyond the realm of commerce and industry.

Franklin also reflected at length on the dangers of militarism and the "anti-people" design of technological systems that required citizens to compete against each other in order to exploit the earth's resources.[19] She contrasted this set of structures with an ennobling approach based on the model of the family household. In her view, artisanal methods permitting workers to engage with and control their product from start to finish were preferable to production lines for obvious reasons – in particular, they afforded a level of human autonomy, personal fulfilment, and ecological sensitivity parallel to that which middle-class women had historically enjoyed in their homes, raising their children.

Above all, Franklin challenged older assumptions that equal educational opportunities and political rights for women constituted the end point of collective struggle. Rather, her powerful arguments about the profit-based privatization of knowledge in universities suggested utopia was far more complicated than it might have appeared one hundred years earlier. More specifically, as Franklin argued in a compelling speech published in 2000, academic institutions needed to defend a conception of knowledge that was grounded in the appreciation of pure research undertaken for its own sake and for the public good. The growing power of private investors, industries, and profit-oriented agencies within universities directly imperilled long-standing understandings of what constituted knowledge and meant, implicitly, that women were gaining a toehold in academic organizations just as those organizations were losing their edge as centres of intellectual enquiry.[20]

   Consistent with Franklin's argument, one of the most influential and popular public intellectual voices on campuses in Canada and around the world during the past decade was that of Naomi Klein, an independent writer and leading activist in anti-globalization protest. Beginning with the publication of *No Logo* in 2000 through her appearance at a G20 event in Toronto in summer 2010 organized by the Council of Canadians, Klein attracted millions to her books, articles, and website. As a left-of-centre intellectual based outside the academy, she advanced a powerful claim that by the early twenty-first century, corporate capitalism was not just exploiting workers and consumers around the world, but also effectively controlling the governments and supra-national institutions that in earlier periods had espoused a broader conception of the public interest.

   Klein was directly influenced by both second-wave feminism and the backlash against it. As an undergraduate at the University of Toronto, she recalled the 1989 massacre of fourteen engineering students at l'École polytechnique in Montreal as a turning point in her life, and acknowledged the impact of that event and the stroke her mother (second-wave feminist filmmaker Bonnie Sherr Klein) suffered on her own development.[21] The core thesis of *No Logo* concerned the corporate branding of individual clothing, food, and drink choices, thus resonating directly with women's movement arguments of the late 1960s and following that "the personal is political."

   Irshad Manji is a third contemporary intellectual force whose trajectory similarly draws on feminist inspiration but whose major focus has been the need for critical rethinking of Islam and, in particular, women's rights within that faith. Born in Uganda, raised in Vancouver, and based since 2008 at New York University, Manji burst onto the Canadian public scene with the 2003 publication of *The Trouble with Islam*, a provocative volume that not only denounced the subordination of women in traditional Islamic education, theology, and community life, but also defended Jewish claims to the land of Israel. The fact that Manji staked her claims as a lesbian, feminist, Muslim woman reflected the extent to which multiple and intersecting identities characterize so many Canadians; in addition, it demonstrated how reconciling those varied identities with the equality rights that feminists had fought to secure in Canada is not always a simple, straightforward task.

   It would be misleading to draw overly optimistic conclusions from the emergence of Franklin, Klein, and Manji as major, albeit quite distinct, contemporary thinkers. While each has demonstrated significant qualities of courage and creativity, which Misztal identifies as central to effective public intellectuals, their prominence remains all the more notable because it has not extended to dozens of other women – at a time when female students from diverse ethno-cultural and immigration backgrounds are numerically eclipsing males in universities across the country, and when women faculty members have been moving upward through professorial and academic leadership ranks.

In her review of developments in Australia, education researcher Jill Blackmore posed what is arguably the central question in this area: if feminist intellectuals seek to challenge (and ultimately change) our understandings of the world, then can they act with any degree of influence in universities that face sustained corporate and privatization pressures?[22] Blackmore's dilemma is all the more pressing given the gradual decline of explicitly gendered social movement activism in Canada, where the high profile attached to the word "women" declined precipitously following the end of constitutional talks surrounding the 1982 Canadian Charter of Rights and Freedoms, the Meech Lake Accord, and, finally, the Charlottetown Accord referendum of 1992. In fact, the National Action Committee on the Status of Women as the umbrella voice of Canadian feminism virtually disappeared from public radar screens after that point, consumed from within by battles over race, sexuality, class, and left/right politics, and from without by the arrival of more conservative times.[23]

Whether the emergence of counter-institutions to universities has provided more opportunities for women intellectuals remains unclear. Websites, blogs, Twitter, and Facebook have demonstrably multiplied the channels available to individuals who want to communicate their ideas, but the scope and number of those streams has reduced the possibility that any new entrant could exert much influence. On one level, web-based writers have operated within an increasingly fragmented and, in some respects, saturated electronic environment in which older notions of broadcasting have been replaced by narrow-band statements to people who likely shared the same basic point of view before they logged on. What is considered common knowledge to one "converted" web community appears in some cases to be unknown, ignored, or defined as fiction by competing ones, meaning the core concept of public wisdom no longer extends beyond a defined boundary of "believers."

Second, existing gender differences in access to leisure time did not disappear with the rise of web-based communication. Time-study research by Statistics Canada has shown that even as levels of formal education and occupational attainment have risen within the population, women have continued to enjoy significantly less free time across their lifespans than men. This pattern is primarily due to the fact that females spend more of their waking hours than males on unpaid work: on average, women assume responsibility for more complex tasks involving other people, notably caring for members of their extended families, than men, which has reduced the availability of leisure hours.[24] It is hard to see how the same constraints that limited the ability of women to engage in older forms of public commentary by writing letters to newspaper editors, for instance, would not affect their ability to participate in web-based discussions of current affairs.

The visual dimension of contemporary communications flows arguably has presented the greatest opportunity as well as the greatest risk for women intellectuals. Those seeking to raise their profiles via newer visual media risk being trivialized and dissected along the lines of body image, hair, clothing, and so on – which in turn threatens to overshadow whatever substantive content they might bring to civic discussion. Yet an optimist can examine the case of Naomi Klein and extract from it a promising example – an intelligent woman dissected her own consumer shopping habits, wrote an international bestseller based on her knowledge and experiences, and continued for at least a decade afterwards to carefully steward her own web presence in a way that showcased authoritative political and economic ideas ahead of personal appearance.

The contributions of Franklin, Klein, and Manji remind us of the extraordinary insight into public as well as traditionally private matters that contemporary intellectuals can provide. Hopefully, their examples will inspire others to step forward and claim voice, thus shedding further critical light on our times.

NOTES

1 See, for example, Jean Bethke Elshtain, *Public Man, Private Woman: Women in Social and Political Thought* (Princeton: Princeton University Press, 1981); and Virginia Held, "Feminist Transformations of Moral Theory," in Charles K. Wilber, ed., *Economics, Ethics, and Public Policy* (Lanham, MD: Rowman and Littlefield, 1998), 151–73.
2 See Ruth Lister, *Citizenship: Feminist Perspectives*, 2nd ed. (New York: New York University Press, 2003).

3 Barbara Misztal, *Intellectuals and the Public Good: Creativity and Civil Courage* (Cambridge: Cambridge University Press, 2007).
4 A.B. McKillop, "Intellectual History," in *The Canadian Encyclopedia*, 2nd ed. (Edmonton: Hurtig, 1988), vol. 2, 1073–5.
5 Michael Hayden, "Hilda Marion Neatby," ibid., vol. 3, 1464.
6 See http://www.american.edu/spa/wpi/sunday-morning-monitor.cfm; consulted 21 July 2010.
7 Lesley Andres and Maria Adamuti-Trache, "You've Come a Long Way, Baby? Persistent Gender Inequality in University Enrolment and Completion in Canada, 1979–2004," *Canadian Public Policy* 33, no. 1 (March 2007), 95.
8 This concern was reflected, for example, in debates in Toronto over boys-only public schools. See http://www.theglobeandmail.com/life/family-and-relationships/all-boys-schools-foster-achievement-culture/article1332995/.
9 See Misztal, *Intellectuals and the Public Good*.
10 See Heather Murray, *Come, Bright Improvement!: The Literary Societies of Nineteenth-Century Ontario* (Toronto: University of Toronto Press, 2002).
11 See Carol Lee Bacchi, *Liberation Deferred?: The Ideas of the English-Canadian Suffragists, 1877–1918* (Toronto: University of Toronto Press, 1983).
12 See http://canadianhistory.suite101.com/article.cfm/flora_macdonald_denison.
13 McClung as quoted in Candace Savage, *Our Nell: A Scrapbook Biography of Nellie L. McClung* (Saskatoon: Western Producer Prairie Books, 1979), 83.
14 http://section15.ca/features/people/2003/01/09/flora_denison/; consulted 29 July 2010.
15 See Lynn McDonald, ed., *Women Theorists on Society and Politics* (Waterloo: Wilfrid Laurier University Press, 1998), 260. McDonald cites the cases of Margaret Thatcher as British prime minister during the period of the Falklands conflict, and Agnes Macphail as a Canadian MP who voted for the declaration of war in 1939.
16 See Yvonne Hirdman, *Alva Myrdal: The Passionate Mind*, trans. Linda Schenck (Bloomington: Indiana University Press, 2008).
17 See http://en.wikipedia.org/wiki/Ursula_Franklin.
18 Ursula Franklin, *The Ursula Franklin Reader: Pacifism as a Map* (Toronto: Between the Lines, 2006), 102.
19 Ursula Franklin, *The Real World of Technology*, CBC Massey Lecture series (Toronto: Anansi, 1992), 76.
20 See Ursula Franklin, "What Is at Stake? Universities in Context," in James L. Turk, ed., *The Corporate Campus: Commercialization and the Dangers to Canada's Colleges and Universities* (Toronto: Lorimer, 2000), 17–22.

21 See http://en.wikipedia.org/wiki/Naomi_Klein.

22 See Jill Blackmore, "Tracking the Nomadic Life of the Educational Researcher: What Future for Feminist Public Intellectuals and the Performative University?" *Australian Educational Researcher* 30, no. 3 (December 2003), 16.

23 See Sylvia Bashevkin, *Women on the Defensive: Living through Conservative Times* (Toronto: University of Toronto Press, 1998).

24 See http://www.nwtsrc.com/content/news/statistics/09_who_participates_in_active_leisure.pdf.

PART THREE

On the Front Lines

9 A Political Scientist in Public Affairs

TOM FLANAGAN

Richard Posner defines a public intellectual as

> someone who uses general ideas drawn from history, philosophy, political science, economics, law, literature, ideas that are part of the cultural intellectual tradition of the world, to address contemporary events, usually of a political or ideological flavor, and does so in the popular media, whether in the form of Op Ed pieces, television appearances, signing full-page advertisements, or writing magazine articles or books addressed to a general audience.[1]

I have done most of those things; but more importantly I was nominated by Lorne Gunter in a *National Post* 1995 contest to determine "the most important public intellectual in Canada."[2] That I was badly beaten in the contest by hockey announcer Don Cherry is a good measure of my stature as a public intellectual!

More seriously, a public intellectual draws on his academic discipline while addressing a larger audience about public affairs. I have attempted to do that, partly through appearances in the media, partly through writing books that try to reach a larger audience than the usual academic targets of professors, students, and university libraries. But I have also participated in public life in ways that did not involve directly addressing the public. I have, for example, been an expert witness in litigation, offering historical evidence in cases involving Aboriginal rights and land claims. Such cases usually generate little media coverage, and as a witness you are not speaking to the public but to the judge who has to arbitrate among competing versions of history. I have also spent several years working for political parties, holding organizational positions such as director of research, chief of staff, and national campaign manager. These were confidential activities (though I wrote about them later); but what happens behind the scenes within political parties obviously has an impact on public debate, because parties take the lead in structuring the perception of issues.

This chapter is about participation in public affairs broadly understood, including all four of my ventures: writing books for a broader public than academic specialists, speaking to judges as an expert witness in litigation, organizing the work of political parties, and writing and speaking as a media pundit. Although these four roles are quite different from one another, they exhibit one overarching similarity as compared to the academic life of teaching and research. To state it as simply as possible, public affairs are fundamentally adversarial, while intellectual life is fundamentally authoritative.

University teaching is highly authoritative. The university puts a professor in charge of teaching a course, with the right and responsibility to assign readings, lead discussions, and evaluate performance. You can let students know it's all right to disagree with you, but you are still in charge, and your decision about what grades to award may have a considerable effect upon students' future lives.

Research is less obviously authoritative; indeed, certain adversarial elements are built into the research process. Post-graduate theses are "defended" rather than "approved," which implies an adversarial process rather than an authoritative judgment. Grant applications and publications are submitted to multiple referees, who often disagree among themselves. Journals publish book reviews and literature surveys designed to promote debate about the value of research contributions. In all these respects, research involves a constant clash of views and perspectives.

And yet there is a higher sense in which authority rules in the world of science and scholarship. Through all their disagreements, researchers are united by seeking to discover something true about the universe, a correspondence between theory and fact. Academic disagreements are supposed to be settled by reference to evidence, not by rhetorical appeals to passion or attacks on personal character. Aristotle's *ethos* (character) and *pathos* (emotion) are the very stuff of political debate, but peripheral to scholarly discussion, which is supposed to be about *logos* (reason).[3] Like everyone else, scientists and scholars care about material success, but they strive above all for reputation – recognition for having discovered some truth about the world. Recognition confers authority.

We say that a distinguished researcher "is an authority" in his field, which testifies to our belief that his statements are well grounded in empirical evidence. In contrast, we say that a government official "is in authority," which doesn't imply that he has any particular expertise, only that he wields the power of the state. Science and scholarship harness adversarial processes for reaching authoritative determinations of what is true and false, for discovering validated theories about the natural universe and the human world.

The realm of public affairs, in contrast, is essentially adversarial, at least in a liberal democracy, where social life and political order are considered pragmatic arrangements for living together, not "true" emanations of reason or divine will.[4] Law is what legislatures decide to pass and what the courts say it means. As the American Supreme Court justice Robert Jackson wrote, "We are not final because we are infallible, but we are infallible only because we are final."[5] Public opinion is never univocal. Responsible media outlets strive to represent a range of views by creating panels on radio and TV, commissioning various columns in print, and requiring reporters to consult multiple sources in preparing news stories. The media never expect you to persuade anyone else, just to represent a point of view so that readers and viewers will have options.

The contest of political parties, moreover, is adversarial in a very special way, because the main purpose of participation in democratic politics is not to be right but to build a coalition large enough to get control of the government. Democracy not only recognizes the legitimacy of opposition but builds it into the system. For example, the leader of the opposition in the Parliament of Canada is paid a ministerial salary, gets an official residence and limousine with driver, and is sworn into the Privy Council. It is his duty, and his party's duty, to oppose the government, which often leads to taking implausible positions (how can the government always be wrong?) for the higher good of ensuring that the government's position is tested in public debate.

Moving from academic life into public affairs is a transition that may take many years to understand fully. Rather like Jeremy Bentham sending reform proposals to Catherine the Great,[6] you begin with the naive conviction that, in virtue of years of study and research, you possess special knowledge that only needs to be put into practice in order to improve the quality of public life. If you are lucky, you outgrow that preposterous conceit and realize that participation is public affairs is like acting in a drama whose plot is unknown to anyone. You play your role in the belief that the endless adversarial jousting will discover more beneficial arrangements for living together than any one intelligence could ever design. In my Hayekian view, politics is a process for discovering new modi vivendi, not for implementing abstract paradigms. The intellectual who specializes in using his individual reason to search for truth encounters "the wisdom of crowds" in the realm of public affairs.[7]

Author

Academic books in Canada usually sell about five hundred copies, mostly to university libraries as well as researchers and students particularly interested in the subject matter. A thousand copies is almost a best-seller for a Canadian academic book.[8] I've written a number of books that have sold in the range of five to ten thousand copies. My first book to experience good sales was *The Diaries of Louis Riel*, published in 1976.[9] Today I wouldn't consider this translation of Riel's notebooks a particularly good book because my knowledge of editing texts was very limited when I did it. But it sold about 8000 copies because of Riel's notoriety. Two subsequent books I wrote on Riel also sold well: *Louis "David Riel": "Prophet of the New World"* (1979) and *Riel and the Rebellion: 1885 Reconsidered* (1983).[10]

These books, as well as my other writings on Riel, were historical in character and did not deal with contemporary public affairs except to argue that Riel should not be granted a posthumous pardon for having incited the North-West Rebellion. I believe, however, that they had some influence on public opinion by portraying Riel as a millenarian prophet and by explaining how the government had in fact responded to alleged Metis grievances. Riel is probably the most recognizable figure in Canadian history, so it matters culturally what Canadians know and think about him.

One thing I have learned is that to have an impact on public opinion through your writing, you have to publish *a lot*. Over a period of almost twenty years, I published three monographs and dozens of articles on Riel and the Metis, while also working with a team that collected, edited, and published everything that Riel ever wrote.[11] One book, no matter how well received, is almost always quickly forgotten. To have an impact, you must establish yourself as a leading authority, and that requires volume. I don't know if Engels was right when he said that quantity can turn into quality,[12] but my experience is that you don't get to quality without quantity.

I also learned that scholarly publications by themselves have little impact unless they are discussed in the media. That doesn't mean a review in the *Canadian Journal of Political Science*; it means reviews and columns in newspapers as well appearances on talk radio and TV shows. It's almost impossible to get that kind of attention unless the book contains an element of controversy. Because the media are in the entertainment as well as information business, they thrive on conflict.

A good example of what I mean is the work that Rainer Knopff and I did on Canadian human rights commissions in the 1980s. Publishing in refereed journals and university presses,[13] we developed the same criticisms of human rights commissions recently popularized by Ezra Levant in *Shakedown*.[14] What Knopff and I wrote had zero impact on public opinion and the political process because it was confined to narrow academic circles, whereas Levant touched off a broad wave of popular concern about the human rights industry.

In contrast, I set out deliberately to influence public policy by writing books about contemporary Aboriginal issues: *First Nations? Second Thoughts* in 2000, and *Beyond the Indian Act: Restoring Aboriginal Property Rights* in 2010.[15] *First Nations? Second Thoughts* was a polemical book, challenging what I called the "Aboriginal orthodoxy" deriving from the Report of the Royal Commission on Aboriginal Affairs. It gored sacred cows right and left, including Aboriginal self-government, land claims, and treaty rights. It won two prizes[16] and was on the *National Post* non-fiction Canadian best-seller list for eleven weeks in the summer of 2000. It was also vociferously denounced by almost every native leader from Phil Fontaine on down. With that level of controversy, it garnered an avalanche of media attention.

The book's effect on public opinion and public policy was more negative than positive. It helped stiffen the resistance against Aboriginal demands for more sympathy, more land, more jurisdictions, and more money without accountability. Certain arguments in the book, for instance, that band councils have an inherent trend to "family factionalism," abetted by representation without taxation, had rarely been made in public before, but have now become conventional wisdom among conservatives, especially in the *National Post*, which devotes a lot of editorial attention to Aboriginal affairs. At first, media accounts referenced my book, but gradually my arguments became familiar enough that the author no longer needed to be identified – a sign that the ideas were making some headway in public opinion.

My most recent book, *Beyond the Indian Act*, is a positive attempt to bring about legislative change in the form of a proposed *First Nations Property Ownership Act*, which would allow First Nations to take over ownership of their lands from the federal Crown and to create individual titles in fee simple on as much or as little of their land as they wished. Both stages of reform would be completely voluntary. The idea of private property for First Nations is a theoretically radical departure from the status quo, made incremental in practice by a voluntary opt-in approach.

Writing by myself, I could never hope to achieve legislative change; but *Beyond the Indian Act* is a collaborative effort, especially with Manny Jules, former chief of the Kamloops band and head of the First Nations Tax Commission, who contributed the foreword to the book and also designed the cover. Jules virtually created the concept of voluntary, First Nations–led legislation, beginning with the "Kamloops Amendment" of 1988, which for the first time authorized Indian bands to levy property taxes on reserve leaseholds.[17] *Beyond the Indian Act* wraps an academic gown around ideas that Jules has been developing for years. The book addresses public opinion, while Jules will work at finding First Nations to request the legislation, so that the government will be willing to introduce it into parliament. Initial indications are positive, but we won't know for several years whether we will succeed in getting the legislation passed.

It is easier to excite outrage than to bring about positive change. An author who writes fluently and has media connections can get people worked up about grievances, but it is another matter altogether to steer the political process towards a specific change. For that you need to link with a group or organization capable of undertaking political action; and at that point your book leaves the realm of pure scholarship and takes on a political aspect. Manny Jules and I generally agree about property rights for Aboriginal people, so that's what we wrote about in *Beyond the Indian Act*. We could undoubtedly find some differences of opinion on other Aboriginal issues if we worked at it, but we don't do that because we are trying to achieve change in one area, not to have the last word about Aboriginal issues in general. Hence, the book is a sort of political compromise, not because it states things we don't actually believe, but because it leaves potentially divisive questions unaddressed. That's one of the differences between pure scholarship (being right) and politics (building support to get things done).

Expert Witness

My publications on Riel and the Metis led to my work as an expert witness in Aboriginal litigation. In the summer of 1986, I received a telephone call from the federal Department of Justice, looking for someone to help the Crown as a consultant and expert witness in litigation over fulfilment of the Manitoba Act. The Manitoba Metis Federation (MMF) was arguing that the land provisions of the Manitoba Act and related legislation had not been properly implemented after 1870. There were many interrelated claims, but the central one concerned section 31 of the Manitoba Act, which required 1.4 million acres of land to be set aside for distribution "to the children of the half-breed heads of families ... towards the extinguishment of the Indian title to the lands in the province." In the view of the MMF, if the land had not been distributed properly, the Metis share of the Indian title was still alive, which meant that the federal government would have to negotiate a modern land-claims agreement with the Metis of Manitoba.

In the course of writing *Riel and the Rebellion*, I had acquired some knowledge of Metis lands in Saskatchewan; but I was far from an expert on Metis lands in Manitoba, having treated that subject only in passing in *Louis "David" Riel: "Prophet of the New World."* In spite of its deep pockets, the Crown often has trouble finding expert witnesses who have already done research on a particular topic, because most researchers who work on Aboriginal issues are part of the Aboriginal political movement and will testify on behalf of Aboriginal litigants but not on behalf of the Crown. So the Justice department was willing to fund a year's worth of research while I took a sabbatical to develop the necessary expertise on the history of Manitoba Metis lands.

This turned out to be one of the most interesting experiences of my life. I spent the academic year 1987–8 on sabbatical in Ottawa, going through records in the National Archives of Canada in order to write the history of the Manitoba Act and its implementation. We originally thought the case would come to trial quickly, but when that didn't happen, the Department of Justice gave me permission to publish my findings in book form, entitled *Metis Lands in Manitoba*.[18] When the trial finally did take place in the spring of 2006, I was on the witness stand for three weeks – one of examination in chief and two of cross-examination – to present all the details of my research. The Crown subsequently won a sweeping victory, getting the trial judge to agree with all of its main contentions.[19]

My work on the Manitoba Metis case led to a number of others invitations to be an expert witness in cases on both Metis and Indian claims. These invitations came from the federal Departments of Indian Affairs and of Justice as well as Departments of Justice in Manitoba and Alberta. Sometimes they came directly from government lawyers, sometimes from private litigators acting for the government. In a number of instances (e.g., the Lubicon dispute) I filed a report that may or may not have affected the government's negotiating policy, but the case never came to trial, so I did not testify.

I did end up testifying in three cases of some importance. In *Blais*, I gave evidence about the implementation of the Manitoba Act, which helped convince the court that the Metis defendant did not have an unextinguished Aboriginal right to hunt moose out of season.[20] *Benoit* concerned a dispute over whether Treaty 8 conferred immunity from taxation beyond that specified in section 87 of the *Indian Act*. I testified about the history of Treaty 8, how it was drafted, negotiated, and signed, showing that no promise about taxation had been included or implied. The Crown lost at trial, but won in the Federal Court of Appeal.[21] Whereas *Benoit* was narrowly focused, *Buffalo* was broad. Its main contentions concerned Indian Affairs' administration of the natural gas revenues of the Hobbema and Ermineskin bands in Alberta, but there were many other claims about the implementation of Treaty 6. It was almost as if the bands had bundled together every grievance accumulated since 1876. As in *Benoit*, my role was to testify about the genesis of Treaty 6, showing what it meant in historical context. My work in *Buffalo* consisted more in critiquing the extensive reports filed by half a dozen experts from the other side than in carrying out an original program of research. As the other side had introduced most of the relevant facts, my job was to put them in a more sensible historical framework. The Crown prevailed in this case in the areas where my testimony was relevant.[22]

My role as an expert witness was to provide historical information and context as a backdrop for the court's assessment of legal arguments. All cases involved factual disputes about what had been said and done in the past, so the judges could not do their legal work without getting a report on the relevant history *wie es eigentlich gewesen ist* (as it really was). It required an appeal in *Benoit*, but the courts eventually got the history right in all these cases.

There is usually a political element in these high-stakes cases, which often arise out of the breakdown of negotiations with government; but as an expert witness you are insulated from the politics. The lawyers reserve the law to themselves and you never talk to the politicians; you are just given an assignment to carry out historical research. I was originally recruited to work on the Manitoba Metis case when the Conservatives were in government, but I was kept on the file after the Liberals won the 1993 election. The Liberals were also in power when I worked for the federal Crown in *Buffalo*. My invitations to work for Alberta and Manitoba all came when Conservative governments were in office. Saskatchewan never asked me to do any work, which may have something to do with the NDP's long spell in government in that province (1991–2007), but I have no direct evidence about this "dog that didn't bark." But I can say that in all my work as an expert witness, there was never any discussion of political factors.

However, invitations to be an expert witness virtually ceased after my second period of activity in party politics, 2001–6. After getting lots of offers in the 1990s, the only invitation I have received recently was to replace Gerhard Ens as a consultant in the CAP-Daniels case, after Ens decided to withdraw.[23] The Crown asked for a history of Metis land and scrip in Western Canada, which builds on what I did in the Manitoba Metis case, plus some other academic publications about Metis history.[24] Again, it's a dog that didn't bark; no one tells me why they're not seeking my services, so I'm not entirely sure of the reasons. I suspect it's because several years of managing campaigns for the man who is now prime minister has made me seem too partisan, and therefore vulnerable to charges of bias during cross-examination.

The common-law judicial process is adversarial, with two sides arguing a question before an impartial judge. In cases requiring outside expertise, each side hires its own witnesses, giving rise to the famous "clash of experts," which the judge has to resolve by assessing credibility and examining the objective evidence introduced along with testimony. Legal teams avoid hiring expert witnesses whom they perceive to be committed to the other side; but beyond that, at least in my experience, they are looking more for reputation and competence than for pre-commitment to their own cause. I was never pressured to torque my findings to support the arguments being made by the Crown. Lawyers sometimes questioned my choice of wording (do you have to be so inflammatory?) or topics (is that really relevant?), but they never asked me to suppress anything. Indeed, it would be pointless to pressure a witness too much, because any departures from evidence would easily be revealed in cross-examination. The more sensible course for an advocate is not to bring a witness into court if he feels his testimony will not be helpful. Indeed, that happened to me once. I was in Edmonton to testify for the Crown in a treaty fishing-rights case, and there hadn't been much of a chance for the lawyer to consult with me beforehand. When we finally sat down to discuss matters, I said I couldn't offer historically valid testimony about the treaty to support the argument he wanted to make. At that point, he sent me home, and I sent him my invoice – no hard feelings.

Going several times through all the work of an expert witness – carrying out research, submitting a written report, testifying in the trial hearing – has increased my admiration for the judicial process as an adversarial approach to approximating historical truth. Each side is allowed to hire the best witnesses it can afford. Prospective witnesses are given months or years to do detailed research on the points at issue. The witness's report is then vetted by the team of lawyers for whom he is working. In my experience, one of the (usually) junior members of the team will spend so much time with the historical evidence that he virtually becomes a historian himself, capable of posing extremely detailed challenges to the report. As a witness, you have to be able to defend everything you have written. Scrutiny faced from legal employers is far more searching than anything encountered in submitting research proposals, articles, or books to academic referees.

The intensity of the challenge goes up another notch when your report is submitted to the other side. Now it is reviewed by another legal team, assisted by their own experts, intent on discrediting your findings or reinterpreting them to support their own arguments. Anyone who publishes in academic life is accustomed to occasional hostile reviews, but this is like having an issue of a journal with multiple hostile contributors entirely devoted to finding the flaws in something you have written. Finally, you spend days or even weeks on the stand, answering under oath questions based on the preparatory work which has engaged the other side for months or years.

One of the most challenging experiences of my life was to be cross-examined in the Manitoba Metis case for two weeks by Jim Aldridge, a Vancouver lawyer with a deservedly high reputation in Aboriginal issues. Having immersed himself in all the details of my long and complicated reports, and the thousands of pages of nineteenth-century documents on which they were based, Aldridge took me through everything line by line, asking polite but probing questions. His manner was so friendly that I had to constantly remind myself that he was not drawing out the strengths of my report but zeroing in on its weaknesses. And indeed he did find spots where I had overlooked or misunderstood relevant documents. As a witness, you have to accept that as a fallible human being you will have made some mistakes that are bound to be discovered by all the smart people working for the other side. You have to admit it when you are obviously wrong and not try to defend the indefensible or make excuses for yourself.

Of course, witnesses for both sides are getting the same treatment for the edification of the court. At the end of the process, the judge should have a highly nuanced understanding of the historical backdrop to the case, including what cannot be established for lack of evidence. I have never been through an inquisitorial system where the court appoints its own neutral experts, but I can't see how it could produce a better result for the judge than the "clash of experts." In complex matters where truth is difficult and sometimes impossible to establish with certainty, I see no replacement for the confrontation of hypotheses presented by experts chosen and prepped by the parties to the conflict.

Only once did I encounter an abuse of the adversarial process, when I was cross-examined for four days on my qualifications in *Buffalo*. Cross-examination on qualifications usually lasts about twenty minutes. One side presents a witness, running through his qualifications as recorded on his curriculum vitae, and asks the court to qualify him as a witness. The other side then cross-examines, probing those qualifications and pointing to areas of relative weakness. The strategy is normally not to prevent a witness from being qualified to testify but to raise doubts about credibility in the mind of the judge – usually a rewarding exercise, since all witnesses are human and thus are stronger in some respects than in others. But in *Buffalo*, the other side mounted an all-out effort to keep me off the stand. They had apparently read everything I had ever written and threw back at me any wording that could possibly imply animus against native people. They even asked if I was a drug abuser, based on some comments in my doctoral dissertation about the relationship between religious mysticism and an oxygen–carbon dioxide mixture sometimes used in psychotherapy to promote free association. The whole experience was made worse because the lawyer conducting the cross-examination had most of his own experience in criminal law and treated me as if I were a dodgy associate of a criminal defendant. Several lawyers to whom I have subsequently described the ordeal said the judge should not have let it go on so long.

And yet, even when the process was arguably abused for a personal vendetta, it did serve a purpose. Cross-examination did highlight some weaknesses in the report. In one place an alignment error in a statistical table had put some entries in the wrong columns, and in another spot I had relied on anecdotal evidence from newspaper accounts when more reliable evidence from government reports might have been available. These slips in handling evidence did not nullify my conclusions, but they certainly deserved to be pointed out. It was unorthodox to do it in cross-examination on qualifications rather than on evidence, but that made it more dramatic and hence more appealing to the other side. Looking back on it, in my written report for the court, I had made some pretty sharp criticisms of the reports submitted by the other side's witnesses, and indeed of the qualifications of some of those witnesses, so I shouldn't have been surprised when I got a rough ride myself. Adversarial processes by definition involve conflict, so you have to take some punches as well as land them. Trying to sanitize the process too much might interfere with the give-and-take that is its greatest advantage.[25]

Political Hack

When I was a student and a young professor, my interest in politics was mainly historical and philosophical, and my choice of research topics was often esoteric. I never dreamed that I would some day get involved with political parties and campaigning. I became seriously interested in contemporary public policy issues as a result of reading Friedrich Hayek, Milton Friedman, and many similar authors in 1976–7. I was in Washington, DC, that year to accompany my wife, who was studying sign language at Gallaudet University, an institution for the deaf. I was revising the manuscript of *Louis "David" Riel: "Prophet of the New World,"* but I couldn't do that all day every day, so I undertook a reading program in classical liberalism. It was originally intended to be for teaching purposes, but it also made me start paying closer attention to public policy. From there I started to read books such as William Gairdner, *The Trouble with Canada*, and Peter Brimelow, *The Patriot Game*,[26] as well as many works published by market-oriented think tanks such as the Fraser Institute. Partisan politics was still far off the agenda, however, because from my new libertarian point of view, the Progressive Conservatives and the Liberals were almost equally unattractive.

I joined the Reform Party in 1990 after a graduate student gave me the party's "Blue Book" to read (I learned later that it had been largely written by another University of Calgary graduate student, Stephen Harper).[27] For the first time, I saw a political party that represented my views on balanced budgets, lower taxes, deregulation, privatization, and many other economic topics. I was less enthusiastic about some of Reform's other positions, such as senate reform and direct democracy, but I was happy to accept them as part of an overall package. I joined the party and gave $100, but didn't do anything else, still not thinking of myself as politically active.

All that changed in the winter of 1991, when Preston Manning asked me to go to work for him as director of policy, strategy, and communications. It was a risky move to offer such a senior position to someone with absolutely no experience in working for a political party, but Manning didn't have a lot of other choices. As leader of a new party vilified as extreme, even racist, he had to take some chances with personnel.

I worked for Reform from May 1990 through December 1992, and later described that brief experience in my book *Waiting for the Wave: The Reform Party and Preston Manning*.[28] I got a crash course in political parties, and I made some contributions to Reform's development, but overall I flamed out badly. I now understand that my basic problem was an overly deductive approach to public policy. I thought of issues in public policy as problems to be solved by applying principles derived from my libertarian gurus such as Hayek and Friedman. I was intolerant of the practical compromises that political parties have to make if they are serious about building a coalition big enough to win. I remember, for example, being quite disappointed when Preston Manning invented a verbal formula that allowed him to accept supply management of dairy products.[29] I thought (and still think) that supply management is one of the worst policies ever adopted in Canada, but it was extremely popular in the only areas of rural Ontario where Reform had some chance of making a breakthrough. Paris was worth a Mass (or at least some overpriced milk).

I might have been able to put up with political pragmatism and occasional opportunism, but the problem was deeper than that. Manning described himself at that stage in his life as a populist, deriving his positions inductively from "the common sense of the common people."[30] I was a Hayekian, deriving positions deductively from what I took to be the timeless truths of libertarian philosophy.

After resigning my Reform Party employment at the end of 1992, and being fired as a Reform adviser in August 1993, I became a media pundit (described in the next section). I stayed out of partisan politics except for collaboration with Stephen Harper, with whom I occasionally co-authored publications. For me it was a literary exercise, but Harper was thinking through the strategy for his return to politics after resigning as a Reform MP in 1997. One of our joint essays became, in effect, his roadmap to power. First presented as a speech by Harper to · the 1996 "Winds of Change" conference in Calgary, it described how a national conservative party could be rebuilt by uniting Western populists, traditional Tories in Ontario and Atlantic Canada, and nationalist (but not separatist) francophones in Quebec.[31] That turned out to be exactly the strategy Harper followed in running for leader of the Canadian Alliance, engineering a merger with the Progressive Conservatives, and finally making a breakthrough in Quebec in 2006. The thinking was entirely Harper's; I just helped give it a persuasive literary form.

The other highlight of our literary collaboration was the notorious "Firewall" public letter, which called on Premier Ralph Klein to resume exercise of Alberta's constitutional jurisdictions, for instance, by opting out of the Canada Pension Plan and creating an Alberta Pension Plan.[32] The idea behind the letter, which was entirely Harper's, was to encourage the "have" provinces to distance themselves from Liberal-controlled Ottawa; he also hoped to start a similar movement in Ontario. My contribution was literary form plus some specific policy ideas. But the "Firewall" movement never really got under way because Stockwell Day got into extreme difficulty as leader of the Canadian Alliance, and Harper decided to re-enter elective politics by running to replace him.

Almost by accident, that decision led to my own return to partisan politics. Along with several other friends, I volunteered to help Harper's leadership campaign get under way; and when the first campaign team we hired didn't work out, I volunteered to manage the campaign myself.[33] Easy to offer when you don't know what's involved! Apart from dropping leaflets door to door for my MP Diane Ablonczy, I had never even worked in a local campaign, let alone managed a national leadership race. So I set out to learn by doing. Fortunately, Harper and I had friends who had much of the necessary knowledge and experience, so I didn't have to tell everyone what to do. My role was to weld all the volunteers, and a few hired people, into a team, keep them focused, and make sure they were doing what they had promised on time and within budget. There were lots of little bumps along the way, but overall the campaign was highly successful. Harper won on the first ballot, and we made a profit of $100,000 to use as seed money for future campaigns and projects.

In the wake of that success, Harper wanted me to go to Ottawa with him as chief of staff in the Office of the Leader of the Opposition. But my wife didn't want to move to Ottawa for the long term, so I said could do it for a year to help him get started. I returned to the University of Calgary in June 2003, but at Harper's request stayed on half-time to build a campaign team for the next federal election, whenever that might come. I had barely started on that project when Harper pulled off the merger with the Progressive Conservatives, so I had to drop national campaign preparations in order to manage his leadership campaign against Belinda Stronach and Tony Clement. By the time we won that race, Paul Martin had become prime minister, and we knew there would soon be a national election. So I stayed on to supervise the breakneck preparations for that race, which began when the writ was dropped on 23 May 2004.

After we failed to win that election, I tried to resign, but Harper asked me to stay on as half-time campaign manager to get ready for another election, which could come at any time in that minority parliament. When we failed to force an election in spring 2005, I finally did succeed in resigning, to be replaced by deputy campaign manager Doug Finley. I then went back to work in the war room as senior communications adviser for the 2005–6 campaign. Mainly what I did was to lead the rapid response group to ensure that we had no more fiascos like the "child porn" media release that had undermined our 2004 campaign.[34] Once the election was won, I was again out of active politics and back to the University of Calgary.

This go-round in politics was much more successful than my Reform years. I made a significant contribution to making Harper Conservative leader and to helping build the campaign machine that brought the Liberals down to a minority government in 2004 and took the Conservatives to minority government in 2006 and 2008 and a majority in 2011. To put this in perspective, when it became obvious that Paul Martin would replace Jean Chrétien, the most common view was that the Liberals would be in power for another generation and that under Martin's leadership the Liberals would win more than two hundred seats in the next election. I take satisfaction in having helped build the team that derailed Martin's "juggernaut."[35]

Working for Harper meant that I had no involvement with policy because, both as candidate and leader, he exercised tight personal control over strategy, policy, and communications. I was his chief organizer, dealing with the more mundane side of politics – raising money, hiring people, finding premises, printing pamphlets, and negotiating contracts with suppliers, including airlines, bus companies, telemarketers, pollsters, and advertisers. I saw my job as creating the machine that could implement whatever strategies Harper decided upon.

While I was preoccupied with that mission, I became quite agnostic about questions of public policy. I was willing to let Harper and his policy advisers debate the merits of various policies, while I was focused on winning the next election. As far as I was concerned, legendary Conservative campaign manager John Laschinger was right: "To those in the backroom, winning is everything."[36] It was raw primate politics, almost as described in Frans de Waal's classic book *Chimpanzee Politics* – males forming coalitions to win rank, and thereby to get more copulations with females in their fertile periods.[37] Human beings play for resource control more than for direct sexual advantage, but the basic idea is the same. Ironically, I had evolved from my original purist view that policy had to be deduced from first principles to an agnostic view in which policy was merely a weapon of political combat.

Not surprisingly, the Conservative Party that I helped propel to victory now espouses many policies that I can't endorse. Supply management, subsidies to business, government bailouts of auto manufacturers, deficit spending in the name of stimulus – the list could go on and on. Of course, the Conservative government in power has also done many things that I do support, such as cuts to the GST and personal and corporate income tax, re-equipping the Canadian Forces, and stopping the movement towards federally funded institutional day care. I didn't get a whole loaf by helping the Conservatives win, but I certainly got half a loaf – and what conservative ever expects to get a whole loaf in the complex and tangled field of public affairs?

More broadly, I believe my political work helped restore competitiveness in Canadian federal politics. Prior to Harper's return to politics as Canadian Alliance leader, pundits such as Jeffrey Simpson frequently lamented the fact that no one could seriously challenge the Liberals, which was making that party complacent and even corrupt.[38] But after the merger of the Canadian Alliance with the Progressive Conservatives, and the building of an efficient Conservative campaign machine, Canadian politics has become competitive again. The 2011 election produced a Conservative majority government faced by a New Democratic opposition of 103 members – the largest opposition since 1979.

So my contribution to Canadian politics was to help make it more competitive – and hence adversarial – by restoring the balance between parties of the centre-right and centre-left. Not exactly a utopia, is it? Adversarial politics is unedifying in many ways – a pervasive spirit of partisanship, a wildly exaggerated question period, negative advertising between elections. Many Canadians tell pollsters they don't like it. I don't like it, either. But I still think it's better than giving one party a lock on power for generations.

Among the Punditi

Like many political scientists, I was occasionally in the media early in my career when something came up touching my expertise. For me in the 1980s, that meant mainly Louis Riel. The publisher of *Reform and the Rebellion* paid for a promotional tour for the book, which led to a lot of media coverage. Perhaps most memorable was winning a CBC radio debate about Louis Riel's trial and execution. The historian Desmond Morton and I, facing literary critic George Woodcock and Metis leader Elmer Ghostkeeper (a former student of mine), managed to convince a CBC audience that Riel had been properly convicted.

But apart from these occasional forays, I wasn't in the media much until after Preston Manning fired me as a Reform Party adviser in August 1993. Being then in my doctrinaire phase (which I now find comical), I was afraid Manning was going to water down the conservatism that I thought the Reform Party should represent, so I decided to go public. I had a vague vision of steering the Reform Party by becoming an independent Reform voice in the media. By then I had been associated with Reform for almost two years, so I had met some journalists and had developed a notion of how to place stories in the media.

Reporters quickly started coming to me once they learned that I was willing sometimes to criticize Preston Manning. I was supportive of Reform more often than I was critical, and much of the time I was simply analytical, but it was enough to get me into the media's collective Rolodex. The 1995 publication of *Waiting for the Wave* (as close to a tell-all book as anyone ever writes in this decorous country) intensified the media attention. I knew I was being used sometimes by reporters who only wanted to disparage Manning, but I also wanted to promote my book and took every opportunity to enhance sales. Not very successfully, by the way – *Waiting for the Wave* sold the fewest copies of all my books intended for a broad audience. I used to joke that Preston wasn't charismatic enough to sell my book, but I now understand that the book was too densely written for popular taste. Also, a book about Reform didn't appeal much to Canada's literary class, unless it was an all-out attack, which mine wasn't.

I haven't kept an exact count, but I suppose that since 1994 I have appeared in Canadian media between one and two hundred times a year. The only exception was in the years 2002–6, when I was working for Stephen Harper. Then I followed his commandment, which I also thought was correct, that his employees should shun publicity and leave the media to the communications department. I have done a lot of things in the media: writing my own op-eds, appearing on radio phone-in shows, acting as a talking head on television panels, and being a source for reporters' interviews. However, I haven't set up my own blog or gone into social media. Maybe that reluctance is a generational thing, but I also think it's in my own interest. I've learned from experience that my initial reaction to breaking stories is often unreliable, especially if based on partial and preliminary information. I prefer to wait to comment rather than rush into print before I really understand what's happening.

I wrote a monthly op-ed for the *Globe and Mail* from 1997 to 2000, then switched to the *National Post*. I wrote for that paper somewhat more than monthly until mid-2002, when I entered my Harper-imposed tunnel of silence. Coming out the other end, I started to write monthly again for the *Globe and Mail* in April 2006, and am still doing that five years later. I try to publish columns that no one else would write, using my knowledge of political science and history. Many pundits are already doing a fine job of commenting on daily events, so I try to be a little different.

I'm also now appearing twice weekly on CBC News Network's "Power and Politics" with Evan Solomon, where I'm trying to introduce a little humour into the discussions. For a lot of Canadian public affairs broadcasting, Marshall McLuhan might have said, "The tedium is the message." I try to liven it up with occasional props, costumes, and flashes of deadpan humour. Occasionally I get it wrong, as in December 2010, when I joked about assassinating WikiLeaks founder Julian Assange and made myself an international target of hate mail, death threats, and media outrage. Most of the time, however, it seems to work, even if it's still a work in progress. The purpose, in addition to having a little fun, is to make my hard-edged conservative ideas seem less threatening to the CBC's largely left-leaning audience.

I also continue to pick up the phone and talk to reporters whenever they call. Sometimes they try to get me to say something critical about (originally) Preston Manning and the Reform Party and (now) Stephen Harper and the Conservative Party. I've learned to recognize this situation and only respond to it now if I feel my comments might be useful. Other times they have a story already written, at least in their minds, and are looking for a specific comment from an academic authority to provide what they see as balance. Again, I've learned to recognize the situation and will sometimes play the game if it's a reporter with whom I have a useful long-term relationship.

Or they may be looking for specific historical, constitutional, or institutional information that I am likely to know as a political scientist. This happens occasionally but not very often, given that the media are more in the entertainment than the information business. And occasionally they want to talk to someone who's been inside a political party and can perhaps give a realistic internal assessment of what's being reported in public.

I often ask myself whether all this media activity is worthwhile. I enjoy it most of the time, as long as it doesn't become so time-consuming that it ruins the day. Most media people are intelligent and well informed about public affairs, so it's interesting and informative to talk to them. I learn quite a bit, because reporters tell me about developments I wouldn't otherwise be aware of. And knowing that I might speak and write about many aspects of public affairs makes me inform myself more broadly and not get trapped in academic specialization. But the question still lingers, what's the point?

Being in the media is like a family reunion where everyone is talking at once. Some people are well informed and others are downright ignorant. Some are moderate and polite while others are extreme and rudely offensive. The milieu is not conducive to serious reflection. The *Globe and Mail* gives me a maximum of 650 words for an op-ed; only rarely do I get to write anything longer. Appearance as a talking head lasts only a few minutes, normally shared with other guests. And these are the best forms of media appearance, where you get to write or speak directly without being filtered by reporters. When you are interviewed for a story by even the fairest and most competent journalist, all that emerges is short quotations and sound bites, often taken out of context, always much less than you attempted to say. And even if the story portrays your comments accurately, the headline, written by an editor who may have his own agenda, sometimes gives readers a distorted view of what you said.[39]

Measured by the standards of academic discourse, the media conversation is poorly structured, superficial, and chaotic. But it's the only public conversation we have that's relevant to politics. It's the agora of modern democracy. Every political office in Ottawa has at least one television set running all the time, turned to the news networks. Every politician, staffer, and civil servant starts the day with a news summary plus reading as many newspapers as possible. Many have their Blackberries set to bring them instantaneous news alerts on topics they're interested in. Even if they don't, someone is sure to email them any important story as soon as it appears on a media website.

It may not be perfect, but it's what we have, and as a conservative I have to respect that. It's a privilege to be granted a voice in the democratic Tower of Babel. My goal is to articulate an unabashed but reasoned conservative world view amidst all the other viewpoints struggling to be represented in the conversation. Occasionally I may persuade someone, but most of the time I, like all the other voices, am speaking primarily to those already disposed to agree with me. What I'm doing, in effect, is to provide others with intellectually grounded arguments for use as political weapons.

In a modern pluralistic democracy, the public forum is adversarial in a multilateral way. Virtually all viewpoints are represented, albeit some much more strongly than others. Very little goes unchallenged for any length of time, particularly now that the mainstream media are heavily influenced by the blogosphere and social media. The process is messy and unsatisfying if you believe the goal of rational inquiry is to establish the truth, but it does force ideas about public affairs to be tested in public. Ultimately political decision-makers, most of whom have little real expertise in anything except getting elected, will be influenced by what they think is true, or at least popular. So it's worthwhile to be a part of the media conversation, even though I recognize the limits on what any individual can accomplish. And, fundamentally, those limits are a good thing, for democracy is not supposed to mean rule by an intellectual elite.

Conclusion

Let me conclude with some observations on the four adversarial processes that I have encountered in Canadian public affairs. Table 9.1 provides an overview of these processes as seen from the point of view of the individual taking part in them:

Table 9.1. Adversarial Processes in Public Affairs

	Publication of books	Expert witness in litigation	Political party worker	Media pundit
Intellectual rigour	Can be high, though must be saleable	Very high because of intense scrutiny	Low for policies, which are determined by political appeal	Low because of very short format
Control of message	High, as long as acceptable to publisher	High, within narrow focus determined by employer	Low, message controlled by party leader	High in op-ed or TV appearance; low when serving as journalistic source
Policy impact	Can be substantial if tied to political movement or mass media	Can be substantial but narrowly focused	Occasionally substantial, but subject to vagaries of politics	Low unless connected to political movement
Level of influence	Usually low unless book becomes widely discussed	Narrow, confined to restricted area of law, but can be important within that area	Wide if working for a major party	Superficial but wide if appearing in national media

Being an expert witness is closest to the academic life. The intellectual rigour of the work is very high, indeed higher than that of much academic research; and the researcher controls what he is doing, albeit within the limits set by relevance to the litigation. The adversarial aspect is intense and highly focused in the "battle of the experts" taking place in the courtroom. Impact on the law can be significant if the case is precedent-setting and if your research helps win the legal battle.

Writing books for the general public is also relatively close to academic life, except that you have to express yourself in a way that is intelligible and interesting to non-specialists. As author, you get to choose your topic and say what you want, assuming it's not libellous and the publisher thinks it's saleable. The book market is pluralistic, so you have to expect critical reviews and denunciation in parts of the media – all of which can be good for sales. A widely discussed book can help nudge public opinion in a certain direction over time. But in the short run a book by itself will have little or no impact on public policy unless it's tied in with a political movement or resonates in the media echo chamber.

Working for a political party holds out the prospect, and sometimes the reality, of getting close to governmental power and being able to influence legislation, regulation, and the appointment of officials. Of course, you have to fight through the intensely adversarial process of election campaigns to get to that stage. But even if you do get close to power, the result will probably be less enticing than the prospect. In a competitive democracy, it is almost impossible to evade the median voter theorem,[40] so your policy views are likely to be implemented only if they are close to the conventional wisdom.

Finally, being in the media gives you wide but superficial influence. Tens of thousands of readers may peruse your 650-word op-ed, and hundreds of thousands of viewers may see your eight-second clip on the evening news. But your opinions are just part of the democratic Babel, and it is virtually impossible to track any influence on government policy arising out of participating in the media. Your contribution is to help keep the democratic conversation going, not to achieve any particular result.

Overall, there is no particular imperative for scholars to participate in public affairs, certainly no more than for other professionally educated people. It's a matter of taste and interest, not moral obligation. The scholar who does choose to participate in public life will find that his research and writing ability, as well his knowledge of his discipline, can be useful assets in carving out a niche for himself. For a person with the right temperament, the activities themselves can be their own reward, and they are sometimes even financially remunerative. But messianic hopes of changing the system are best parked at the entrance. If you do decide to play in this league, you'll be in with thousands of teammates and opponents who couldn't care less that you are the acknowledged authority on John Stuart Mill's early life, or the theory of justice, or the effects of proportional representation on party competition. You'll be in there hitting and getting hit with everyone else, no one knowing for sure where it's all going. It's a long way from academic life.

NOTES

1 http://www.cceia.org/resources/transcripts/130.html.

2 http://www.canada.com/national/nationalpost/news/story.
   html?id=6ac60088-625d-4f18-87cb-e34e3dced5f5.

3 Aristotle, *Rhetoric*, 1356a.

4 J.L. Talmon, *The Origins of Totalitarian Democracy* (London: Norton, 1952).

5 *Brown v. Allen* (1952), http://www.jrank.org/quotations/pages/835/
   Robert-H-Jackson-Robert-Houghwout-Jackson.html.

6 Mary Mack, *Jeremy Bentham: An Odyssey of Ideas, 1748–1792* (London:
   Heinemann, 1962), 362.

7 James Surowiecki, *The Wisdom of Crowds* (New York: Doubleday, 2004).

8 Joan McGillvray, editor at McGill-Queen's University Press, to Tom Flanagan, email message, 19 Apr. 2010.

9 Thomas Flanagan, ed., *The Diaries of Louis Riel* (Edmonton: Hurtig, 1976).

10 Thomas Flanagan, *Louis "David" Riel: "Prophet of the New World,"* 2nd ed.
    (Toronto: University of Toronto Press, 1996; 1st ed. 1979); *Riel and the Rebel-
    lion: 1885 Reconsidered*, 2nd ed. (Toronto: University of Toronto Press, 2000;
    1st ed. Saskatoon: Western Producer, 1983).

11 George Stanley et al., eds, *The Collected Writings of Louis Riel*, 5 vols.
    (Edmonton: University of Alberta Press, 1985).

12 Friedrich Engels, *Anti-Dühring* (1877), part 1, chap. 13, http://www.
    marxistsfr.org/archive/marx/works/1877/anti-duhring/ch10.htm.

13 Thomas Flanagan, "Policy-Making by Exegesis: The Abolition of
    Mandatory Retirement in Manitoba," *Canadian Public Policy* 11 (1985),
    40–53; Thomas Flanagan, "Insurance, Human Rights, and Equality Rights
    in Canada: When Is Discrimination 'Reasonable'?" *Canadian Journal of
    Political Science* 18 (1985), 715–37; Thomas Flanagan, Rainer Knopff, and
    Keith Archer, "Selection Bias in Human Rights Tribunals: An Exploratory
    Study," *Canadian Public Administration* 31 (1988), 483–500; Rainer Knopff
    (with Thomas Flanagan), *Human Rights and Social Technology* (Ottawa:
    Carleton University Press, 1989).

14 Ezra Levant, *Shakedown: How Our Government Is Undermining Democracy in
    the Name of Human Rights* (Toronto: McClelland & Stewart, 2009).

15 Tom Flanagan, *First Nations? Second Thoughts*, 2nd ed. (Montreal: McGill-
    Queen's University Press, 2008; 1st ed., 2000); Tom Flanagan, Christo-
    pher Alcantara, and André Le Dressay, *Beyond the Indian Act: Restoring
    Aboriginal Property Rights* (Montreal: McGill-Queen's University Press,
    2010).

16 The Donner Canadian Prize for the best book of the year in Canadian pub-
    lic policy; and the Canadian Policy Science Association's Donald Smiley
    Prize for best book of the year in Canadian politics, both awarded in 2001.
17 Flanagan et al., *Beyond the Indian Act*, 142–6.
18 Thomas Flanagan, *Metis Lands in Manitoba* (Calgary: University of Calgary
    Press, 1991).
19 *Manitoba Métis Federation et al. v. A.G. of Canada et al.*, 2007 MBQB 293.
20 Upheld by the Supreme Court of Canada, *R. v. Blais*, [2003] 2 S.C.R. 236,
    2003 SCC 44.
21 *Canada v. Benoit*, 2003 CAF 236 (2003).
22 *Buffalo v. Canada*, 2001 CAF 282 (2001).
23 *Daniels et al. v. HMTQ et al.*, Federal Court file no. T-2172-99.
24 E.g., Thomas Flanagan, "The History of Metis Aboriginal Rights: Politics,
    Principle, and Policy," *Canadian Journal of Law and Society* 5 (1990), 71–94.
25 Readers interested in this topic will want to consult Arthur J. Ray, *Telling
    It to the Judge: Taking Native History to Court* (Montreal: McGill-Queen's
    University Press, 2012). I had not seen this book at the time of revising this
    chapter (June 2011).
26 William D. Gairdner, *The Trouble with Canada* (Toronto: Stoddart, 1990); Pe-
    ter Brimelow, *The Patriot Game: Canada and the Canadian Question Revisited*
    (Toronto: Key Porter, 1988).
27 Reform Party of Canada, Blue Book, 1988, p. 26. At http://contentdm.
    ucalgary.ca/cdm4/document.php?CISOROOT=/reform&CISOPTR=197.
28 Tom Flanagan, *Waiting for the Wave: The Reform Party and Preston Manning*
    (Toronto: Stoddart, 1995); 2nd ed. repub. as *Waiting for the Wave: The Reform
    Party and the Conservative Movement* (Montreal: McGill-Queen's University
    Press, 2009).
29 Ibid., 30.
30 Ibid., 22.
31 Stephen Harper and Tom Flanagan, "Our Benign Dictatorship," *The Next
    City* (January 1997), 35–40, 54–7.
32 Stephen Harper et al., "Open Letter to Ralph Klein," *National Post*, 24 Jan.
    2001.
33 Tom Flanagan, *Harper's Team: Behind the Scenes in the Conservative Rise to
    Power*, 2nd ed. (Montreal: McGill-Queen's University Press, 2009), 39.
34 Ibid., 179–80.
35 Susan Delacourt, *Juggernaut: Paul Martin's Campaign for Chrétien's Crown*
    (Toronto: McClelland & Stewart, 2003).
36 John Laschinger and Geoffrey Stevens, *Leaders and Lesser Mortals* (Toronto:
    Key Porter, 1992), 6.

37 Frans de Waal, *Chimpanzee Politics: Power and Sex among Apes* (Baltimore: Johns Hopkins University Press, 1982).
38 Jeffrey Simpson, *The Friendly Dictatorship* (Toronto: McClelland & Stewart, 2001).
39 E.g., my interview reported in Peter Zimonjic, "Ex-Harper aide: Turn AG loose on MPs' expenses," *Toronto Sun*, 28 Apr. 2010. The headline wrongly gives the impression I think there's a lot of misspending by MPs waiting to be uncovered, while the story accurately reports what I really said: "Flanagan said he's less concerned with the estimated one-fifth of the board's budget used to pay for MPs' expenses than he is with the remaining $400 million. 'I think there's all sorts of antiquated stuff that is not a case of individual members misusing their allowances but rather of a sluggish institution that hasn't really been open to public view for a long time or maybe ever.'"
40 Anthony Downs, *An Economic Theory of Democracy* (New York: Harper & Row, 1957). Downs showed that, given certain assumptions, political parties competing for power tend to position themselves towards the middle of whatever ideological spectrum prevails.

10 Personal Success versus Public Failure: The Muting of Canada's Academic Intellectuals

STEPHEN CLARKSON

Since the summer of 2010, I've been thinking a good deal about the disconnects in my life in the light of being honoured by a wonderful award for the contributions I had made to Canadian political economy ("I hear you've been upgraded," was the way my life partner's son put it with warm irony), so I propose to address this book's theme – which is broadly about those who produce ideas for public consumption – from the vantage point of my own experience in Canadian academic life both in generating ideas and in communicating them.

When I was invited to join the University of Toronto's Department of Political Economy in 1964, I brought with me from my graduate years a mix of notions about the constructive role that academics should normally play in their society. A number of my tutors at Oxford were known as "TV dons" because the ideas they were toying with in our tutorials were likely to be heard on the BBC the next Sunday as they discussed the great issues of the day for the British public's edification.

Later at the Sorbonne a few of my professors would often join their doctoral students after our weekly general seminar to take part in a "manif" – a mass demonstration – on the Boulevard St Germain protesting against General de Gaulle's handling of France's war in Algeria against the terrorist Front de libération nationale. Beyond taking to the streets in times of trouble, our teachers were regularly visible in the media. One of our professors was a recognized fascist who attacked the government on its other flank, urging de Gaulle in the right-wing press not to abandon the "pieds noirs," the French who were still hanging onto their colony in the name of France's civilizing world mission. Some academics appeared in socialist papers denouncing these same imperialist proclivities, while still others held forth in Catholic or liberal dailies staking out various positions between these extremes.

From the far left to the far right, the French operating premise was the same. Whether intellectuals were occupying university chairs or writing novels, it was as normal for them to participate in their national community's cultural, philosophical, and political life as it was to publish a philosophical tome or mount a play. Whenever Jean-Paul Sartre did one or the other, his action would generate its own critical reverberations in the media, whose intense discussions came close to approximating the mythical perpetual-motion machine – a vibrant, excited, intense, often self-absorbed conversation about the nation's constantly evolving concerns.

So when I turned up on St George Street to lecture on comparative politics for the princely sum of $7000 a year, it seemed natural to get involved in the intellectual discussions that were then roiling around the country. Although my specialty was Sovietology, I accepted an invitation from the economist Abe Rotstein to join the editorial board of the *Canadian Forum*, a literary cum political monthly that had been published since 1920 to air current issues. During term time I would often have lunch upstairs at the Faculty Club's political-economy table, where my colleagues – economic historians, business professors, political scientists, economists, and political theorists – gathered every day to munch their sandwiches and chat about issues both small (the Maple Leafs' game the night before) and large (whether foreign direct investment was good for the Canadian economy). On the positive side of this issue, the economic historian John Dales might explain the argument he was developing that protectionist policies promoted population growth at the expense of individual wealth. Or Harry Eastman would insist with his elegant disdain that tariffs were a self-defeating public policy dooming Canadian industry to be forever unproductive. Or Ed Safarian would insist that his own research on branch-plant managers was showing that they behaved no differently from domestic firms, given the same policy environment.

Enriched though I was by these collegial exchanges, I gravitated to a more diverse, but more engaged group of academics from philosophy and theology, sociology and history, as well as politics and economics, who wanted to change the face of Canada. It may have been a bit pretentious to call ourselves the University League for Social Reform (ULSR), but we held intense meetings to discuss each other's papers, many of which were then edited into books,[1] some of whose chapters had far-reaching effects on the course of Canadian political thinking and public policy.

I remember, for instance, the excitement pulsing along our ugly cement-block corridor in Sidney Smith Hall the day that the economist Mel Watkins received a manuscript from Stephen Hymer, a younger Canadian doing his doctorate in economics at Yale. Watkins rushed to his political-scientist colleague Peter Russell to urge him to include this essay in *Nationalism in Canada*, the ULSR's second volume, which Russell was editing. Hymer's chapter, "Direct Foreign Investment and the National Economic Interest," caused a breakthrough in the debate over economic nationalism by linking Eastman's and Safarian's micro-economic focus on how firms behave with such macroeconomic concerns as the balance of payments and exchange rates. More important, it provided the theoretical germ that inspired the Task Force on Foreign Ownership and the Structure of Canadian Investment that Prime Minister Lester Pearson had set up on the advice of his former finance minister, Walter Gordon. Ed Safarian and Abraham Rotstein joined five other economists from around the country under Watkins's direction to generate a comprehensive assessment of foreign investment's impact on the Canadian economy. The resulting Watkins report (*Foreign Ownership and the Structure of Canadian Industry*), to which I contributed a notably unnotable piece of research, transformed Canadians' understanding of their chronically uncompetitive economy by explaining why branch plants, as "miniature replicas" of their US parent firms, were doomed to be inefficient. While the Watkins report touched too many sensitive nerves for Pearson to handle, it broke the ground for the federal government's subsequent Gray Report of 1972 (*Foreign Direct Investment in Canada*), which laid out the rationale for Ottawa's subsequent – if half-hearted and unsuccessful – efforts to regain some national control over the Canadian economy.

I edited the ULSR's third volume – *An Independent Foreign Policy for Canada?* – which had chapters by some scholars who praised and essays by others who attacked the Pearson government's backing for US foreign policy. Our particular concern was Ottawa's providing not just military supplies but diplomatic support for the American war in Vietnam by taking its side on the putatively neutral International Commission on Supervision and Control and its reluctance to stand up to Washington by extending official recognition to the People's Republic of China, which had already been in power for two decades. One Canadian international-relations scholar later rated this volume as one of the ten

most important books on Canadian foreign policy and another demonstrated that its critique had a decisive impact on the reorientation of
Canadian diplomacy that was effected under Pierre Trudeau.

It would of course be impossible to prove that Pierre Trudeau's Third
Option (to reduce Canada's economic dependence on the US market by
diversifying its trade partners), the Canada Development Corporation
(to buy back control of formerly Canadian companies), or the Foreign
Investment Review Agency (to screen proposed takeovers of other Canadian firms) would not have seen the light of day without the ULSR's
initiatives. Still, there is this little doubt that in the late 1960s and early
1970s this feisty group of Toronto academics made significant contributions to how the Canadian public thought about its major challenges
and how its politicians enacted public policy.

I was still researching and writing in my first academic field, the
Soviet theory of underdevelopment, preparing a manuscript that the
University of Toronto Press would ultimately publish in Canada and
Macmillan would bring out in the United Kingdom, but it did not seem
untoward for me to sit on the board of the Ontario Welfare Council and
later on that of the Social Planning Council of Toronto. Still less did I
feel out of step for joining forces with a handful of my university colleagues to found Praxis Corporation, an activist institute dedicated to
promoting social change. Abe Rotstein managed to get Beland Hond-
erich, the Toronto *Star*'s publisher, to give us some financial support. I
persuaded my priest at St Thomas's Anglican Church to let us use an
empty house belonging to the parish as our rent-free home base. We in
turn provided office space for such activist initiatives as an anti-poverty
organization. We gave start-up finances to the young lawyer-turned-
activist John Sewell, who was organizing welfare tenants in a rundown
neighbourhood called Trefann Court. Our most effective collaboration
was with Alan Powell, the working-class Welshman who was teaching
in the University of Toronto's sociology department in one part of his
life and organizing a coalition of citizens groups and ratepayers' associations to resist the planned Spadina Expressway that threatened to
disrupt the vibrant life of many communities in midtown Toronto.

Our somewhat inchoate concerns about the dangers facing Toronto
were given greater coherence when, at one of our weekly brown-bag
lunches, a joyously opinionated American named Jane Jacobs joined
our discussions. Ms Jacobs had become a household name among urban progressives for leading a successful fight to stop the Lower Man-
hattan Expressway, which would have destroyed the lively community

of Greenwich Village. By the time she left New York City for Toronto, hours before one of her sons was to be drafted into the US Army, she had published *The Death and Life of Great American Cities*, which became an instant classic by overturning the prevailing orthodoxy of urban designers who were still prescribing high-rise developments for poor people and thruway grids for cars. Her infectious conviction that people were generally right and politicians, bureaucrats, and – yes – academics were generally wrong clarified our own notions of what we needed to resist if we were to save Toronto from following the path of urban decay and ghettoized violence that had recently seen Harlem burn in New York and Haight-Ashbury ignite in San Francisco. It was my involvement in this intellectual ferment that pushed me into a few years of intense partisan engagement.

When Walter Gordon retired from politics, I flew up from Columbia University, where I was enjoying a year's fellowship, to contend – unsuccessfully – the nomination for Walter's seat in the Toronto riding of Davenport for the 1968 federal election that Pierre Trudeau had triggered following his selection as leader of the Liberal Party. In the wake of the enthusiasm Trudeau had generated, Liberals in Toronto – very directly inspired by Jane Jacobs's thinking – decided to launch a municipal political party, and, to everyone's surprise but especially my own, I found myself nominated to be the fledgling party's mayoralty candidate. Ours was a long, intense campaign which generated considerable national interest in part because I was articulating a comprehensive urban-reform platform that Jane subsequently judged to have broken the logjam and cleared the way after my defeat for the subsequent mayoral victories of David Crombie and John Sewell, which did redirect Toronto's development along more people-friendly and community-oriented lines.

These were heady days for the public-spirited professor. Some, like the mathematician Chandler Davis, helped organize massive teach-ins that were held in sports arenas and broadcast around the country and the continent to educate the public about the Vietnam War's horrors. Some, like the classicist Alan Samuel, launched publishing houses so that the growing ranks of playwrights, poets, novelists, and non-fiction writers could get their works published and sold in the bookstores. Quite a few wrote opinion pieces for the newspapers' op-ed pages. A good many were active in political parties, generally the New Democratic Party. Some, like Howard Adelman, were entrepreneurial, getting huge mortgages under federal housing programs to set up such experiments in social living as Rochdale College. Others, like James Eayrs, who hosted a weekly public-affairs television program on the CBC, extended their teaching beyond the classroom to communicate regularly with the public through the mass media.

When the ULSR book I edited on Canadian foreign policy was published, I put together a number of half-hour programs that were aired on the CBC's morning radio service. When I invented a powerful new simulation-based teaching technique, a CBC television producer happily made a documentary of my classroom-in-action for his national program. When I had something to say for the general public, I could make a cross-country speaking tour organized by the Canadian Club and engage with citizens, whether in a hotel ballroom in Halifax, a parish hall in Moose Jaw, or a basement pub in Victoria.

We would have scoffed at using the words "public intellectual" to designate a separate species of homo sapiens: all academics could engage in the public sphere to make our society better, "better" being defined according to their individual lights, whether left, right, or centre. And many did. Very few of us were brandishing placards outside the US consulate protesting against American imperialism. Some of the most important Canadian intellectuals were actually quite shy. The completely uncharismatic professor of theology George Grant had a huge impact because of the power of his short polemic *Lament for a Nation*, which made a philosophical case for Tory nationalism. Others were exhibitionists, like the English professor Marshall McLuhan, whose insights about how TV had created a global village entranced the whole world.

All this is to report that responsible scholars forty years ago felt no compunction about behaving like active citizens. There was a sense that university academics – along with writers like Margaret Atwood and her friend, the irreverent artist Charles Pachter – were releasing the country's creative potential and building a generous society with its own culture, fired by a dynamic, self-directed economy, a feeling which Trudeau had tapped into in 1968 with his "just society" slogan. True, a prevailing optimism gripped Canada during the years before and after 1967, when it celebrated its centenary. There was also a fear that the United States might drag the world into a nuclear holocaust with the Soviet Union – unless a social revolution did not first erupt there. But supporting this socio-cultural energy was a university ethos which accepted the participation of professors in their community life and a media system that was open to the transmission of the ideas being spawned on the country's campuses.

These professional and cultural conditions did not last. As provincial governments expanded their post-secondary education systems in order to multiply the number of students doing bachelor, master's, and doctoral degrees, our universities hired huge numbers of American professors, since Canada was not producing enough PhDs to meet the sudden demand to staff new campuses and expand old ones. These US scholars naturally brought their values with them and so helped shift the Canadian universities' professional ethos from a European to an American mould. When in this period of transition a rising American was hired by York University to chair its political science department, he gave his new colleagues a list of the four most prestigious US journals, such as the *American Political Science Review* or *International Organization*, in which they should publish – or perish. Many mid-career American scholars used such Canadian postings as way stations to better positions back home, and this man did not stay long at York. But the publish-or-perish syndrome took root, and some of the younger US immigrants, who did choose to make their careers in Canada and contribute to its scholarly life, also came up against this narrowly professionalized ethos.

I saw this transformation at first hand when sitting on a promotion committee to consider the dossier of an Africanist who had joined our department from Berkeley and was up for tenure. Sandy Lakoff, one of the migratory professors whom we had hired from Harvard and who would soon go on to greater glory in California, asked disdainfully why Jonathan Barker was wasting his time editing a special issue for the young *Canadian Journal of African Studies* instead of submitting articles to the leading *American Journal of African Studies*. Although Jonathan won his tenure nonetheless, my point is that these new professional norms militated even against the involvement of professors in their adopted country's scholarly life.

I next came face-to-face with this new American imperative in a personally more brutal encounter. The occasion was the launching of the book I had written about my campaign for the mayoralty of Toronto, which Alan Samuel had published. Because my departmental chair was an expert on municipal administration, I gave him a copy of *City Lib: Parties and Change* and invited him to lunch. This did not lead to the lively exchange I had been expecting. Instead, my academic boss opened fire. First, he felt I had missed the boat with *City Lib* by not comparing the Liberal Party's failure to penetrate Toronto's politics with "the extensive US literature on American cities' experience with federal political parties." Next he made it clear that my activism was not acceptable, whether stirring up trouble through Praxis or writing op-eds (although it was apparently fine for him to be a backroom adviser to the Conservative government of Ontario). And, just to make it clear that, had I not myself already been granted tenure, I would be looking for work elsewhere, he opined that my teaching was not, as he graciously put it, "a red-hot Mama."

Around this time my marriage exploded, leaving me as single parent of two very young daughters. I realized that of my four main activities – parenting, teaching, research, and public engagement – I would have to drop the latter. Teaching and research I could largely do from my home base. Public engagement involved endless meetings, generally at night, so I had to bring my involvement as an activist academic to an end just as the socio-cultural conditions accepting academic participation in the public sphere also disappeared.

The broader societal significance of this change became clear to me at one point in the 1980s when Ed Neufeld, a former colleague in Political Economy, who had joined the federal government's Department of Finance as a senior economist and had then moved to be chief economist at the Royal Bank of Canada, gave a seminar in our – his home – department. By way of prologue to his talk, he listed a range of burning public issues – free trade, native peoples' rights, the women's movement, federal-provincial conflict, public-sector privatization – and asked why social scientists in general and political scientists in particular were so silent on them in public. When it came to the discussion period, Peter Russell weighed in with the answer. The structure of professional incentives, he bluntly stated, militated against scholars taking part in public debates. It hurt you professionally to participate in public discourse, because these appearances were deemed unprofessional. Writing for the general public or, even worse, having a best-seller would generate envy, then scorn for having "popularized" scholarly research. What helped you – whether for getting hired in the first place, getting tenure subsequently, or getting salary increases year by year – was earning professional brownie points. These came from two types of peer-reviewed publications: peer-reviewed articles in internationally reputed – which generally meant American – journals and books accepted by the publishing houses of better universities, which typically required three academic readers' positive assessments of a manuscript before it could be published.

In the new professionalized academy, public involvement generally counted against you, particularly behind closed doors, where your project could be sunk and your career path put in jeopardy without your knowing who had fired the torpedo. Sitting 10 years ago on the adjudication committee that was selecting which 50 of some 150 research-project applications would get financial support from the Social Sciences and Humanities Research Council (SSHRC), I was astonished to hear my francophone colleagues marking down the proposal from a very prominent Quebec political scientist because he had not published in English and in "international" journals. These were the criteria for professional success in Quebec but not necessarily for social relevance. It would have been better for him professionally to publish in the *American Political Science Review* and be noticed by few Quebeckers than in the *Revue Québécoise des Sciences Politiques*, where he could expect his ideas to be read and quickly reverberate through the Quebec media.

For some decades now, the process of alienating university professors from public discourse starts with their academic training. When they are choosing the thesis topic on which they will devote three or four seminal years and get their first experience in scholarly research, they need to find a niche in the academic literature which they can fill in such a way as to satisfy not only their academic supervisor but a final committee consisting of three or four other specialists in this tiny field. Subsequently, when preparing their theses for submission to a university press, hiving off chapters for submission to learned journals, or proposing a new research project for funding from scholarly research councils, young professors' audience remains equally narrow – their own colleagues in their own discipline, whose judgment will determine their professional future. As a result, scholars write not for the general public but for a limited and fragmented audience: not even for fellow sociologists as a discipline, but for experts on the Asian diaspora; not even for fellow anthropologists in general, but for specialists in native burial rites.

There are still cases of older professors who have the urge to communicate with the broader public. They can and do so at no professional risk because they are already established or even retired. But even for them, it is far easier to commune with their own, often globally spread-out, academic family of researchers than try to find an outlet that will take their concerns to Canada's general public.

Some of the academy's social scientists are tapped by government, whether to do research for royal commissions, public enquiries, or in-house studies. These government needs for policy advice are also met by think tanks which commission favoured professors to research specific issues. In this way the business-financed C.D. Howe and Fraser Institutes produce an impressive flow of studies arguing conservative and ultra-conservative positions respectively, while the Institute for Research on Public Policy, which gets some of its money from the federal and provincial governments, is by and large more centrist. Government does get value for its money, but little of this work goes beyond policy specialists. Virtually all of this knowledge production is commissioned from academics whose points of view are what the think tank or bureaucrat wants to hear. The public gets little access to this back-channel consulting, and any such mainstream output – particularly of economists whose bias against government regulation pervades the assumptions built into their models and informs their policy recommendations – is rarely rigorously challenged from rival perspectives. Ideologically conditioned or not, little of this back-channel consulting is made available to the public in a form it can ingest.

The consequences of the Canadian academy's alienation from the public came into high relief in the mid-1980s over the issue of "free trade," which was boldly put on the agenda by the former finance minister Donald Macdonald when he was appointed to chair what became the landmark Royal Commission on the Economic Union and Development Prospects for Canada. Macdonald made it clear that he favoured an economic integration agreement with the United States as a solution for Canada's problems facing a wave of US protectionism, so it was no coincidence that those economists who did not subscribe to this idea were weeded out of the commission's roster of experts by his research director. When MacDonald's free-trade recommendation was eagerly accepted by Prime Minister Brian Mulroney and a deal with Washington negotiated, the subsequent intense public debate was notable for three characteristics. Civil society – environmentalists, pensioners, cultural organizations, native peoples, feminists, and trade unions – was fervently opposed. Big transnational corporations, led by the Business Council on National Issues (BCNI) were fervently in favour. But little was heard from the Canadian academy.

True, professors organized conferences and published books – John Crispo pro free trade and Duncan Cameron contra.[2] But the broader academy had little traction. The kind of informed discussion about the consequences of tilting the public playing field in favour of footloose corporations and against environmental or social-justice values was heard in the seminar room, while the media broadcast shouting matches between polarized and polarizing debaters. With the notable exception of the Simon Fraser University political economist Marjorie Cohen, who regularly took on the BCNI's spokesman Tom d'Aquino on television and in public meetings, the academic intellectual was absent from public discourse about a historical, society-changing decision that was ultimately made in the issue-distorting rough and tumble of the 1988 federal election.

Reinforcing this tragic contradiction between the Canadian academic system's growth and the decline in its public presence was the equally contradictory phenomenon of the growth in our media outlets and the decline in their intellectual content. The federal political parties' bipartisan hostility to the CBC – the Trudeau Liberals considered Radio Canada to be too Péquiste in its leanings and the CBC's English networks a nuisance, while the Conservatives under Brian Mulroney and later Stephen Harper considered the CBC to be too Liberal – led to its steady financial attrition. Constant pressure to cut staff and compete with the private sector for advertising revenue and therefore ratings have militated against CBC television's engagement with ideas, although CBC radio provides meagre doses of real thought to a shrinking demographic.

A parallel, government-sanctioned concentration of the newspaper sector has reduced the space that the printed press chooses to make available for informal discussion. While Conrad Black gave a powerful forum to right-wing commentary and ultra-conservative harangue by creating the *National Post*, its presence in the daily paper market did not spur its competitors to turn to the university campus to raise their ideational quality. As a recent editor of the *Globe and Mail* put it to a group of my colleagues whom I had invited to lunch with him, "My readers are not all A students." His meaning was clear: Canada's self-proclaimed national paper was to be dumbed down, not beefed up. Better to publish Margaret Wente day after day as long as she provoked dozens of readers to write angry letters-to-the-editor than to invite, say, a Quebec theologian to comment on new stirrings among young Catholics in the francophone church. Such essays would, of course, be welcome in *Le Devoir*, but Quebec culture has a deep – and very French – respect for intellectuals, a socio-cultural difference which gives professors a far more common presence in the francophone media than their counterparts enjoy in the rest of Canada.

As for public speaking, organizations like the Canadian Clubs now book their speakers through agencies which steer clear of professors lest they be *too* intellectual in their performance. The probability is that the kind of dynamic professors who win teaching awards for their engaging capacity to make the discussion of ideas a riveting experience for their students are far better communicators than the average CEO or federal minister who doggedly reads a text that was drafted by a speech agency. There are many academics who have enough self-confidence and would gladly bring their expertise to a broader public if given the chance.

This does not mean that all professors are silenced. The news media have a burning need for fifteen-second clips by experts to comment on breaking stories, and the editor of this book, Nelson Wiseman, is the Canadian media's most consulted professor on Canadian politics. Other authors in this collection, Janice Stein and Tom Flanagan, are prominent liberal and conservative commentators on international issues and Canadian electoral politics. Peter Russell himself along with Patrick Monahan from Osgoode Hall Law School are regularly consulted on constitutional matters. Tad Homer-Dixon at the University of Waterloo has become a globally recognized expert on environmental catastrophes who can get his views published whenever he has something to say. The former Olympic runner and present sports scholar Bruce Kidd is regularly interviewed on anything to do with sports policy or the Olympics. But these stars underline the general rule that the Canadian public is deprived of getting stimulation from the hundreds of academics who are not already celebrities and whose salaries it pays through the tax system.

I understand the recent emergence of the "public intellectual" as a societal response both to the constricted academic *supply* of ideas to the public sphere and to their reduced *transmission* through the public media. These factors have fostered the conditions in which a small roster of professionalized intellectual stars can flourish. Jack Granatstein retired from York University many years ago but, thanks to a good agent and his powerful personality, can readily place his views as a conservative military historian in *Maclean's* magazine or the *Globe and Mail*. John Ralston Saul is more in the French mode of intellectual, since, without any university base, he made a name for himself as a provocative writer and speaker who can attract large paying audiences. Maude Barlow – also in this book – has a national and now an international presence thanks to having built a movement sustained by thousands of students-paying members.

By the turn of the century, new information technology had multiplied TV channels both for broadcasting and for "narrowcasting" to specialized audiences, but the frenetic compulsion to attract viewers with scenes of physical violence or verbal confrontation has done nothing to increase the quality of public discourse in this country, still less in the United States, which sets the standards for English Canada's media. The World Wide Web allows all scholars to post their publications on sites that can be accessed from all over the world and so gives them a wider audience, but this does not mean that the general public profits as a national community. Such new social networks as YouTube, Twitter, and Facebook have created a highly fragmented, globally connected public domain in which everyone with access to the Internet can find an expert or be one. Whether these new media break down the present public-intellectual star system remains to be seen. But what remains *unseen* is the sad reality that the Canadian public through its taxes has paid for the construction of a vast and impressive professional academy which serves the interests of government and the corporate sector but from which it receives negligible intellectual value.

In my view, Canada cannot afford this waste of resources. I myself pushed the SSHRC to give bonus points for applicants who did manage to get the results of their previous research transmitted in the public domain, and it did take some steps in this direction. As universities now have to compete in recruiting students, their administrators realize that, every time one of their faculty members appears on television, their campus brand gets some precious free publicity. But this does not mean that university presidents have the power or the courage to challenge the stubbornly professionalized norms in each of their discipline-bound departments, whose bottom line remains the peer-reviewed publication.

To pick up the personal note on which I began, I look back on my own career with a sense of profound dismay. I can be considered a personal success because I have received wonderful awards for my writing and my teaching and enjoy a rich life with my family, friends, and students. Nevertheless, I feel that we who joined the academy have failed to make our society a better place for Canadians. To be sure, some battles were won along the way – particularly for tolerance among immigrant groups in our biggest cities and for women's, natives', and gay rights. But overall, our society has become more unjust, our environment is more poisonous, our economy more subject to forces we decline to control, our attitudes to labour and the disadvantaged more dismissive, and our politics more vicious.

The muting of the professor is only one factor, but it helps explain how Canada among other Western countries has reversed the previous century's slow progress towards human emancipation. I believe that, had Canadian academics been able to participate vigorously in their own country's debates and decisions, the public discourse would not have degenerated, and our governments' policies would have been able to improve, not worsen, the quality of Canadians' life and move the notion of a Just Society from a mere slogan closer towards reality.

NOTES

1 Abraham Rotstein, ed., *The Prospect of Change* (Toronto: McGraw-Hill, 1965); Peter Russell, ed., *Nationalism in Canada* (Toronto: McGraw-Hill, 1966); Stephen Clarkson, ed., *An Independent Foreign Policy for Canada?* (Toronto: McClelland & Stewart, 1968); Trevor Lloyd and Jack McLeod, eds, *Agenda 1970: Proposals for a Creative Politics* (Toronto: University of Toronto Press, 1968); Ian Lumsden, ed., *Close the 49th Parallel etc: The Americanization of Canada* (Toronto: University of Toronto Press, 1970); Alkis Kontos, ed., *Domination* (Toronto: University of Toronto Press, 1975); Alan Powell, ed., *The City: Attacking Modern Myths* (Toronto: University of Toronto Press, 1972); Mel Watkins, ed., *Dene Nation: The Colony Within* (Toronto: University of Toronto Press, 1977); David Shugarman, ed., *Thinking about Change* (Toronto: University of Toronto Press, 1974); William Leiss, *The Limits to Satisfaction: An Essay on the Problem of Needs and Commodities* (Toronto: University of Toronto Press, 1976).
2 John Crispo, ed., *Free Trade: the Real Story* (Toronto: Gage, 1988); Duncan Cameron, ed., *The Free-Trade Deal* (Toronto: Lorimer, 1988).

11 Polling for Democracy

MICHAEL ADAMS

When I was invited to contribute to this volume I hesitated, not seeing myself as a public intellectual. Public intellectuals do their own thinking. As a pollster, I tend to scavenge other people's thinking: asking questions, aggregating the responses, and reporting on what they have said. Nor did I have any great insight to offer about public intellectuals as a class, although I did toy with the hypothesis that Canada has too many publics – regional, demographic, and psychographic – to really elevate our intellectuals into national public figures in the way that, say, France or even the United States might.

These disclaimers notwithstanding, I think there might be some value in reflecting on how polling and related punditry have evolved over the course of my career, and what contributions they might make to the kinds of social and policy discussions that public intellectuals often try to spark or advance. I have come to believe that the data we pollsters produce can catalyse discussion and action among the engaged public, and that in this sense, the data pollsters gather – especially if they gather it through a thoughtful and rigorous process – can fulfil some of the same functions as persuasive prose from an accessible academic or a respected journalist. In other words, I think public opinion data itself might be a kind of public intellectual presence in our society: not the singular voice of an expert individual, but the collective voice of the society or some group within it.

My sense of the value of survey research has changed a great deal over time. I have always been fascinated by it, but as a young man I was more interested in the "insider" quality of polling. In high school, I dreamed of being Lou Harris to some Canadian version of JFK. I aspired to sit around a war-room table in the middle of the night, the trusted alchemist of public opinion, parsing the numbers and trying to understand what the general public was really trying to tell us, and what we should do about it. Devising brilliant political strategies for a charismatic, idealistic politician seemed to my young mind the highest use to which public opinion data could be put.

As I got older and founded my own research company, I was less attracted to the idea of political battle, but still assumed that the audience for my research would be a small group of expert insiders – a business seeking to woo a new market segment, a human-resources officer trying to court or retain the best and brightest, or a government department trying to determine how best to serve its citizens. For many years I and my colleagues gathered survey data with these small audiences in mind, offering our clients a window onto public attitudes through the use of the random sample, the innovation for which George Gallup became famous after he correctly predicted the outcome of the 1936 presidential election in the United States with his small but representative samples of the American voting public.

Intermittently, I and my fellow pollsters would conduct election horse-race polling, competing to have the most accurate analysis of what the public was thinking and how the race would play out. The public and therefore the media were interested in these numbers, and punditry began to come with the territory of polling. (My first encounter with television punditry was during the 1984 federal election as a leaders' debate commentator on a panel hosted by CBC star journalist Barbara Frum.) Still, intoning each day's electoral horse-race numbers was a fairly mechanical affair, as it still is. Pollsters merited the name "public intellectual" about as much as the meteorologist on the evening news did: both offered valuable information and a little analytical nuance as necessary, but neither was likely to offer the Big Idea of the day.

It was not until I wrote my first book, *Sex in the Snow*, that I came to appreciate how intrigued members of the general public were by the attitudes of their fellow citizens – not just about how they were going to vote next week, but what they wanted for their society and how they saw the world around them. It has not always been taken for granted that people want to know what other ordinary citizens – not just experts, elites, and public intellectuals – think.

I had assumed early in my career that those who would be most interested in our research findings were those who had something commercial or political to gain from understanding society better. Before we began working on *Sex in the Snow*, which featured not just ordinary polling but a more complex methodology that measured social values, I and my colleagues found the analytics to be fascinating and our clients found it extremely illuminating. But I had to be talked into writing a book about it: I didn't imagine that the average Canadian – even the average curious, readerly Canadian – would want to read about our segmentation analyses. True, not everyone wanted to read about Canadian social values. But the publisher was right about public interest and I was wrong: the book sold over 24,000 copies, which came as a happy surprise. Perhaps I shouldn't have been surprised that engaged Canadians would be attracted to the data. Public opinion research holds a mirror up to society; most of us, passing a mirror, can't help but take a peek. During this time some of my colleagues also began wading deeper into social and political analysis. Allan Gregg went beyond the standard talking-head role and began hosting a public affairs show on TVOntario. Others, such as Frank Graves and newly minted poll sponsor and interpreter, former Reform Party leader Preston Manning, have appeared with some regularity in op-ed pages. They, too, recognized the demand for information about public opinion not only among elites but among engaged citizens.

By the time I began writing about our research for the general public, Environics had been using the social-values method for over a decade, surveying Canadians about concepts that did not appear in ordinary polling and using their answers to slot them into segments or "tribes," as we called them.[1] As the tribes became more widely known, friends and acquaintances began to ask me a funny question: "What am I?" They wanted me to put them in a tribe, to offer them an on-the-spot sociocultural diagnosis based on my knowledge of their personalities and beliefs, like someone guessing people's weight at a county fair. Sometimes I would tell people to go and fill out our abbreviated values survey online. Sometimes I would give my "expert" assessment on the spot, reminding them that we were more in the territory of the Amazing Kreskin than that of social science. (Admittedly, I rarely tell anyone I think they are an Aimless Dependant, especially after dark.)

What I took from this recurring experience was that thoughtful people are not only curious about the world, they are curious about themselves. To study survey data – whether our social-values data or political horse-race polling – is to learn about yourself in the context of your society. When people asked me "What am I?" they were, of course, not expecting some penetrating existential insight. They were asking "Where do I fit in this society? Who is like me? Who is unlike me? What do I share with my fellow citizens? What do you see in your conversation with a random sample that I can't see in my conversations with friends and family, or in reading the analyses of newspaper columnists?" (This was 1997, long before the social-media explosion, which still does not offer a random sample but does give ordinary people much more information than they had before about what others like them are saying and doing.)

It is my sense – though I cannot prove it – that pollsters enjoy greater prominence and respect in Canada than they do in many other societies. If this is true, it is not because the quality of our polling is better, but because pollsters' role in our society is different and perhaps more necessary: because of Canada's geographic size and social diversity, we have a limited number of ways to get to know each other as Canadians, and polls are one obvious way of getting a snapshot of the whole society. Survey data can help us try to imagine what it's like to be somebody else in our society: an immigrant, someone living in another region of Canada, someone whose economic circumstances are different from our own. It can also help us see where our own attitudes and interests fit in a broader social context. Am I in the mainstream or am I an outlier?

Survey data can also help us to see ourselves, for all our internal diversity, as a society distinct from other societies. The work of mine that received the most attention was my 2003 book *Fire and Ice: The United States, Canada and the Myth of Converging Values*. In addition to its fortuitous timing (the book came out at a time when the Chrétien government and the Bush administration were travelling in opposite directions on a few high-profile issues, including the Iraq War), the book seemed to attract people with both its cross-national (Canada-US) comparison, and its longitudinal comparisons (looking at both societies over time). These two approaches answer a couple of questions that any society – but especially at a time of rapid political and technological change – is bound to seek answers to: who are we, and what are we becoming? Many public intellectuals reflect on those questions by bringing deep understandings of historical context to bear on contemporary issues, or by sharing their expertise about the workings of other societies. In my case, I simply marshalled the social-values data we had gathered on behalf of our clients over the years, and made an argument about what I thought the numbers were saying when taken together and seen from 35,000 feet.

If *Sex in the Snow* caused me to realize how curious engaged Canadians were about where they fit into the values landscape of their society,

Fire and Ice convinced me that engaged Canadians cared deeply about the values that united Canada and made it distinct from other societies – even those as ostensibly similar to us as our nearest neighbour and largest trading partner. Of course, some commentators disagreed strongly with the conclusions I drew in *Fire and Ice*, but for the most part their claim was not that Canada was without shared values that distinguished them from Americans, but that my research had focused on the wrong ones. Much more important than whether Canadians and Americans felt the same about gender equality or the acceptability of everyday violence, some argued, was whether we believed in concepts like "democracy" and "the rule of law." Although I spoke to people with vastly different ideas about "shared values" in Canada, I found that most engaged people had some interest in reflecting on values that might serve as some kind of connective tissue among citizens, and also in how our values might be evolving over time and what this meant for our laws and institutions. The more I spoke to people about our research, the more convinced I became that public opinion research was not only an invaluable tool for marketing managers, politicians, and public servants, but also a means of fostering introspection and empathy in a diverse democratic society.

It was this growing sense of the value of survey data as a tool for enhancing our civic life that caused me to found the Environics Institute, a non-profit entity whose mission is to survey those not usually heard from, posing questions not usually asked. The first time I was inspired to conduct a survey not for current or prospective clients but simply to contribute to the national dialogue was in 2006. A number of events in the news, from terrorist attacks in the United States and Europe to the arrests of eighteen men in Mississauga (the "Toronto Eighteen" as they came to be known) had sparked considerable debate about the links between Islam and extreme political ideologies, and whether Muslim immigrants were integrating successfully into societies in Western Europe and North America. The more newspaper columnists and assorted talking heads (some said to be "representatives" or "spokespeople" of the Muslim community in Canada) debated the state of Muslims and other religious minorities in Canada, the more I wanted to hear from Canadian Muslims themselves. "If we want to know what these people think," I thought as the experts offered their hypotheses, "why don't we ask them?"

Of course, it is not as simple as that. You can ask one person to express in their own words what they think about an issue. You cannot ask 1500 people what they think without designing a process that excludes some of the complexity of how we each see the world. Survey researchers wield a significant amount of power in designing questionnaires, establishing the frames through which people will be able to express their opinions, and then in picking storylines out of the piles of numbers that emerge from the interview process. Like any human-designed tool of measurement, survey research has its biases. (Still, it is less biased than a self-proclaimed "representative" of almost a million people speaking on the evening news. And it is certainly less biased than a handful of young men plotting violence "on behalf" of their co-religionists.) The question of bias is not easily dismissed, especially when one is trying to create a portrait of a minority group that might be hard to reach because of language or geographic distribution or socio-economic status, and that might not be experienced in expressing their views and values to strangers calling them on the telephone without advanced notice or a proper introduction.

The holy grail for me as a pollster is to produce data that has been gathered through a thoughtful, rigorous process – and is therefore accepted as valid, so that the data become a solid empirical platform for flexible, creative discussion. People may derive a huge array of conclusions from the same survey data, and this is satisfying because the data have advanced the discussion in some way; but if the discussion drifts into squabbling about methodology, the big picture – and the value of the study – are lost. A representative sample of a larger population is a powerful means of giving voice to ordinary people, and, despite its imperfections, it is one of the most accurate means we have of understanding our society and the subgroups that constitute it. The collective voice of a group, expressed through survey data, is an illuminating contribution to many social and policy debates. Just as we need public intellectuals to explain, frame, and contextualize, we need some way to access the voices of ordinary people so they are not misrepresented or co-opted by those whose interests are served by the claim that "the people" support them, whether in a mature democracy or an emerging one.

While the survey of Canadian Muslims was the first major project of the Environics Institute, perhaps our most ambitious project has been the Urban Aboriginal Peoples Study (UAPS). I believe this study is the strongest example to date of the kind of role survey data might play in our national conversation in the years to come.

The Environics Institute wanted to amplify the voices of Aboriginal people living in Canadian cities, since this is a large and growing population, but one that seems to take up little space in our national dialogue and imagination. Few institutional leaders give voice to the perspective of this half of the country's Aboriginal population, as urban Aboriginal people themselves told us in the survey when we asked who, if anyone, spoke for them effectively. We were determined to at least get a good snapshot of Aboriginal peoples in Canada's cities to lend some visibility to this group, not just for non-Aboriginal Canadians, but for Aboriginal peoples themselves in both urban and rural settings, including reserves.

We spent two years working with an advisory circle of Aboriginal and non-Aboriginal academics and experts – and implementing substantive changes to the methodology design – in order to ensure that our sample would be credible. We spent several more months working with an Aboriginal coding firm (to ensure that respondents' verbatim statements were faithfully represented in our analytical frameworks) and reflecting on the findings with our advisory circle and other experts.[2] The worst-case scenario for this study would have been the rejection of the data: to have three years, thousands of thoughtful interviews, and hundreds of thousands of dollars be consumed in bickering about statistical details. Only by taking those details seriously could we arrive at a study where the vast majority of commentators – including the main national Aboriginal organizations and an array of respected academics – acknowledged the validity of the data, and could then use the numbers to spark rich discussions about the experiences, identities, values, and aspirations of Aboriginal peoples living in Canadian cities. The UAPS is now a presence – I might even say a voice or a set of voices – in the Canadian conversation, especially among those who are engaged with Aboriginal issues. It is a catalyst for debate and policy ideas, and it is a mirror in which the over half a million Aboriginal people living in Canadian cities can see themselves and think about who they are becoming and where they fit into a larger social picture.

My role in this study was to convene subject-area experts and to participate in a process whereby we slowly arrived at a study and a data set we collectively saw as valid, original, and important. Although participating in this study – and to a lesser extent speaking and writing about it – has been a source of immense professional satisfaction to me, my main job in this study and in the rest of the work of the Institute is not the work of a public intellectual, but of a convenor and intermediary, maybe even a knowledge impresario. My role has been to offer others, some of them public intellectuals – from John Ralston Saul to Tom

Flanagan to Calvin Helin to David Newhouse – a foundation of data from which to formulate ideas and arguments about how to support Aboriginal peoples as they strive for success in our cities and beyond.

I was once told by an eminent Canadian who thought I was a little too free-wheeling in my own commentary about survey data that I should keep my mouth shut and let the numbers speak for themselves. Keeping my mouth shut has never much appealed, and the numbers don't speak for themselves – they need to have a story told about them, with someone connecting the dots. (As the business journalist Alan Webber has put it, "Facts are facts; stories are how we learn.") But as I move into the next phase of my career, I am increasingly focused on generating good numbers through which others can tell their own stories and develop their own theories. In my own career, I have gone from wanting to share insights about public attitudes with expert clients, to wanting to share those insights with the general public, to wanting to generate good data and help others find insight and value in the numbers.

I will continue to offer my analyses of the latest polling numbers and certainly of our social-values data, but my analyses will coexist with those of many others. Getting on TV with the most interesting numbers was once a sought-after objective among me and my peers, and having great fresh data to share is still a thrill. But in a networked age of information overload, announcing numbers through broadcast media does not have the power it once did to get attention and spark dialogue and even change. Public engagement processes, like the one the Environics Institute is currently undertaking to share UAPS data with urban Aboriginal communities across the country, now seem more likely to turn numbers into ideas and action.

As I write these words in the fall of 2010, I cannot help but reflect on the current context in this country. Survey research and program evaluation by the federal government is down from $30 million to $8 million; all government departments are banned from subscribing to syndicated tracking studies that enabled public servants to understand social change (and me to write my books about evolving attitudes and values). Most recently, Canadians have been informed of the replacement of the compulsory long form with a voluntary census in 2011. (The 2006 census, incidentally, allowed us to develop a sampling plan for the Urban Aboriginal Peoples Study.) The effect of this decision will not be felt tomorrow, but it will be in the years ahead as policy think tanks, academics, and public servants find they do not have reliable data to determine if our social and economic life, and particularly that of vulnerable minorities (new Canadians, young Canadians, poor Canadians, Aboriginal peoples, visible minorities, Canadians with disabilities), is improving or deteriorating.

In effect, we are currently being asked: "Why should a society try to know itself?" If public policy debates descend into conflicting opinions devoid of sound data, our public agora will look more like the comedy and tragedy of the Rush Limbaugh show and every debate will be just a matter of your anecdote and opinion versus mine. (As I heard one social scientist quip, the plural of anecdote is not data.)

Public intellectuals, private citizens, and others are now faced with the question of what constitutes intellectual leadership in a climate where information and expertise are themselves being undermined. This is a long way from the dream of the German mathematician and philosopher Leibniz, whose faith in the rational was so deep that he hoped for a future in which "when there are disputes among persons, we can simply say: Let us calculate, without further ado, to see who is right."

NOTES

1 A mention of our social-values work is an opportune time to note that my work in the public forum is underpinned by the work of a large number of people at Environics. "My" data and some of the related insights come from the methodological, analytical, and managerial capacity of the company I founded: Doctors David Jamieson (our chief scientist), Barry Watson, Keith Neuman, and Donna Dasko have made invaluable contributions, and my colleague in writing projects, Amy Langstaff, has helped me to articulate many of our findings over the years. Partners such as Jan Kestle (Environics Analytics), Claude Theoret (Nexalogy Environics) and Jen Evans (Sequentia Environics) in new branches of the Environics family also help amplify and analyse the voices of Canadians in their own fascinating ways and share the results.

2 Research has a fraught history among Aboriginal peoples in Canada. There is a long history of non-Aboriginal researchers studying Aboriginal peoples without appropriate consultation and without sharing the data they have gathered, often in order to impose paternalistic "solutions" on the population that has been studied.

12 A People's Intellectual

MAUDE BARLOW

I do not usually see myself as a public intellectual, but rather as an activist who uses the public realm of ideas to promote my beliefs and campaigns. However, for the purpose of this essay, I will use the term as I understand it.

For me, the public intellectual is someone who helps give voice to those who may lack the power of access to address their issues in the traditional venues of the public arena. For example, while the Internet has without question given a new opportunity for the traditionally voiceless, the mainstream media in Canada are still largely closed to all but a handful of dissenters from the dominant ideology of our time. Most of Canada's mainstream media are controlled by parent corporations with interests in telecommunications and broadcasting and in promoting the goals of competitiveness, foreign ownership, and media concentration. A 2007 survey of 600 journalists from corporate-owned media in Canada found that 60 per cent of them said the values and politics of their corporate owners had an effect on the day-to-day editorial agenda of their news organization.

Ask any union, environmental, or social justice group in Canada and they will tell you that their voices are more unwelcome than ever in our mainstream daily newspapers and television and radio stations.

The public intellectual also promotes the public's right to know and fights to give the public access to information on the processes behind elite-driven policy decisions, processes many in power would prefer to leave unexamined. (In this way the public intellectual differs from the traditional academic, although he or she may be an academic as well. The public intellectual enters the realm of everyday life seeking to bring the knowledge of academia, art, law, politics, economics, or science to the general public so that this knowledge will serve a greater good and will advance the interests of the whole population, not just a small cadre of specialists.)

This struggle between power-holders who seek to contain information and those who demand its dissemination is not recent. In a 1976 report on the governability of democracies for the Trilateral Commission, called *The Crisis of Democracy*, the late American author and National Security Council official Samuel P. Huntington deplored the "excess of democracy" that had broken out in wealthy countries and called for a greater degree of moderation in democracy. He wrote approvingly that President Truman had been able to govern the country with the "co-operation of a relatively small number of Wall Street lawyers and bankers" and noted that a "governable democracy" requires apathy and non-involvement on the part of the populace.

Bernard Ingham, former press spokesman for Margaret Thatcher, was less circumspect when in the same year he held a briefing for US correspondents. "Bugger the public's right to know," he said. "The game is the security of the state, not the public's right to know." This attitude is appalling to the public intellectual, as I would define the term. A healthy democracy requires the optimum participation of its citizens and provides the processes and institutions to encourage their active inclusion. At the Council of Canadians, we spend a great deal of our time attempting to get a hold of government documents of interest to Canadians and fight government secrecy and the withholding of information.

A public intellectual knows that issues of class, race, and gender have played a large part in denying universal access to power and the public arena of ideas. As a result, whole communities have been left out of the official history of states and their development. The public intellectual seeks to tell their story.

Howard Zinn, the late American scholar, historian, and public intellectual, wrote his path-altering *A People's History of the United States* precisely because he felt that the true stories of the lives of ordinary people, particularly those left out of the power structures of their time, were not represented in most state histories. In telling the history of a country, he warned, it was essential not to accept the memory of the state, and therefore likely of the state's elite, as the memory of the people. When a history of a country is presented as a history of a family, it conceals the fierce conflict of competing interests between conqueror and conquered, slave and slave master, worker and owner, thus silencing those left out of the telling of the story.

Noting that Nobel Prize–winning philosopher Albert Camus said the most important job of the public intellectual is not to be on the side of the executioners, Zinn devoted his life as a public intellectual to "disclosing those hidden episodes of the past when, even if in brief flashes, people showed their ability to resist, to join together, occasionally to win."

Building a Movement of Resistance

Resisting, joining together, building a movement for social and environmental justice, occasionally winning, giving a space for those voices so often left out of the public discourse – that is the mandate of the Council of Canadians. My work and any influence I have on public policy and political discourse comes directly from this organization I have had the honour of chairing for almost two decades. Unlike many public intellectuals who operate alone, I have the privilege of working with a brilliant and dedicated group of experts, academics, and activists who share my vision of social change and who have committed their lives to it. When I become engaged in a campaign or issue, it is understood that I have an army of dedicated and talented colleagues with me. My ideas do not stand alone, as with others who might be called public intellectuals; I consider it the first duty of a public activist to find like-minded allies and form the kind of long-term bonds that will lead to true change.

Twenty-five years ago, a group of well-known Canadians came together to voice their concern over the talk of a free trade agreement between Canada and the United States negotiated by Ronald Reagan and Brian Mulroney and create a new organization dedicated to preserving hard-won rights in Canada. Contrary to still-lingering myth, Council of Canadians founding members like Margaret Atwood, Pierre Burton, Mel Hurtig, Walter Gordon, Sheila Copps, Marion Dewar, Jim Laxer, and Bob White were not opposed to trade or trade rules per se; we came together rather out of a conviction that a combination of economic globalization – by that time on the ascendancy – and the "cold shower of competition" promised by Mulroney and his business allies would threaten Canadian cultural programs, universal social security, domestic control over our natural resources, and any hope of an independent foreign policy.

At first, the council was run a bit like the elite institutions it criticized, but soon it began to morph into a true social movement with many thousands of members. Today we are almost exclusively sustained by our close to 65,000 members, bolstered only by a few foundation grants supporting our international water-justice work. We also have more than seventy chapters across the country where activists come together to oppose bad government policy and promote policies and campaigns they have defined.

The creation of a broad civil-society movement together with the collaboration in networks with like-minded groups in Canada and around the world has changed the way we do politics and reflects what I think are the politics of a true public intellectual. In the first years, we lobbied powerful politicians, parliamentary committees, and institutions, bringing in experts and relying on the arguments and research we presented for success. We assumed that if we presented airtight cases, we would be given a space in the policy deliberations.

But it soon became clear that a powerful new player, a big business lobby then called the Business Council on National Issues (now called the Canadian Council of Chief Executives) had arrived on the scene and had special privilege in the halls of power, whether under Conservative or Liberal rule. On the eve of ratification of the Canada-US Free Trade Agreement, Brian Mulroney had declared before a blue chip corporate audience in New York City that Canada was "open for business," and soon, we saw, all the rules would change. Our perspective, even though it arguably represented at least half the Canadian population on issues such as the role of business and free trade and a clear majority of Canadians on issues such as public health care and the right to water, was not only no longer welcome, we were often treated with contempt when we presented our case before committees.

Physicist and educator Dr Ursula Franklin caught the essence of the shift when she said that she once thought that politicians in power were well meaning but ill informed, and that if she made a strong and informed case before them, she would sway their thinking or at least open their minds to her argument. However, more recently she has come to believe they are very well informed indeed but perhaps not so well meaning. It similarly became clear to me in those first years of the neoliberal experiment that we had to do more than make a compelling case, no matter how well documented our arguments were on, for instance, climate change, or the effects of falling foreign aid budgets on the global South. To make any headway, we had to build public support and get our case to the media, who in turn would put pressure on the politicians.

So we created what we called our Citizen's Agenda, a project based on the belief that ordinary citizens, when well informed, can influence their governments and other institutions in a way that a restricted group of "experts" never can and that, in fact, only informed voters were going to be able to challenge the hegemony of influence in the halls of power now enjoyed by the private sector in Canada. Central to the Citizen's Agenda is the key public-intellectual principle of promoting the public's right to know. Thus, an important component of our work is taking the research and information of experts, be they scientific studies, legal arguments, or complicated trade agreements, and "translating" them into language that everyone can understand; hence the title of books and reports such as *Profit Is Not the Cure: A Citizen's Guide to Saving Medicare*, or *The World Trade Organization: A Citizen's Agenda for Change.*

The Citizen's Agenda is based on the firm belief that ordinary citizens, in other words, non-experts in a given field, are perfectly capable of understanding even the most complicated science or law or trade deals, written for the purpose of affecting public policy. Too often, the language of official documents is intimidating to the public and discourages their active participation. Our job is to make these documents and issues accessible to the widest possible number of people, including those least traditionally likely to become involved in public policy.

To this end, we train chapter members to promote our campaigns in their local communities, lobby local politicians, hospital board officials, members of Parliament, and so on, hold town hall meetings, write op-eds and letters to local newspapers, and become public speakers. We have a sophisticated communications team that puts out regular press releases and op-eds, publicizes our campaigns, writes reports, fact sheets, and even comic books, creates YouTube and viral videos and tweets, publishes a tri-annual magazine for our members and maintains a brilliant interactive website. I personally have published sixteen books, chapters for many others, dozens of reports, and hundreds of op-ed commentaries, all to promote my and the council's vision to the widest possible audience. In recent years, our work for trade, the environment, and social justice has gone international, leading us to work with like-minded groups around the world.

Taking Action

I do not judge progress on an issue or the success of a campaign by whether we won or lost it, and I doubt if any public intellectual does. This is all about the hearts and minds of the public. Winning is sweet indeed, but for me, the true test of progress is the building of a movement and the creation of a space for public dialogue and debate in an arena that was formerly the exclusive domain of a privileged few. For instance, even though popular opinion was on our side on both the Canada-US and North American Free Trade Agreements, because of the power aligned against us, we were unable to stop their passage or even have them modified. But we did not stop building our case that unregulated trade and investment deals were removing the ability of governments to maintain domestic policies that promote social and environmental security, and we were able to help our colleagues in Latin America halt the Free Trade Area of the Americas, the proposed expansion of NAFTA, in its tracks. Similarly, the World Trade Organization Doha Round has been stalled for years now, in part due to a strong alliance between global civil-society groups and countries of the global South no longer willing to do the bidding of the powerful countries of the North.

One story illustrates how as a public intellectual/public activist, I helped take an obscure investment agreement with the highly specialized and very dense language of trade officials and make it into the stuff of popular resistance. In 1996, I was told that Canada was a leading proponent of an OECD-sponsored international investment agreement called the Multilateral Agreement on Investment. Civil-society groups in the South were very concerned because this deal would have given transnational corporations the right to sue governments that tried to take back some control over local resources or impose conditions upon the operations of these foreign companies in their territory.

Puzzled that the government of Jean Chrétien, who had campaigned when in opposition against the secrecy of such deals, would be involved in an international deal I had never heard of, I called the office of then trade minister Roy McLaren and was told it did not exist. Mere months later, colleagues and I received a copy of the MAI in a brown paper bag. The very day we made it public, the Liberal government put up a website extolling its virtues. True to our belief in the public's right to know, we sought to find out more on the history of the MAI in Canada through access to information, and lo and behold, we discovered that the Department of Foreign Affairs and International Trade had been meeting with key leaders in the business community on the deal since 1993 and that it was near completion.

An angry activist can be a force to be reckoned with. With a colleague, I wrote the book *The MAI and the Threat to Canadian Sovereignty*, which became a best-seller within weeks of publication. We formed a large coalition of groups to oppose the MAI, co-chaired by the Council of Canadians and the Canadian Labour Congress. I set out on a cross-country speaking tour attended by huge crowds in every community. We broke the areas of concern – environment, social programs, security, workers, and so on – up and farmed out research on each sector to experts in our movement. Using this research, we prepared popular material explaining the MAI to Canadians and a handbook for local municipal politicians, which our chapters used to obtain dozens of local resolutions expressing concern or outright opposition to the MAI by city councils. These collectively resulted in a resolution against the MAI at the Federation of Canadian Municipalities' 1996 annual meeting. Literally hundreds of "MAI-Free Zones" were set up in schools and universities, in seniors' residences and hospitals. Hundreds of groups signed our petition to the government and we met with newspaper editorial boards across the country.

With the national CBC in tow, I went to the October 1997 OECD MAI summit in Paris, where civil society set up an international network to defeat the MAI. The CBC carried our protest as the lead story for three nights running. We soon had a global petition against the MAI signed by thousands of civil-society groups around the world. Governments in Canada and Europe were stunned at this unexpected opposition to an obscure investment agreement they considered the exclusive purview of their trade experts and lawyers. In April 1998 talks were suspended, and in December of that year, government officials pulled the plug on the MAI. I debated a furious Donald Johnson, the former Liberal cabinet member who was now OECD president, and told him the days of putting up a "no ordinary people" sign over these deals was over.

A *Globe and Mail* editorial chastised the government for its attempts at "globalization without representation," and in a front page article reported that the MAI campaign was the first Internet victory for global civil society. The *Financial Times* said the fear and confusion on the part of negotiators was like a scene from the movie *Butch Cassidy and the Sundance Kid*, where the hapless politicians were being chased by hordes of vigilantes – vigilantes, the paper noted, who had "drawn blood." The Fraser Institute launched an angry attack at the "spineless" Liberals for allowing civil society to derail their policies and warned that they would be better prepared the next time.

Critics were right to take this new movement seriously. The international coalition that came together to defeat the MAI stayed together to mount the protest that shut down the November 1999 WTO ministerial meeting in Seattle, Washington, and went on to form Our World Is Not for Sale, an international network of over 150 major union, environmental, development, social justice, peasant, indigenous, and farm organizations opposed to the World Trade Organization and other unjust trade and investment regimes. This network has relentlessly researched and critiqued the WTO and its impact on millions of displaced workers and farmers as well as its poor environmental record. It has been a powerful presence at every WTO gathering since.

In Canada these concerns surfaced again when, in March 2005, the Paul Martin government signed a new business agreement, the Security and Prosperity Partnership (SPP) for North America, with American and Mexican Presidents George W. Bush and Vincente Fox. Its mandate was to promote prosperity in North America by integrating security measures across the continent based on the "war on terror" measures of post-9/11 America, as well as harmonizing the processing procedures and standards for all goods and services that are traded across the borders of the three countries. Of course our concern was immediately that, with George Bush in the White House, the harmonization would all be in one direction – downward.

Once again, the talks were held behind closed doors and there was no role for parliament, as this deal was never slated to go for ratification before the legislative bodies of the three countries. Once again, the big business community was the only sector consulted by and advising the governments, this time in the form of the North American Competitiveness Council, made up of the CEOs of thirty prominent corporate leaders of major North American corporations. Once again, the Council of Canadians pulled together a network to expose the SPP and its agenda. I wrote a book on the secretive deal called *Too Close for Comfort: Canada's Future in Fortress North America*, and went out on the road again across the country to sound the alarm. While the mainstream media were slow to pick up on the resistance to this deal, all hell broke loose when, at the August 2007 "Three Amigos" summit in Montebello, Quebec, union leaders exposed several masked, rock-wielding undercover police officers masquerading as protesters. The footage from this confrontation was shown around the world.

When Barak Obama became president, he expressed his distaste for the secretive history of the SPP and let it officially expire. In August 2009, the American SPP site was updated to say: "The Security and Prosperity Partnership for North America is no longer an active initiative. There will not be any updates to this site." Unlike the demise of the MAI, the end of the SPP garnered no media attention in Canada, but it was another blow to the belief that these deals, which ultimately affect everyone, are the sole domain of a small cadre of bureaucrats, selected elected officials, the big business community, and hand-chosen experts. The victory over these deals negotiated behind closed doors was a victory for democracy.

Affecting Change

For me, the lessons learned from these examples are clear. In dealing with any issue of public policy, it is essential to enlist the support and direct involvement of as many other groups and individuals as possible and, as well, bring in the expertise of those outside the inner circle. It is also essential get the research out in accessible form to the groups and sectors likely to be impacted. Government secrecy must be challenged and as much information as is possible must be made available to the widest possible audience. That audience, those citizens, must be trusted to know what to do with the information. I am never-endingly amazed at the creative ways in which communities and individuals express their opposition to bad policy.

To do this work, it is also essential to know that change is possible. Tetteh Hormeku, director of the African arm of Third World Network, says that such a belief in the face of the hegemony of the current economic and development model is the most radical notion of all. It is important for me to include here other Canadian public intellectuals/ activists who are making a huge difference to our country and our world simply because they hold fast to a dream of how we could create more sustainable and just societies.

Dr David Schindler is a world-renowned freshwater scientist and Killam Memorial Professor of Ecology at the University of Alberta who uses his clout in the scientific community to reach out to Canadians about the water crisis in Alberta and Canada. A prolific writer, speaker, and media guest, he uses his extensive knowledge to lobby for change in public policy. His discovery that detergent phosphates were responsible for the pollution of Lake Erie led to ground-breaking legislative protections for the lake. Fellow Albertan Andrew Nikiforuk is a journalist and commentator who wrote the immensely influential book *Tar Sands: Dirty Oil and the Future of a Continent*. He, along with key First Nations leaders like Clayton Thomas Muller and George Poitras of the

Environmental Indigenous Network, have taken the struggle against the Alberta tar sands to international audiences.

Bruce Campbell has directed the Canadian Centre for Policy Alternatives for many years, producing consistently high-quality books and reports and the monthly journal *The Monitor*, all in the service of a movement. He is also a highly respected author himself. Tony Clarke directs the Polaris Institute, which has been a leader in exposing corporate control over public policy. Tony is a prolific author as well and is also deeply involved in the campaign against the tar sands. Pat Mooney of the ETC Group is a world-respected authority on biotechnology and corporate food production whose combination of impeccable research and dogged determination has kept generations of Canadian government officials on their toes. David Suzuki is, of course, a leading Canadian public intellectual whose foundation leads the way in green alternatives.

People around the world know Naomi Klein's voice; millions actively seek out her books, columns, and speaking engagements. Stephen Lewis has moved untold millions to action with his passionate writing and speaking on the plight of HIV/AIDS victims in Africa and has set up a foundation to directly effect change. Journalist and bestselling author Linda McQuaig has written extensively on the need to protect Canada's social programs and the dangers of too-close ties to US policies. Her weekly Toronto *Star* column is widely read and quoted.

Political economist and York University professor Jim Laxer has inspired generations of students with his vision of social justice and many best-selling books. His brother Gordon is also an economist and professor at the University of Alberta and founder of the highly influential Parkland Institute in Edmonton. A prolific author as well, Gordon Laxer's vision of the need for energy security in Canada has actually influenced legislation in several provinces. Danielle Martin is a family physician and founding chair of the prominent group of health-care professionals Canadian Doctors for Medicare. She has become a leading voice in the debate on the future of health care in Canada.

These and many other activists, academics, and writers in Canada need to be honoured for putting their own careers second to the common good and their belief in a country and a society that can do better. It is my great honour to work alongside them in our struggle for economic, social, and environmental justice. Most important is their collective commitment to provide a safe place for those traditionally without a voice in our society, the mark of a true public intellectual.

13 Canadian Economists as Public Intellectuals

PIERRE FORTIN[*]

There is an old tradition, among economists, of getting involved in public discussion of maladies such as high unemployment, faltering growth, wealth inequality, disorderly public finances, or a deteriorating environment. In the twentieth century, the list of highly influential public intellectuals would certainly include economists John Maynard Keynes in Britain, John Kenneth Galbraith and Paul Samuelson in the United States, Edmond Malinvaud in France, and Harold Innis in Canada.

Fewer Public Intellectuals among Economists Today than in the Past

In North America, the implication of academic economists as public intellectuals seems to have declined in recent decades. Table 13.1 is an attempt to explain why. Beginning in the 1970s, PhD students in economics understood that, in order to be successful in their discipline, it was much better for them to be good problem-solvers and mathematicians than have a broad knowledge of economic facts and a thorough knowledge of the economic literature. Knowledge of the psychology or sociology of human behaviour was rarely mentioned, despite the great emphasis it had received from the best economists of the last two centuries, such as Mill, Wicksell, Pareto, Keynes, and Samuelson.

*I thank two anonymous referees for their perceptive comments and helpful suggestions.

Table 13.1. Opinion of PhD students in top North American economics departments on the importance of various skills for success in the economics profession

Date of survey	1985	2002
Implied average age of respondents in 2013	54	37
Percentage who think the following skill is very important:		
Being good at problem solving	65	51
Being excellent in mathematics	57	30
Being interested in, and good at, empirical research	16	30
Having a broad knowledge of the economics literature	10	11
Having a thorough knowledge of the economy	3	9

Note: Seven departments were surveyed – Harvard, MIT, Princeton, Yale, Columbia, Stanford, and Chicago.

Sources: David Colander and Arjo Klamer, "The Making of an Economist," *Journal of Economic Perspectives* 1, no. 2 (Fall 1987), 95–111; and David Colander, "The Making of an Economist Redux," ibid. 19, no. 1 (Winter 2005), 175–98.

The rise of formalism, widespread ignorance of economic history and economic facts, and the absence of a broader culture in economics and other social sciences would not seem to constitute a good preparation for effective intervention in public life. Comparing opinion surveys in 1985 and 2002, table 13.1 fortunately gives some hope for the future. It suggests that thirty-seven-year-old economists today are less bent towards formalism and more empirically oriented than their fifty-four-year-old predecessors. Whether this will help increase the number of public intellectuals in the younger generations of research economists remains to be seen.

Fewer Public Intellectuals among Economists in Canada than in the United States

What about Canada specifically? High-level public intellectuals seem to be fewer among Canadian than among American economists. I see two reasons for this. The first is that scientific recognition and faculty promotion in recent decades has come increasingly from refereed publications in international journals of high standing. However, only one such journal is Canadian – the *Canadian Journal of Economics*. The majority of leading journals are American. They have little interest in applied research on the Canadian economy. Many among new generations of young Canadian research economists believe that investing in Canadian studies is a loss of time from the standpoint of career advancement.

The second reason that there are fewer Canadian than American economists who are public intellectuals is that Canadian institutions do not facilitate exchanges between universities and government to the same extent as American institutions. In the United States, world-class academics such as Galbraith, Arrow, Okun, Tobin, Solow, Eckstein, Nordhaus, Feldstein, Boskin, Stiglitz, Yellen, Frankel, Blinder, Summers, Diamond, Mankiw, Bernanke, and Romer are admired not only for their scientific achievements, but for the major contributions they have made to public policy while they held government jobs.

Supporting Evidence

In other words, the formal training towards the PhD degree, the dynamics of international reputation building, and limited opportunities for exchanges between universities and government may deter many Canadian research economists from investing in knowledge of the Canadian economy and developing an interest in Canadian public policy.

What is the evidence for this? One piece is the 1993 paper I prepared for the Canadian Economics Association's twenty-fifth anniversary symposium.[1] I showed that, between the late 1960s and the early 1990s, research by Canadian academic economists had shifted markedly from applied research on the Canadian economy (1) towards pure theoretical research, and (2) towards applied research on the United States and other foreign economies. In my own area of specialization, macroeconomics, a large portion of the current research done by Canadian academics is based almost exclusively on US data.

A contemporary indication that Canadian research economists are less interested in public affairs and policy than their US counterparts is the disproportion in the number of economics blogs between the two countries. In the United States, there are currently over 250 economics blogs worth following. Several top economics blogs involve leading American research economists. Nobel laureate and *New York Times* columnist Paul Krugman currently runs the most popular economics blog in that country, called *The Conscience of a Liberal*.[2] Other examples are *Vox* (Alberto Alesina, Olivier Blanchard, Esther Duflo, Barry Eichengreen, Jeffrey Frankel, Carmen Reinhart, Shang-Jin Wei), the *Becker-Posner Blog* (Gary Becker, Richard Posner), *Grasping Reality with Both Hands* (Brad DeLong), *Economix* (Ed Glaeser, Simon Johnson,

Casey Mulligan, Uwe Reinhardt), *Econbrowser* (James Hamilton), the *Baseline Scenario* (Simon Johnson), *Freakononomics* (Steven Levitt), *Greg Mankiw's Blog* (Gregory Mankiw), and the *Nouriel Roubini Blog* (Nouriel Roubini). In contrast, I count only three economics blogs that are run by Canadian research economists: *Worthwhile Canadian Initiative*, *Eclect-Econ*, and *Martin Coiteux sur l'économie*.

Some Active Public Intellectuals among Canadian Economists

Blogging is clearly not (yet!) the most important way an intellectual interested in public affairs and policy can participate effectively in the agora. Other activities include doing speeches, writing books, publishing columns or op-eds in newspapers and magazines, appearing on television, doing studies for government departments, government agencies, or think tanks, and participating in government commissions or task forces.

The key point to remember is that nature abhors a vacuum. If too few research economists get involved in public policy discussions, their knowledge is not made widely available. This then leaves the floor open for ideologues and charlatans to take over debates and increases the risk that bad policy decisions are the outcome. We are made worse off as a nation. I am not denying here that there are biases of various kinds among economists. I am just saying that if more of them – from all persuasions – get involved, the probability that better policy decisions will ensue will be greater.

Although too few Canadian economists who are practising public intellectuals are involved in public policy discussion, I think it is fair to say that the contribution of those who actually are is of high average quality. A leading and inspiring figure in past decades has been Gilles Paquet, initially of Carleton University, and later of the University of Ottawa. Paquet is a first-rate economic historian and a pioneer of behavioural economics in Canada. He has been for many years a pillar of the Canadian Economics Association and of the Royal Society of Canada, and a major participant in a large number of public policy debates in Canada. Another marvellous example was the late Doug Purvis, of Queen's University. He was not only a first-rate research macroeconomist, but also a very influential public intellectual who was involved in myriad public activities until his untimely death in 1993. Since then, the Doug Purvis Prize has been awarded annually to the author(s) of a highly significant written contribution to Canadian economic policy.

The list of past winners of the Purvis Prize contains the names of some of the most active public intellectuals in current generations of Canadian economists: Craig Riddell, Jon Kesselman, John Helliwell, Ralph Winter, Brian Copeland, Erwin Diewert, David Green, and Kevin Milligan (all from the University of British Columbia), Ron Kneebone, Ken McKenzie, and Scott Taylor (University of Calgary), Jack Mintz, Michael Trebilcock, and Michael Baker (University of Toronto), David Laidler (University of Western Ontario), Tom Courchene (Queen's University), myself (University of Quebec at Montreal), Frances Woolley (Carleton University), Gérard Bélanger (Laval University), and Bev Dahlby (University of Alberta).

John Maynard Keynes's Ideal of "Master-Economist"

What does it take for an economist to be successful as a public intellectual? My answer to this question will be based on my personal experience both as a research economist and as a public intellectual. My academic research has focused on economic growth and fluctuations, monetary and fiscal policy, public finance, social policy, and the economies of Canada and Quebec. As a public intellectual, I have been chief economic adviser to a provincial premier, chair of government task forces on business investment, income security, and agriculture, participant in debates on inflation and Bank of Canada policy, author or co-author of over forty reports for public and private organizations, adviser to the Quebec Assembly of Catholic Bishops, economic columnist for the most widely read French-language Canadian magazine (*L'actualité*), and speaker on various topics in a large number of forums.

My life as a public intellectual has been inspired mainly by the wide-ranging involvement of John Maynard Keynes in British and world affairs. In the following excerpt, drawn from his eulogy of an older British economist, Alfred Marshall, Keynes gave the following summary of the kind of ideal that inspired him and that he sought to emulate:

> The master-economist must possess a rare combination of gifts. He must reach a high standard in several different directions and must combine talents not often found together. He must be mathematician, historian, statesman, philosopher – in some degree. He must understand symbols and speak in words. He must contemplate the particular in terms of the general, and touch abstract and concrete in the same flight of thought. He must study the present in the light of the past for the purposes of the

future. No part of man's nature or his institutions must lie entirely outside his regard. He must be purposeful and disinterested in a simultaneous mood; as aloof and incorruptible as an artist, yet sometimes as near the earth as a politician. Much, but not all, of this ideal many-sidedness Marshall possessed. But chiefly his mixed training and divided nature furnished him with the most essential and fundamental of the economist's necessary gifts – he was conspicuously historian and mathematician, a dealer in the particular and the general, the temporal and the eternal, at the same time.[3]

This is also the kind of ideal that I and many others have tried to pursue in our academic work and public involvement.

Free Trade, Inflation, Minimum Wage, and Childcare

To be more specific, I would say that the most important requirements for success as a public intellectual are a solid scientific reputation, independence from political ideologies and economic interests, clarity and simplicity of expression, and the ability to connect scientific results with people's concerns. Let me give four concrete examples of areas where I have been involved in public policy discussion: free trade, inflation targeting, minimum wage policy, and universal childcare.

A major factor behind the Canada-US Free Trade Agreement of 1988 was the solid bipartisan political support that it had received from Quebec, beginning with Premier Lévesque's speech at the biennial meeting of state governors and provincial premiers in Boise, Idaho, in November 1984. Lévesque's view was that economics is just like sports. If you want to win gold, you'd better have your athletes and businesses compete against the world's best. (Remember, 1984 was an Olympic year. Gaëtan Boucher and Sylvie Bernier had just won gold in Sarajevo and Los Angeles.) In preparation for this speech, I had been involved with others in reviewing all the standard arguments in support of free trade, ranging from comparative advantage to economies of scale, which the premier did appreciate. But in the end, the simple parallel with the Olympic Games is what produced the final "click" for free trade.

In 1991, the government and the Bank of Canada signed an agreement specifying that, from 1995 on, the bank would achieve an inflation rate target of 2 per cent. There were indications that, upon renewal of the agreement in 2001, a number of bank officials wanted the target to be lowered to 1 per cent. I thought that this very low target rate would force the bank's monetary policy to maintain the national rate of unemployment at a permanently higher level on average over time. This is because maintaining inflation at a very low level would have required average wage increases to be very low too, and therefore absolute wage cuts to be more widespread. Since workers resist wage cuts fiercely, a permanently higher unemployment rate would have been needed to "discipline" them into accepting those wage cuts. I rushed to measure how important resistance to wage cuts was in Canadian wage-settlements data. I found that it was indeed very strong, which confirmed my apprehension. I then came out against any decrease in the inflation target below 2 per cent and suggested instead that it should be raised a bit, perhaps to 3 per cent.[4] Needless to say, my findings and policy recommendation were rejected by Bank of Canada researchers out of hand. I later learned that the chairman of the US Federal Reserve, Alan Greenspan, somehow got hold of my results and took them seriously. For this (and obviously other) reasons, he never agreed to set an official inflation target for the United States, and he allowed actual inflation to average 2.5 per cent during his terms in office. Meanwhile, in Canada, the government fortunately rejected outside suggestions that the inflation target be decreased and have kept it at 2 per cent until today.

Another area where I have been involved is provincial minimum wage policy. Surprisingly enough, in the early 1990s, American economists David Card and Alan Krueger found that minimum wage increases in some US states did not have any significant negative effect on the number of low-wage jobs. This seemed to contradict my earlier estimates based on Quebec data from the 1970s, which had found that the disemployment effects of the provincial minimum wage were large. A bit of thinking suggested a solution to this empirical paradox. If the minimum wage is initially low – maybe 35 per cent of the average wage, as was the case in the United States in the 1980s and 1990s – then the increase will affect few workers and will therefore have only a small effect on jobs. But if the minimum wage is already high – maybe 55 per cent of the average wage, as in Quebec in the 1970s – then a large number of workers will be affected and the negative impact on jobs will also be large. This reasoning suggested that setting the minimum wage halfway between 35 and 55 per cent of the average wage – perhaps around 45 per cent – could offer a good compromise between two objectives: increasing the incomes of low-wage workers and avoiding wholesale job destruction.[5] The Quebec government took this suggestion seriously, and since 1998 the Quebec minimum wage has been relatively stable, around 46 per cent of the provincial average wage.

Recently, I have been participating in a public discussion about Quebec's universal childcare policy. In the past fifteen years, Quebec has been offering an educational childcare (EC) program to all children aged 0 to 4, initially at a reduced fee of $5 a day and then at $7 since 2004, mainly through regulated early childhood centres (*centres de la petite enfance*) and family-based childcare. Before- and after-school programs have also been made available at $7 a day to all primary-school children. Quebec's $7-a-day EC program currently attracts 50 per cent of all preschool children at an annual cost to the provincial government of $10,000 per subsidized place. However, the EC program is so popular, its impact on mothers' labour-force participation is so strong, and its favourable tax-revenue feedback to provincial and federal treasuries is so large that my colleagues Luc Godbout and Suzie St-Cerny and I have been able to estimate that the program more than pays for itself. We have found that every $1 of provincial spending on EC generates $1.50 of additional tax revenue: $1.05 for the provincial government and $0.45 for the federal government.[6] These findings shed light on the question of whether other parts of Canada should follow the universal, Scandinavian-type family policy that Quebec has adopted, or should stick to EC programs that are targeted purely at at-risk children. My view is that Canada does not need to choose between universality and targeting, but that it can have both at a bargain price. If universality indeed generates more tax revenue than expenditure, then with federal-provincial cooperation the difference can be used to finance the high-quality targeted interventions that are deemed most useful.

These four examples of personal involvement in public policy discussion raise a question about where I stand on the right-to-left political spectrum. My positions on free trade and the minimum wage could be labelled "right-wing," whereas my stands on monetary policy and universal childcare could be seen as "left-wing." Outside of Quebec, I was once called "perhaps the most influential left-wing voice among Canadian academic economists of his generation."[7] This was clearly an exaggerated statement – albeit flattering, of course. At about the same time, in Quebec, one left-wing writer was shouting: "Cet hiver, je vais chauffer aux conneries de Pierre Fortin. De quelle ostie de planète de débranchés il vient, ce Fortin-là?"[8] So, where do I really stand? I am probably a double agent. When your ideal society is one that should be both competitive *and* just, and when you are concerned about wealth creation as well as wealth sharing, you are bound to appear to lean sometimes to the right, and sometimes to the left. Right-wingers are naturally led to think you are a left-winger, and left-wingers that you are a right-winger. Nothing you can do about it.

Conclusion

Public intellectuals are independent thinkers who have acquired and continue to maintain a solid disciplinary reputation, make their knowledge accessible to the public, address broad social and economic problems with respect, but without shunning controversy, and come up with concrete prescriptions for public policy.

Unfortunately, because the training towards the economics PhD has become very formal in recent decades, the percentage of research economists who are also public intellectuals in North America seems to have decreased. This trend may be stopped or begin to be reversed among the new generation of more empirically oriented young economists, but we do not know yet. The decline in the percentage of research economists who are practising public intellectuals has been even more pronounced in Canada than in the United States. The dynamics of international reputation building and limited opportunities for exchanges between universities and government have probably deterred Canadian research economists from investing in knowledge of the Canadian economy and developing an interest in Canadian public policy. I have presented various bits of evidence in support of all these conjectures.

Nevertheless, Canadian research economists who are involved and influential in public affairs and public policy form a small, but vigorous community. I have reported a few instances of personal involvement in public policy discussions that suggest a number of necessary conditions for success in this area. Here is my preferred list of conditions:

1 "Memento quia pulvis es et in pulverem reverteris."[9] Be humble, candid, and straightforward. Aim for the simplest, down-to-earth way of presenting a subject or an argument. Avoid the pomposity of an academic parvenu.
2 Remain an independent thinker. Make your values known, but do not be the tagalong puppy of a narrow ideology or a political party. A public intellectual is the obverse of a mercenary. If you disagree with someone, say so, and say it clearly, firmly, and respectfully.

3 Continue to do basic research and publish in good scientific journals. Your background research is the source of your knowledge and influence. Without it, your human capital will depreciate rapidly, and with it your reputation as an intellectual. You do not have the choice between being a good research economist or a successful public intellectual. Remaining the former is a necessary condition for becoming and remaining the latter.

4 Work hard to improve your writing and speaking abilities, and make sure readers and listeners understand what you say. Cut the jargon and express yourself in clear and concise prose. It is a struggle, but it is a must. (Make sure you have done the math behind every statement, but do not show it off.)

5 Limit your interventions strictly to matters you really know something about. If you do not know, say so. Never take any liberty with the truth. Use short cuts if you want, but never take advantage of your deeper understanding of economic reality to dupe the public.

6 Assume the public is intelligent. Show them respect. If they do not understand what you say, take that to be your fault, not theirs. Take account of the context in which they receive your message. In the morning, they are in a hurry; in the evening, they need rest and entertainment. It is your responsibility to adapt your presentation accordingly, and to bridge the gap between the analytical-deductive nature of your arguments and their experience, intuition, and emotions. They want to learn, but they also like to laugh and to cry.

7 Say "we" rather than "you." If you say "we," you are one of them. The public will then be receptive even to your criticism. If you say "you," you distance yourself from them. They will be unforgiving. (This is, by the way, how I think Pierre Trudeau lost his touch in Quebec. At one point, he switched from saying "we, French Canadians" to saying instead "you, French Canadians.") Unrelenting, systematic, unbalanced, and contemptuous criticism of Canada and Canadians (the "we") is suicidal. It will only lead the public to stop listening to you and reject any policy proposal you will make, however appropriate it may actually be.

8 The public pays attention to the economy mainly when there is some unhappy turn of events: the price of gas shot up to $1.50; six hundred apparel workers lost their jobs in Huntingdon; the Caisse de dépôt lost $40 billion during the financial crisis; Shell is closing its Montreal refinery. If you write or talk about such events, make sure your explanation does not become a justification. Do show

your concern (which, I hope, will be genuine) about the suffering of people who have been hurt by these events, even if they were unavoidable or are even beneficial from a broad macroeconomic perspective.

9 Never forget that well-being depends on much more than enjoying a high income. Being in good health, having a job, being in love with your partner, trusting your neighbours, going out with your friends, vacationing with your family all have an income dimension, but their meaning for human happiness goes much beyond the money involved.

10 One basic law of reading and listening is that the longer the book, the article, or the speech, the less read or listened to it will be. Never begin a speech by announcing: "I will be brief," as many academics do. People will know that you are expressing uneasiness at having a presentation that you already know to be too long. Be brief, without saying it.

11 Contrary to many trained economists, people in general are more concerned about equity than about efficiency. Deal with the efficiency aspects of the problems you address, but also with their implications for equity.

12 End your presentation with a concrete conclusion or policy prescription.

NOTES

1 Pierre Fortin, "Where We Were, Where We Are: The First Eight Meetings and the Last Four," *Canadian Journal of Economics* 26, no. 1 (February 1993), 55–69.

2 According to a 2010 survey reported by the social networking news site Wikio, at www.wikio.com/blogs/top/business.

3 "Alfred Marshall, 1842–1924," *Economic Journal* 34, no. 135 (September 1924), 311–72.

4 Pierre Fortin, "Inflation Targeting: The Three Percent Solution," *Policy Matters* 2, no. 1 (February 2001).

5 Pierre Fortin, "Salaire minimum, pauvreté et emploi: À la recherche du compromis idéal," *Regards sur le travail* 7, no. 1 (Fall 2010), 73–91.

6 Pierre Fortin, Luc Godbout, and Suzie St-Cerny, "Economic Consequences of Quebec's Educational Childcare Policy," paper presented at the Meetings of the Association Francophone pour le Savoir (ACFAS), Research

Chair on Taxation and Public Finance, University of Sherbrooke, May 2011.

7 Henry Milner and John Richards, "Seeing Quebec – and Not Only Quebec – with Clear Eyes," *Inroads* 18 (Winter/Spring 2006), 4–6.

8 François Avard, "Vidanges lucides," in Avard, *Avard Chronique* (Montreal: Les Intouchables, 2008). The title of this article (in English, "Lucid trash") refers to the manifesto *Pour un Québec lucide*, issued by a group of 12 Quebeckers led by former premier Lucien Bouchard in October 2005. Available online in both French and English at www.pourunquebeclucide.org.

9 "Remember that you are dust, and unto dust you shall return" (originally from Genesis 3:19). Said at the imposition of ashes on the foreheads of the Christian faithful on Ash Wednesday, the start of Lent.

14 The Unbalanced Discussion of Aboriginal Policy

JOHN RICHARDS

At the core of politics in a democratic society is the art of building a winning coalition. Often this requires leaders choosing words to blur disagreements among allies, and to exaggerate disagreements with competing coalitions. It is a necessary art; without it, democracy is impossible. While successful practitioners of the art display skill and intelligence, they are not engaged in what most of us mean by intellectual activity. Intellectual life accepts that exacerbating disagreements is acceptable behaviour, that debate should continue until the last objection is answered, and implicitly accepts that resolution may be unattainable. The conceit of the public intellectual is that he has undertaken sufficient intellectual labour to know the truth about a particular matter to a reasonable approximation, and simultaneously that his conclusions should guide public policy despite the fact he (usually) enjoys no mandate to govern.[1]

This essay proceeds as follows. First, I attempt to define the ambiguous territory occupied by public intellectuals, and to make the case that they have a useful role to play. Second is a case study of the role played by public intellectuals in the evolution of Canadian Aboriginal policy. My conclusion is that they are not doing their job: they have produced an unbalanced dialogue. It would be disingenuous not to mention the fact that I have actively contributed to this "unbalanced" dialogue over the last decade and bear some responsibility for its inadequacies.

What Is a Public Intellectual?

On the one side are elected politicians and advocates promoting the agendas of particular interest groups. Here goals turn on access to public budgets and power. On the other are intellectuals who earn their living by research, writing, and teaching. Not to be cynical, their goal is the discovery and dissemination of truth. Whether there exists a territory between them is debatable. Perhaps it does not really exist; perhaps those purportedly residing on it are better defined as advocates, as intellectuals, or – in the view of cynics – as verbose quacks.

While admitting it is marshy and subject to erosion, I here make the case that this middle ground does exist and its occupants often contribute something of value. Public intellectuals include wise journalists and essayists, some among those who write and speak for major policy institutes, some university professors, some business and religious leaders, some ex-politicians – plus the occasional novelist, poet, and elected politician. The criterion for inclusion is to have undertaken some intellectual labour, and provided they have done it, there is no reason to exclude from this list select Aboriginal elders or incisive members of groups that gather over coffee in small-town cafes to discuss the state of the world.

Let me illustrate by introducing three individuals. None has written anything significant on Aboriginal affairs, but each has made good use of his public intellectual role.

Joseph Facal, a former PQ cabinet minister, now a professor at the Université de Montréal, was among the group of prominent Quebeckers who, several years ago, issued a manifesto (*Pour un Québec lucide*) calling on Quebeckers to adopt a set of productivity-enhancing public policies. Most are of the "short term pain, long term gain" variety. Facal has elaborated on the manifesto in an ambitious book (Facal 2010) that ranges over the following subjects: a defence of Quebec sovereignty (based on the need for credible commitment to maintenance of Quebec's francophone character and an end to destructive fiscal game-playing pursued by both Ottawa and Quebec City); a defence of Quebec's European cultural heritage (as opposed to a multicultural relativism that he argues is "eating away" [*ronge*] Quebeckers' and Canadians' self-confidence); the value of early childhood programs (a defence of Quebec's expensive early childhood program, albeit he wants to raise the $7 per day fee); K–12 education reform (that emphasizes the basics and flushes out the jargon and non-academic policies imposed by the *pédagogistes* currently in control of the education ministry); an end to cheap domestic electricity rates (currently set far below international rates), plus a strategy of hydroelectric exports to the United States; and better-quality post-secondary institutions (financed by higher tuition fees). He concludes with a discussion of public inconsistency in simultaneously electing politicians who promise generous public services and defeating those who insist on raising the taxes necessary to pay for them.

As a tenured professor of political science specializing in public administration, Stéphane Dion was one among other intellectuals. As the debate over the 1995 referendum on Quebec sovereignty erupted, his barrage of short essays in the Montreal press made the case for federalism and rebutted sovereignist arguments. They were among the most cogent briefs on behalf of a *"non"* vote. Subsequently recruited by Jean Chrétien into the federal cabinet, he hovered between the role of public intellectual and politician. His open letters to Lucien Bouchard (and others) were a continuation of his role as pamphleteer (Dion 1999). At their best, they evoke *The Federalist Papers*; at their worst, they evoke the brief of a clever lawyer seeking to bury uncomfortable counter-arguments.

As minister of the environment in Paul Martin's minority 2004–6 government, Dion became passionately convinced – if he had not been before – of the case for reducing greenhouse-gas emissions. Martin was defeated in the 2006 election, and the Liberals turned to Dion. As leader, he insisted that the Liberals campaign in the 2008 election on the case for a radical reshaping of the tax system in order to phase in an ambitious federal carbon tax, similar in design to the newly introduced BC carbon tax. This was a decision inspired by the conclusions of a public intellectual not a pragmatic politician. The Liberals lost the election, and Dion lost his leadership of the Liberal Party. Adding to his stature as public intellectual if not pragmatic politician, Dion has continued to speak and write extensively on the theme of pricing carbon emissions.[2]

Third, Conrad Black, cosmopolitan conservative. His lengthy biographies of several famous personalities (Maurice Duplessis, Franklin Delano Roosevelt, and Richard Nixon) are exercises in "great man" history, history that sees the broad directions of society as a function of the decisions of a few. Based on the quality of his books and the fact that he wrote without the advantages of a professor's salary, Black might be labelled a "private intellectual." Black's ambition extends beyond rehabilitating the reputations of Duplessis and Nixon, or elevating Roosevelt over Churchill; he wants to influence the present.

Black employs satire and invective as blunt instruments, somewhat in the style of Christopher Hitchens. Black (2009) on climate change: "an insane scam." On this subject he is superficial. On many other subjects, there lies, behind satire and invective, astute observations on the state of the world. Take, for example, his analysis of strategic decisions being made in Ankara:

> For decades, Europe has played Turkey as a 50-pound fish on a 20-pound line, reeling it in when Turkey was needed and rejecting the Turks as a Muslim rabble at other times. The predictable has happened, as Turkey is now enjoying greater economic growth than any other country in (or partly in) Europe. It is an Islamic regime that is casting aside Kemal Ataturk's guardians of secularism, the army and the judiciary, who became thoroughly corrupt in the 70 years that they have held the clergy at bay. Turkey has virtually turned its back on Europe and on its former allies, Israel and the United States, and is now asserting influence over its former Arab satrapies. How far it will vanish into the Islamic world, where no matter what happens it will be a force for comparative moderation, is an open question. (Black 2010)

Very few Canadians have thought hard about Islamic politics; even fewer can summarize their conclusions as well as Black does here.

I selected this sample of three public intellectuals to make two generalizations. First is the incompatibility between the public intellectual's insistence on stating ideas clearly and his achieving short-term political success. Had Machiavelli's career as a diplomat been uninterrupted, no doubt he would have suppressed his penchant for playing the role of public intellectual. The pragmatic analyst of governing in Renaissance Italy would merit a footnote in Italian Renaissance history.

Facal's book *Quelque chose comme un grand peuple* is a somewhat analogous attempt by an out-of-office politician to prevail on matters over which he did not prevail while in office. This is not to say his proposals are doomed. Indeed, championing policies coherently in print as a public intellectual may, in time, do more to bring them about than Facal's having remained an active politician.

Synthesizing ideas from many disciplines and placing the exercise within a specific political context is a useful activity. Inevitably, governing entails such syntheses: cabinets must allocate scarce budget resources; they must choose among legislative initiatives. Neither interest-group advocates nor academics nor most politicians offer much help to the public in deciding whether their leaders' syntheses make sense.

The most obvious illustration of the trade-off between lucid argument and short-term political success was Dion's attempt to persuade Canadians to be consistent about greenhouse gas emissions. In opinion polls Canadians have repeatedly stated the importance they attach to reducing such emissions, but faced with a policy (an escalating carbon tax) that had the potential to achieve results, most Canadians baulked at the inconveniences entailed, and voted for parties to the left of Dion (NDP and Bloc) or to his right (Conservatives). Whatever divided Dion's opponents, they agreed on the value of obfuscating the case for pricing carbon emissions, and opposed imposition of a carbon tax. The conclusion to draw from Dion's failure is first that public intellectuals have not done enough to persuade Canadians that pricing emissions is a necessary policy response, and second, that until this is done, no politician can win majority acquiescence to a reorganization of the tax system to price emissions.

As for Black, the elitism in much of his writings will prevent his ever achieving elected office in Canada. Which is not to deny the effectiveness with which, as public intellectual, he has obliged Canadians to entertain unpopular and unfamiliar ideas.

The second generalization is that all three write well. To play the public intellectual role effectively a prerequisite is the ability to write readable prose. Facal's book is not an easy read but, relative to the opaque texts written by demographers, economists, education theorists, and others, it is *lucide*. Dion is at heart an earnest pamphleteer who tirelessly insists on the rightness of his case and the errors of his opponents. He does so in a manner that may be overly earnest; he is eminently clear. Black's orotund prose is so well crafted that it is a pleasure to read, whether or not one agrees with him.

Aboriginal Policy and the Failure of Public Intellectuals

Complex policy problems – such as Aboriginal affairs – may be "managed" for decades with little progress. The practising politicians and advocacy groups reach an equilibrium that they perceive as tolerable. While there may be no perfect resolution available, there may well be initiatives that could move matters to a more satisfactory equilibrium. Such initiatives inevitably entail losers as well as winners and the losers often have the political clout to block innovation for years stretching into decades. The rationales for major policy initiatives usually derive from the ideas of several academic disciplines, not just one. Hence, "pure" intellectuals expert in one discipline only are not likely to contribute much. There is a role for the public intellectual who has devoted time and effort to master relevant aspects of several disciplines, who attempts a synthesis, and who keeps options alive in the public sphere when politically there is no short-term likelihood of implementation.

There is no guarantee that any particular public intellectual generate the "right" answer. But without some translation of specialized discourses into the public discourse, political debate is reduced to a dialogue of the deaf: the tactical obfuscations of politicians, the briefs put forward by advocates for particular interests, and the articles of academics specialized in their respective disciplines – much of whose prose is incomprehensible to anyone lacking advanced degrees in the relevant field of study.

This is not the place to elaborate on the sins of the past or on various socio-economic gaps between Aboriginals and other Canadians. Before proceeding, however, we need two detours, one historical and the other demographic.

A Historical Detour

In the century between Confederation and the "white paper" of 1969, the strategy pursued in Ottawa was to assimilate the indigenous population, with the expectation that, over time, Aboriginal cultures would fade to folkloric status. Extrapolating from his distaste for Quebec nationalism, Pierre Trudeau proposed that Aboriginals – like Quebeckers – should possess the identical rights and obligations of all Canadians, neither more nor less. In one polemical article written during his time as public intellectual before entering politics, Trudeau compared Quebec nationalists to "kings and sorcerers" of an Indian tribe who "want to make the whole tribe return to the wigwams" (Trudeau 1964). In his first year as prime minister, he devoted considerable energy to this file, which culminated in the white paper's recommendation to dismantle reserves and the Department of Indian Affairs (as it was then called). Aboriginal leaders vigorously opposed this initiative and, since it was not central to Trudeau's concerns, he passed on to other matters.

Third World nationalism came to fruition in the third quarter of the twentieth century as European empires crumbled. That former European colonies achieved independence meant little to indigenous, largely pre-agricultural tribal communities living within these newly independent states. As Alan Cairns (2000) has summarized, in the fourth quarter of the century, indigenous elites used the same arguments as had a previous generation of anti-colonial leaders. Maori leaders in New Zealand, indigenous leaders in India's north-eastern tribal states, leaders of Arctic nomads in Scandinavia and Russia, and Canadian Indian/First Nation leaders demanded the ability to manage their affairs autonomously.

Controversy following the white paper induced Canadian elites to acknowledge, far more fulsomely than before, the wrongs of forced assimilation and discrimination. A prominent example was Thomas Berger's inquiry into the proposed Mackenzie Valley pipeline. His report recommended against construction and asserted the importance of "special status" for Aboriginals (Berger 1977, 4). A good account of the rise of white guilt in the years following the white paper is Gordon Gibson's (2009) unjustly ignored book *A New Look at Canadian Indian Policy*. Early in the 1970s, Gibson was an aide to Trudeau. There are parallels here to an analogous shift in majority US opinion with respect to race relations in the decade following the *Brown* school desegregation decision. Shelby Steele (2002) summarizes that shift as "white guilt" replacing "white racism" as the "propriety norm of respectable society."

One result of the Canadian shift to "white guilt" was addition of section 35 to the 1982 Constitution Act: "The existing Aboriginal and treaty rights of the Aboriginal peoples of Canada are hereby recognized and affirmed." At the time, many had opinions but no one knew what were the "existing Aboriginal and treaty rights." In some regions (north of 60 degrees and most of British Columbia) there were no existing treaties to interpret. Where treaties existed, they defined rights and obligations in words whose meaning and scope were usually ambiguous.

Since 1982, the courts have given a very broad interpretation to treaty rights, and instructed governments to negotiate where treaties do not exist. The ensuing negotiations have consumed vast intellectual resources and generated very little in terms of agreements signed. On the other hand, the insertion of the courts into the dynamic has effectively neutered Ottawa as a source of Aboriginal policy. Ottawa has become the dispenser of money. Delivery of on-reserve services (education, housing, social assistance, and health) has devolved to individual bands, approximately six hundred in number – along with the cash required. As Jean Allard (2002), a Metis activist from Manitoba, wryly observed, "liberal white guilt ... could be assuaged with tax dollars" (126). In general, neither band councils nor Ottawa nor provinces tax band members living on-reserve. Virtually all band revenues derive from federal transfers. These small First Nation governments now administer per capita revenues ten times the per capita average for Canadian municipalities, and do so without a professional civil service or the normal checks and balances associated with non-Aboriginal governments in Canada (Graham 2012).

The Royal Commission on Aboriginal Peoples (RCAP), which reported in 1996, is not an exception to Ottawa's retreat from policy initiatives. RCAP was not a practical guide to policy, but an exercise in cultural anthropology. It elaborated a theory of mutually impenetrable indigenous and white settler cultures in which Indians / First Nations and settler communities would live in parallel, having limited interaction with one another. A prominent image of the report was that of the two-row wampum, drawn from a 1613 treaty between the Dutch and the Mohawk. Two rows on the wampum symbolize "a birch bark canoe ... for the Indian people their laws, their customs, and their ways. The other, a ship, is for the white people and their laws, their customs and their ways. We shall each travel the river together ... in our own boat. Neither of us will try to steer the other's vessel" (Canada 1996, 10).

A Demographic Detour

The Canadian census defines the Aboriginal population in several ways; the most widely used is based on self-identification. Individuals can self-identify as belonging to one of three groups: (1) North American Indian or First Nation (Mohawk, Ojibwa, Cree, and so on), (2) Metis (descendants of communities formed from the intermarriage of Indians and *coureurs de bois* engaged in the fur trade), or (3) Arctic Inuit. Self-identification as an Aboriginal in the census does not necessarily mean Aboriginal ancestry. Another census definition is based on an individual indicating that he or she is a "registered Indian" under provisions of the Indian Act, a Canadian statute dating from the late nineteenth century. The great majority of those who self-identify as Indian/First Nation are also registered Indians. Only registered Indians have the right to live on designated reserve lands and receive the associated benefits.

According to the most recent available census, in 2006 4 per cent of Canadians self-identified as Aboriginal. Nearly two-thirds of them identified as Indian/First Nation, a third as Metis, and the remainder as Inuit. Despite the large fiscal incentives to live on a reserve, nearly half of the registered Indian population choose not to do so. Overall, three in ten Aboriginals live on a reserve, two live in rural non-reserve communities, two in a small city (population under 100,000), and three in a large city. The Aboriginal population share is rising, particularly in

western Canadian provinces, home to over half the Aboriginal population. In these provinces, Aboriginals constituted 13 per cent of school-
age cohorts in 2006.

As late as the mid-twentieth century, Aboriginals were overwhelmingly rural. This is no longer true. There is a parallel between Aboriginals "going to town" and the rural-to-urban migration by the children
and grandchildren of slaves in the United States in the first half of the
twentieth century. African Americans have changed the character of
urban America. Urban Aboriginals are doing the same in western Canadian cities. As with black Americans, Aboriginal migration has been
accompanied with a great deal of migratory "churn" as families move
back and forth between rural and urban communities.

An Unbalanced Discourse

A decade ago two academics, David Newhouse and Evelyn Peters
(2003), edited a book of essays about the urban Aboriginal experience.
There was more hope than reality in their choice of title, *Not Strangers in
These Parts*. In terms of on-reserve Aboriginal leaders, federal and provincial politicians, and most academics, urban Aboriginals *are* strangers. Since 1982, professors – Aboriginal and non-Aboriginal – have been
offering courses on Aboriginal law in every law college across the country, and have inundated law journals with their interpretations of court
decisions on treaty rights. The Assembly of First Nations, the peak association representing approximately 600 chiefs, enjoys a high media
profile. On the other hand, the media ignore associations, such as the
Metis National Council, National Association of Friendship Centres,
or Congress of Aboriginal Peoples, representing other, largely urban,
Aboriginals.

What have Aboriginal and non-Aboriginal public intellectuals added
to the discussion? From Aboriginals addressing a general audience
have come exercises in political philosophy on the potential to create
parallel societies having minimal interaction with the "settler society."
See, for example, Taiaiake Alfred (2008) or Dale Turner (2006). From
non-Aboriginal public intellectuals has come a replay of the collec-
tive- versus individual-rights debates provoked a generation earlier
by the insistence of Quebec nationalists that Confederation afforded
them collective rights to protect and enhance French as *la langue commune* in Quebec, and ultimately to secede from Canada. Indeed some of
the participants in the discussion of collective Aboriginal rights – Alan

Cairns, Will Kymlicka, Charles Taylor – were participants in the earlier discussion.

John Ralston Saul is a prominent example of a public intellectual straddling both debates. He waxed eloquent in the 1990s about Canada as a Siamese twin, where the French and British had learned to cohabit (Saul 1998). He elevated Louis-Hippolyte La Fontaine and Robert Baldwin, two politicians who effected a certain reconciliation between Upper and Lower Canada in the wake of the 1830s rebellions, as the Romulus and Remus of Canada. Saul has now grasped the fact that Aboriginals matter in modern Canada and has changed his mind about Canada as a Siamese twin. I quote from the flyleaf of his latest book – "We are not a civilization of British or French or European inspiration. We never have been." What then are we?

> Our intuitions and common sense as a civilization are more Aboriginal than European or African or Asian ... Our leaders endlessly mull over our institutional and cultural inheritance from British parliamentary democracy, British and French justice, the Enlightenment, British liberalism, Western individualism with its important variations, US populism, Judeo-Christian moral questioning, Athenian principles of citizenship and democracy, Western European philosophy, Western social democracy, Western capitalism, in particular its US form. Frankly, once you get below the surface, I see very little in the way we use all of these that would ring familiar bells in Britain, France or elsewhere in Europe or the United States. (Saul 2008, 3)

I have quoted at some length to give a sense of the breathless enthusiasm with which Saul insists Canadians have filtered everything European through the Aboriginal concern with the collective. This is nonsense. For much of our history Canadians disparaged Aboriginal culture. Saul's essay is a Torontonian equivalent of the *engouement* in eighteenth-century Parisian salons for *le bon sauvage*.

While the majority writing on Aboriginal policy – among both "pure" and public intellectuals – view favourably the insertion of section 35 into the constitution and subsequent judicial interpretations, there exists, not surprisingly, a counter-tradition that, like Trudeau writing on Quebec, fears erosion of Canada as a society united by the ideal of all citizens bearing equal rights and obligations. A prominent example is Tom Flanagan (2000). He is prepared to accommodate First Nation governments, but is sceptical of their potential. His policy recommendations turn primarily on enabling registered Indians, as individuals, to exercise individual property rights.

The best of the counter-tradition is the previously mentioned book by Gordon Gibson, yet another politician turned public intellectual. He insists that he is writing about registered Indians, not the larger Aboriginal population that includes off-reserve Indians/First Nations, Metis, and Inuit. The error of the white paper, in Gibson's eyes, was to propose the phasing out of reserves. To do so was unilaterally to deny legitimacy to all historical collective rights. He offers an admirable survey of the dozen key post-1982 court decisions, culminating in *Delgamuukw*, the 1997 Supreme Court decision that defined a broad Indian title to traditional tribal lands.

Gibson surveys those who have grappled with the appropriate limits to collective rights in the context of a liberal society. In the range of scholars discussed, he puts to shame most academics. He summarizes the argument of philosophically inclined political scientists, including Kymlicka, Taylor, and Cairns. His range extends from Flanagan to Alfred. Gibson presents Calvin Helin (2006), from an elite Tsimshian family in northern British Columbia, whose book *Dances with Dependency* is a tough-minded analysis of the social damage wrought by on-reserve dependence on Ottawa-financed social assistance disbursed by band councils. Allard appears in the book: his proposal is that Ottawa transform much of its annual cash transfer to band governments into "updated treaty money" paid to individuals.

Gibson's recommendations are pragmatic. Collective Indian/First Nation rights exist and should be honoured, but that is only the beginning. What matters is the individual Indian. Many – not all but many – of them want to participate in the mainstream economy of urban Canada. What is required here is more effective provision of public services than is possible via small band governments. He wants a voucher system enabling parents living on-reserve to choose between a reserve and nearby provincial school, provincial administration of welfare applying provincial eligibility standards, provincial administration of on- and off-reserve health services (subject to negotiations with band councils), and a form of guaranteed annual income.

With the exception of Newhouse and Peters, those so far mentioned are primarily engaged in the implications of section 35 and the "industry" that has grown up around its interpretation. Even Gibson, whose book is the subtlest of those discussed, devotes only one chapter to analysis of his pragmatic recommendations.[3]

In sum, this is an unbalanced discourse. Little of it examines the Aboriginal condition independently of the law or acknowledges that half the Aboriginal population is now urban. Let me list a few provocative questions:

- If treaty making and interpretation is the heart of the matter, why have so many Aboriginals "gone to town"? Do they like their urban lives or do they want to return to their rural – on-reserve in the case of those who are registered Indians – communities of origin?
- Does urbanization imply abandonment of Aboriginal identity or adaptation of identity into something new, an urban Aboriginal sensibility that may in time supplant traditional Aboriginal cultures?
- Why are Metis, who have no – or at most minimal – section 35 treaty rights, faring much better in terms of education levels and incomes than those who identify as Indian/First Nation? Why are off-reserve Indians/First Nations faring better in these terms than those on a reserve?
- About 80 per cent of Aboriginal children attend provincial schools (40 per cent of children living on-reserve plus all Aboriginal children of families living off-reserve). Some provincial school systems are achieving much better Aboriginal education outcomes than others. Why? The worst education outcomes are found, in general, on-reserve. Why?
- In Manitoba and Saskatchewan, three in ten among school-age cohorts are Aboriginal. What will be the economic and social fate of these provinces if these children fare no better in school than did their parents?
- Why did the on-reserve Indian/non-Aboriginal life expectancy gap fall by half from 1975 to 1990 but remain stagnant since? Why is the Nunavut suicide rate ten times the national average and what should be done about it? What about foetal alcohol spectrum disorder? What about the high on-reserve incidence of violence against women?
- Welfare utilization on reserves remains very high, about one-third of the on-reserve population. What should be done to lower it?

The basic reason, I suggest, that few Canadian politicians address these questions coherently is the Canadian equivalent of Steele's "propriety white guilt." Belief in cultural incompatibility (between indigenous and settler culture) and support for a very broad interpretation of treaty rights have come to define what it means in mainstream Canada to avoid the suspicion of racism. Most elected politicians are reasonably

well intentioned and want "to do something" about improving Aboriginal conditions, but abstain from innovation for fear of being labelled
racist.

High on the list of things "to do," most politicians acknowledge pri-
vately, is structural reform of on- and off-reserve education. This would
entail reorganization of on-reserve schools into some form of professionally run school districts, early childhood education programs targeting Aboriginals on- and off-reserve, better measurement of Aboriginal
children's education progress through grades K–12, easier mobility of
children between reserve and provincial schools, more native teachers,
and – after undertaking these structural reforms – more money for native students from Ottawa and provincial education ministries. The Assembly of First Nations is highly sceptical of this agenda. At both the
federal and provincial level, politicians are fearful of the charge of racism if they deviate from "propriety." Hence, most conclude, it's better
to "do nothing." A similar charge applies to Canadian academics. It's
fair enough that law professors discuss the potential of treaties and anthropologists the restoration of indigenous cultures, but where are the
experts in school administration analysing better Aboriginal education
outcomes in some school systems relative to others?

Champlain's Dream, the magnificent academic biography of an astute
early observer of the gulf between Aboriginal and settler cultures, does
not vilify one side or eulogize the other. The author, David Hackett-
Fischer (2008) summarizes Champlain's account of what, as a young
man, he saw of Spanish barbarity towards the indigenous population
in the Caribbean, and later accounts of what he saw of torture inflicted
by his Huron allies on captured Iroquois warriors. Perhaps not coinci-
dentally, the author is an American not a Canadian academic. There is
an element of "white guilt" prevalent in Canadian academe that makes
it unlikely any historian in a major Canadian history department would
write a book that gives prominence to torture inflicted by indigenous
populations on one another.

Conclusion

I conclude with a few causes for guarded optimism.

As a generalization, among Aboriginal public intellectuals, the men
insist on simple solutions; the women are more pragmatic and subtle.
As law professor, judge in Saskatchewan, and provincial officer in British Columbia responsible for the protection of children, Mary Ellen

Turpel-Lafond has written extensively about family violence, in particular violence among Aboriginals. Racism and poverty figure in her
analysis, but hers is not a utopian argument in which the settler society
is the source of all problems.

Some policy institutes are beginning to rebalance the discourse. Inevitably, these publications are mongrels that reflect multiple academic
and ideological parents. To assess the actual performance of reserve-
based governments in the three Prairie provinces, the Winnipeg-based
Frontier Centre for Policy Analysis (Quesnel 2010) regularly publishes
an Aboriginal Governance Index. Michael Mendelson at the Caledon
Institute of Social Policy has written (2009) on the theme that stand-
alone small schools run by individual bands can never achieve decent
results; there is a need, he argues, for the equivalent of school districts
to manage schools across multiple reserves. Helen Raham (2010), former research director at the Society for the Advancement of Excellence
in Education, has analysed best practices in Aboriginal education in
school districts across Canada. John Graham (2012), at the Institute on
Governance, has made the public administration argument to the effect
that efficient delivery of public services is impossible under the present system of reserve governance – large per capita transfers to band
governments, no taxation of members, lack of professional administrators. Whether the population is Aboriginal or not is irrelevant to his
argument. I add to this list the contribution that colleagues and I have
made by publishing numerous monographs, most with the C.D. Howe
Institute, most on aspects of Aboriginal education.[4]

A final example of a policy institute rebalancing the discourse is
the Environics Institute, headed by Michael Adams. His comparative
advantage over other public intellectuals is an ability to conduct sophisticated opinion surveys. In 2009, the institute organized the most
comprehensive survey to date of what the urban half of the Aboriginal population think about their lives (Environics Institute 2010; Richards 2010). The survey does not answer all the above questions, but it
makes a start. Why move to the city? Three reasons emerge with equal
frequency: to be closer to family members already in the city, to have
better access to education options for themselves and their children,
and to get a job. Do you like your urban lifestyle? Seventy-one per cent
consider the city in which they live to be "home"; 65 per cent like living
in their city "a lot." Only 22 per cent plan to go back to their "community of origin" – as opposed to the 50 per cent who intend to stay; the
remainder have yet to decide. Do you identify as Aboriginal? Overall,

77 per cent say they are "very proud" to be Aboriginal, and despite reporting some discrimination, 79 per cent insist they never downplay their Aboriginal identity.

I have no objection to analysing the implications of section 35 and treaties – provided that discussion does not crowd out everything else. Which over the last generation it has. Whatever the fate of treaty negotiations, the urban share of the Aboriginal population will continue to grow for the reasons Environics' respondents gave. Over the next generation, the hopes and fears of urban Aboriginals – their journalism, novels, plays, films, songs, and paintings – will define Canada to a far greater extent than our unbalanced public discourse has acknowledged. It remains to be seen whether the emerging urban Aboriginal identity reflects hopes realized or frustrated.

NOTES

1 I thank Jean-Claude Bazinet, Alan Cairns, and Gordon Gibson for critiquing earlier drafts. I thank also my wife, Christiane, for insightful, sceptical comments.
2 A representative recent example is his article for the *Tocqueville Review* (Dion 2011).
3 Gibson has recently become *very* pragmatic, acting as adviser to the Gitxsan Hereditary Chiefs, who are negotiating what he describes as an alternative to the standard treaty model: "The Gitxsan would vote, pay taxes and be governed by the usual federal, provincial and local authorities just like everyone else in [BC]. At the same time, the Gitxsan Alternative would allow them to retain their culture and internal relationships, and would explicitly recognize their very considerable property and cultural rights stemming from the common law as articulated by the Supreme Court of Canada in its *Delgamuukw* decision" (Gibson 2010, 38).
4 See Richards (2011) comparing Aboriginal education outcomes in Quebec to those elsewhere in Canada. A more rigorous empirical treatment of Aboriginal education performance is Richards, Vining, and Weimer (2010). The most recent C.D. Howe monograph is an analysis of life satisfaction or "happiness" results from the Environics Institute survey (Gross and Richards 2012).

REFERENCES

Alfred, Taiaiake. 2008. *Peace, Power, Righteousness: An Indigenous Manifesto*. 2nd ed. Toronto: Oxford University Press.

Allard, Jean. 2002. "Big Bear's Treaty: The Road to Freedom." *Inroads* 11.

Berger, Thomas. 1977. "Synopsis of Volume Two." *Mackenzie Valley Pipeline Inquiry.* https://www.neb-one.gc.ca/ll-eng/livelink.exe?func=ll&objId=234849&objAction=browse.

Black, Conrad. 2009. "A teeming rain forest of irrelevant climate claims." *National Post*, 28 November.

Black, Conrad. 2010. "Europe reaped what it sowed." *National Post*, 15 May.

Cairns, Alan. 2000. *Citizens Plus: Aboriginal Peoples and the Canadian State.* Vancouver: UBC University Press.

Cairns, Alan, and Tom Flanagan. 2001. "An Exchange." *Inroads* 10.

Canada. 1996. *People to People, Nation to Nation: Highlights from the Report of the Royal Commission on Aboriginal Peoples.* Ottawa: Royal Commission on Aboriginal Peoples.

Dion, Stéphane. 1999. *Straight Talk: Speeches and Writings on Canadian Unity.* Montreal, Kingston: McGill-Queen's University Press.

Dion, Stéphane. 2011. "The Fight against Climate Change: Why Is Canada Doing So Little?" *Tocqueville Review* 32 (2): 21a–46a.

Environics Institute. 2010. *Urban Aboriginal Peoples Study.* http://www.uaps.ca.

Facal, Joseph. 2010. *Quelque chose comme un grand peuple.* Montreal: Boréal.

Flanagan, Tom. 2000. *First Nations? Second Thoughts.* Montreal, Kingston: McGill-Queen's University Press.

Frontier Centre for Public Policy. 2009. *The Third Annual Aboriginal Governance Index.* http://www.fcpp.org/publication.php/2807.

Gibson, Gordon. 2009. *A New Look at Canadian Indian Policy: Respect the Collective, Promote the Individual.* Vancouver: Fraser Institute.

Gibson, Gordon. 2010. "The Gitxsan Alternative." *Inroads* 27.

Graham, John. 2012. "Dysfunctional governance: Eleven barriers to progress among Canada's First Nations." *Inroads* 31.

Gross, Dominique, and John Richards. 2012. "Breaking the Stereotype: Why Urban Aboriginals Score Highly on 'Happiness' Measures." *Commentary* 354. Toronto: C.D. Howe Institute.

Hackett-Fischer, David. 2008. *Champlain's Dream.* New York: Simon & Schuster.

Helin, Calvin. 2006. *Dances with Dependency: Indigenous Success through Self-Reliance.* Vancouver: Orca Spirit Publications and Communications.

Mendelson, Michael. 2009. *Why We Need a First Nations Education Authority Act.* Ottawa: Caledon Institute of Social Policy.

Newhouse, David, and Evelyn Peters, eds. 2003. *Not Strangers in these Parts: Urban Aboriginal Peoples.* Ottawa: Policy Research Institute.

Quesnel, Joseph. 2010. *Fourth Annual Aboriginal Governance Index.* Winnipeg: Frontier Centre for Policy Analysis.

Raham, Helen. 2010. "Improving Outcomes for Off-Reserve Students." Conference organized by University of Saskatchewan.

Richards, John. 2010. "A Study That Makes Urban Aboriginals Visible." *Inroads* 27.

Richards, John. 2011. "Aboriginal Education in Quebec: A Benchmarking Exercise." *Commentary* 328. Toronto: C.D. Howe Institute (also available in French: "L'éducation des autochtones au Québec: Un exercice d'analyse comparative").

Richards, John, Aidan Vining, and David Weimer. 2010. "Aboriginal Performance on Standardized Tests: Evidence and Analysis from Provincial Schools in British Columbia." *Policy Studies Journal: The Journal of the Policy Studies Organization* 38 (1): 47–67. http://dx.doi.org/10.1111/j.1541-0072.2009.00344.x.

Saul, John Ralston. 1998. *Reflections of a Siamese Twin: Canada at the Beginning of the 21st Century*. Toronto: Viking Canada.

Saul, John Ralston. 2008. *A Fair Country: Telling Truths about Canada*. Toronto: Viking Canada.

Steele, Shelby. 2002. "The Age of White Guilt and the Disappearance of the Black Individual." *Harper's Magazine* (November), 233–42.

Trudeau, Pierre Elliott. [1964] 1968. "Separatist Counter-Revolutionaries." In *Federalism and the French Canadians*. Toronto: Macmillan of Canada (reprinted and translated from original in *Cité Libre*).

Turner, Dale. 2006. *This Is Not a Peace Pipe: Towards a Critical Indigenous Philosophy*. Toronto: Toronto University Press.

15 "Brave New Ethicists": A Cautionary Tale

MARGARET SOMERVILLE

My first reaction when, many years ago, I was called a "public intellectual" was to reject the label. However, on looking up the term in the *Oxford English Dictionary* it was clear that, provided I was an "intellectual" – which is debatable – the "cap fit," so I had no choice but to wear it: "**Public intellectual** *n.* an intellectual who expresses views (esp. on popular topics) intended to be accessible to a general audience ... **Intellectual** *n.* possessing a high degree of understanding; given to pursuits that exercise the intellect."

My reluctance was connected with an attitude prevalent in the academy in the late 1970s, when I was first appointed at McGill University, that serious scholars did not participate in the public square, at least not through the general media, and that serious scholarship was harmed and demeaned by their doing so. Such participation was seen as vulgarization of the knowledge that they were privileged to hold in trust, and they were regarded as vulgar, in the non-complimentary sense of that word. As one of my colleagues put it to me, "You are dangerously on the edge of total flake [he also used the term b--- s---], Margo."

I was appointed as a professor in both McGill's faculty of law and faculty of medicine. Such joint appointments were rare at the time and mine was, as far as I know, the first at McGill to bridge law and medicine. My background was in both pharmacy and law, so I could understand and speak both professional languages. Although we didn't recognize it at the time, we were in the early days of mind-altering breakthroughs in science and medicine that would raise ethics and values issues for individuals and society unprecedented in human history. We were also at the beginning of developing what we would call today the transdisciplinary research methodologies that we needed to deal with these issues.

On 3 December 1967, South African surgeon Christiaan Barnard conducted the first heart transplant on fifty-three-year-old Lewis Washkansky. The world reeled. Here was a man alive thanks to the beating heart – the organ whose functioning separates life and death – of a dead man. Was this surgery ethical? Had the surgeon murdered the donor in taking his heart? When was someone dead? What was the definition of death? Were there legal or ethical wrongs with respect to the heart transplant recipient? Was this procedure in breach of important values that underpin the profession of medicine or, more broadly, society?

These questions raised issues that were not just relevant to the individuals involved or the medical profession; they also raised issues about some of society's most important foundational values and, therefore, needed broad public input in the decision making about what was and was not ethical. I believe that the first heart transplant can be regarded as the birth of the field of scholarship and professional practice we now call bioethics – the "big bang" of bioethics.

That field has expanded exponentially since that time, because the science and medicine to which it relates has expanded exponentially. It is now so large that we have specialization within it: genethics (the ethics of genetics and molecular biology); neuroethics (the ethics of mind and brain science); epiethics (the ethics of epidemiological research and practice); assisted human reproduction ethics; nanotechnology ethics; clinical ethics; health policy ethics; ethics at the end of life; the ethics of the allocation of and access to health-care resources; research ethics; environmental ethics; and so on. The decisions made in these areas about ethics affect the public; consequently, members of the public have an interest in having their voices heard by the decision makers or, even, in participating in the decision making. But to do that the public needs information. The media are an important conduit to transmit the necessary information to the public so their voices are informed and they can engage in informed decision making. To obtain this information the media frequently consult academics, such as myself, and report our responses. As a result, we end up entering the public square.

And much has changed in attitudes in the academy to such participation. Rather than being decried, it is encouraged as part of our "contribution to the community" and seen as assisting the taxpayers, who contribute a large part of our salaries and research funds, to see what their investments produce. As well, universities, rather than decrying such publicity, now welcome it, in general, as helping to raise the university's profile in the public's consciousness.

Another important way in which academics enter the public square is as witnesses before parliamentary or legislative committees and as advisers to non-governmental organizations and international institutions such as the United Nations and its constituent bodies – for instance, WHO, UNESCO, UNICEF, and the UN Office of the High Commissioner for Human Rights.

I believe that the principal function of a public intellectual who is an ethicist is to facilitate the public's informed engagement in "ethics talk" in the public square, the modality through which we find and maintain our shared collective values. If we accept that role for ethicists, it brings certain requirements that they must try to ensure are fulfilled.

The "talk" must be comprehensible to the average member of the public; both sides of an issue need to be explored; minority voices must be given an opportunity to speak and be heard; on the other hand, so-called "hard" minorities must not monopolize the "talk" to the exclusion of "soft" majorities; we need to keep in mind that just because a majority adopts a certain position does not automatically mean that position is ethically sound.

The ethically relevant facts in any given situation need to be identified, as do the values implicated by those facts; when values conflict, in that not all can be honoured, a choice must be made as to which take priority; and that choice must be ethically justified, that is, the breach of the values that are not honoured must be able to be ethically justified.

Public intellectual ethicists can have a useful role to play in the process described above, but they need to be careful not to act as moral police or secular priests. Their role in the public square is not to be decision makers, but to assist those who are the rightful decision makers to make ethically informed decisions.

Social-Ethical-Legal Values in the Public Square

That said, one is often walking on eggs as an ethicist in the public square. Many of the issues we are called to advise or comment on are highly controversial and polarized.

If you read the newspapers, listen to documentaries on radio, or watch the news on TV you'll see numerous reports on topics such as access to health care, especially expensive new treatments; euthanasia and physician-assisted suicide; withdrawal of life-support treatment; palliative care; treatment of seriously disabled newborn babies; infant male circumcision; abortion; polygamy; same-sex marriage; children's human rights with respect to their biological origins, biological identity, and family structure; prenatal genetic screening; assisted human reproduction and new reproductive technologies; "designer babies"; human-embryo stem cell research; cloning; "manimals" – embryos with both human and animal genes; artificial sperm and ova – making embryos from two same-sex adults; synthetic biology; transplant tourism; xenotransplantation – the use of animal organs in humans; the use of animals in research; being soft/hard on crime and drugs; needle exchange clinics; safe injecting sites; capital punishment; law and ethics governing armed conflict; the ethics of robotic warfare; the ethics of the use of outer space; business ethics; corruption; conflict of interest; environmental ethics; aid to developing countries; and so on.

All these issues involve social-ethical-legal values in the public square.

And how we deal with each of them is important, not only in itself, but also in determining the values on which our Canadian society will be based. These are highly controversial issues at the heart of the present "culture wars" in postmodern Western democracies, and the outcomes of those wars will determine which values will form the basis of our societal-cultural paradigm. That is true because many of these issues involve values that are connected with life, birth, or death, the events around which we have always formed our most important individual and collective values.

These values, together with our principles, attitudes, beliefs, myths, and so on, make up the societal-cultural paradigm on which our society is based – that is, the "shared story" that we tell each other and buy into in order to form the glue that binds us together as a society.

"Culture Wars"

What our collective values should be is currently a source of conflict – some call it "culture wars." These wars are often described as having two sides doing battle: a traditional, conservative, often religious side versus a postmodern, liberal, moral relativist, often secularist side.

This division into two well-defined camps can be useful as a shorthand way to discuss these values issues, but it is an oversimplification, especially in relation to many of our current values issues, such as those I listed above, viewed as packages. Many variations in what constitutes one person's "values package" as compared with another person's package are possible. Moreover, even with respect to one issue there can be a range of different positions. Take, for instance, abortion. At one pole on a spectrum, some people believe there should be no restrictions on it; at the other pole, others believe that it should be completely banned; and in between there is a wide range of positions with a different justification for each. In other words, the reality is far more mixed and complex than two "camps," and it's important to recognize that, as it tells us that although we might disagree with "the other side" on some issues, we can agree with them on others.

That recognition is also important because, as I will propose, I believe searching for those agreements – what I call searching for a "shared ethics" – is crucial in pluralistic, multicultural, multi-religious, secular, postmodern, democratic societies like Canada, to finding a values structure that will allow each of us as individuals and all of us as a society to flourish in the sense of realizing the fullness of our human spirit. It is completely unrealistic to believe we can find a fully shared ethics. Rather, the idea is to find what we have in common ethically with respect to various issues so that we can experience ourselves as belonging to the same moral community in relation to those particular issues. As those experiences accumulate we will be more able to find common ground than we can in any other way.

But that requires mutual respect; a freedom to speak one's "truth," as one sees it; a willingness to listen – audi alterem partem, to hear the other side; and a recognition that all voices have a right to be heard in the public square, and, in particular, that the general public have a right to be involved in the debates that will establish our shared societal values.

I believe that a central role of an ethicist as a public intellectual is to facilitate the "ethics talk," especially in the public square, that will conform to the conditions I've just listed and that can help us to find some "shared ethics." But to do that, the ethicist must first be true to herself and her values and beliefs, and that can be a daunting requirement, as I have discovered personally, because it can require courage, in particular, to speak in support of what one sees as wise and ethical, when that contravenes currently accepted ideas of what others believe constitutes wisdom and ethics.

Very often the resulting clashes involve questions of the imposition of political correctness. Many people, including many politicians, are very fearful of being labelled "not politically correct." Their fear is not unreasonable, as I will explain, but it is dangerous for society's values when that fear silences them, and it's dangerous for society when not all voices can speak or be heard. It is anti-democratic and that under-mines democracy itself. In comparing intellectuals and politicians, Ca-nadian journalist Jeffrey Simpson makes an important point about their different roles and goals. He writes:

> An intellectual lives in truth, or in the pursuit of it; a politician lives in truth's shadows while pursuing power.
>
> A person can be intelligent in politics, but cannot be an intellectual, because an intellectual, if true to the world of ideas, must be fearless, whereas a politician usually lives in fear of defeat for himself, party or government.[1]

One example of my views that led to a great fuss, as I will shortly describe, was my public square comments on the topic of "children's human rights with respect to their biological origins, biological identity, and family structure." This issue involves our metaphysical environ-ment that includes our shared values, and is a matter in relation to which we will continue to have a great deal of difficulty in finding a shared ethics, because it intersects with same-sex marriage, single par-enthood, access to assisted reproductive technologies, and, to a lesser extent, with adoption, all matters on which there is no consensus. The question I asked in exploring this topic was "Do children have a right to a mother and a father, preferably their own biological parents?" That question would have been regarded as rhetorical even just ten years ago. Now it is explosive. It is a politically incorrect question.

Political Correctness

Let me now turn to political correctness and my experience of it as an ethicist in the public square. I'm sometimes seen as controversial for my views on certain topics, because those views are not politically cor-rect. Political correctness is, I propose, a serious threat to the proper functioning of public intellectuals. It operates through fear, whether of being shamed, shunned, excluded, or punished in some way. Indeed, I had an interesting experience in this regard at the 2008 Learned Socie-ties Congress that was held at the University of British Columbia.

The custom at the conference is to invite the previous year's CBC Massey lecturer as one of two keynote speakers, and I was appearing in this capacity as a result of a postponed invitation arising from my 2006 Massey Lectures.

Professor Noreen Golfman, from Memorial University, the president of the Federation of Humanities and Social Sciences, which convened the congress, received complaints from people who object to some of my views and the values they reflect, to the effect that it was inappropriate to have invited me as a keynote speaker. (I note that the CBC received similar complaints for having invited me to deliver the Massey Lectures, including, I understand, a complaint lodged with the Canadian Radio-television and Telecommunications Commission (CRTC), the regulatory body governing broadcasting in Canada.)

When asked by a *Globe and Mail* reporter why she had done this, Professor Golfman replied that "the Congress never got any news coverage, so she and her committee thought perhaps it might, if they had a controversial speaker." Professor Golfman also told the reporter that inviting me "shows we [the congress organizers] are not afraid of taking risks with our speakers." The next day the story was on the front page of the *Globe and Mail*.

I believe it's very important to protect our universities as spaces where the most open dialogue possible can be engaged in and for us to be aware that those spaces are at substantial risk of being shut down on some of our Canadian university campuses through the impact of political correctness. That should be of great concern to all academics, no matter what their personal values or views on the matters at issue, to universities, and to Canadian society.

Let me, however, make four preliminary points:

- First, I do not believe freedom of speech is an absolute right. Any speech that clearly constitutes ethical or legal wrongdoing may be restricted. Speech is no less subject than other activities to the necessity of "freedom in fetters" in order to maintain the conditions that make freedom possible.
- Second, I'm using the term "politically correct" as a shorthand term to cover a variety of identity-based social movements and the neo-liberal values and moral-relativism philosophy that they espouse. I am not using it, as can sometimes happen, to describe people or their views or values derogatorily, which is not to say I agree with all of them.
- Third, I believe the vast majority of people want to avoid harm and do good, but when our values conflict, we don't always agree which ones should be given priority in order to achieve that outcome, which engenders conflict among us. It is essential, no matter how intense that conflict, that we always act with mutual respect.

- Fourth, we should keep in mind the concept of moral regret. It requires that when, for reasons of ethics, something we do or stand for offends or hurts others – for instance, my opposition to same-sex marriage – even though we believe that we are required to do or stand for what we believe to be ethical, we should still deeply regret that our doing so causes others pain.

It is sometimes said that "all movements go too far," but that might be necessary for them, including politically correct, identity-based social movements, to have any impact at all. However, that being the case, they need to pull back or to be pulled back at a certain point, if they are not to do more harm than good.

My specific concern is that the various politically correct movements and the moral relativism that accompanies them have "gone too far," with very harmful impact on freedom of speech, on freedom of association, and on academic freedom in our universities, in general, and on the exercise of these freedoms by public intellectuals, such as myself, in particular. In discussing this, I'd like to speak from another personal experience.

The Ryerson University Events[2]

In 2006 I accepted an invitation to receive an honorary doctor of science degree from Ryerson University. When that was announced a powerful storm of protest erupted from the activist gay community and their supporters across Canada, demanding that, because of my views on same-sex marriage, the university withdraw its offer of the degree. (I will explain, shortly, the reasons why I oppose same-sex marriage.) That, in turn, generated an even bigger media storm across Canada in defence of freedom of speech.

The Paradox of Intense Tolerance

One element of this "perfect storm" that erupted was many people expressing to me their deep concern about "what's happening in our universities." An aspect of that concern is that an extreme of moral relativism can lead to a loss, on the part of university students, of substantive values, certainly shared ones, or even "ethics nihilism," in the sense that ethics becomes nothing more than personal preferences.

Postmodernism is now de rigueur in the humanities and social sciences. Postmodernists adopt a relativistic approach. In ethics, moral relativism translates into a view that there is no grounded truth; rather what is ethical is simply a matter of personal judgment and preference. Moral relativism means that values are all of equal worth and which take priority, when they conflict, is merely a matter of each person's perception and preference. That approach deconstructs values – they lose their substance. The result, paradoxically, is that "the equality of all values," itself, becomes the supreme value. This stance ultimately leads, at least in theory, to extreme or *intense tolerance* as the "most equal" of equal values. But does that happen in practice?

That is where political correctness enters the picture. It excludes politically incorrect values from the "all values are equal" stable. The intense moral relativists will tolerate all values except those which they deem to be politically incorrect – which just happen to be the ones that conflict with their values.

Political correctness operates by shutting down non-politically correct people's freedom of speech. Anyone who challenges the politically correct stance is, thereby, automatically labelled as intolerant, a bigot or hatemonger. The substance of their arguments against a politically correct stance is not addressed; rather people labelled as politically incorrect are, themselves, attacked as being intolerant and hateful simply for making those arguments. This "derogatorily label the person and dismiss them on the basis of that label" approach is intentionally used as a strategy to suppress strong arguments against any politically correct stance and, also, to avoid needing to deal with these arguments.

It is important to understand the strategy employed: Speaking against abortion or same-sex marriage is not characterized as speech; rather, it is characterized as a sexist act against women or a discriminatory act against homosexuals, respectively, and, therefore, as, in itself, a breach of human rights or even a hate crime. Consequently, it is argued that the protections of freedom of speech do not apply.

Another part of the same strategy is to reduce to two the choices of position that are available: One must be either pro-choice on abortion and for respect for women and their rights or pro-life and against respect for women and their rights. The possibility of being pro-women and their rights and pro-life is eliminated.

The same approach is taken to same-sex marriage: One is against discrimination on the basis of sexual orientation and for same-sex marriage, or against same-sex marriage and for such discrimination. The option of being against such discrimination and against same-sex marriage, as I am, is eliminated.[3] That approach is not accidental; it is central to the strategy that has been successful in Canada in maintaining a complete void with respect to having any law governing abortion and having same-sex marriage legalized.

Yet another strategy is to label people who have views that are not politically correct as religious (sometimes, even when they are not) and to dismiss them and their arguments on that basis without responding to the substance of their arguments. In other words, an ad hominem attack is used.

I propose that the way in which political correctness is being used is a form of fundamentalism. The characteristics of fundamentalism are, first, that fundamentalists want to impose their views on everyone else. Second, fundamentalists take an either/or approach – either my beliefs or yours. They refuse to accommodate both sides of a divide, even when that is possible and easily done. Rather, they deal with conflict between two sides of a debate by eliminating the other side. And, third, they engage in proselytizing in an effort to have their views prevail. For instance, the advertising campaign with the slogan "There's probably no God. Now stop worrying and enjoy your life," on buses in Britain and Canada, is a relatively recent example of such proselytizing, in this case by fundamentalist neo-atheists, that attracted a great deal of media and public attention. We might like to regard fundamentalists as irrelevant and ignore them. But we need to keep in mind that, because of their nature, fundamentalisms are a danger to democracy and, hence, to our Western democratic societies.

Moral Relativism and Political Correctness in Practice

The issue that sparked the "Ryerson controversy," legalizing same-sex marriage, is an example of what "pure" moral relativism and intense tolerance, as modified by political correctness, mean in practice.[4]

While I abhor discrimination on the basis of sexual orientation and agree that same-sex marriage could be a powerful message of the wrongs of that, I oppose same-sex marriage because of its impact on children's rights.[5] In choosing between adults and children, I believe we should give priority to children. I argue that children need and have a right to both a mother and a father, preferably their own biological parents, unless the "best interests" of a particular child require otherwise, as in many adoptions.

Marriage limited to the union of a man and a woman establishes that right; same-sex marriage eliminates that right for all children (which is why I oppose the redefinition of marriage), but support civil unions (which do not have that impact). My approach clashes head-on with that of the morally relativist, politically correct stance that supports same-sex marriage – namely, that "personal preference with regard to founding a family establishes what constitutes a family."

The Ryerson protestors sought to "deal" with me by labelling me. I was described as guilty of a hate crime; the new Ernst Zundel (a German Holocaust denier living in Canada, and, like him, I should be deported – they were grateful that I came from Australia and could be sent back there); a neo-Nazi; and a member of the Ku Klux Klan. My views had no place in the university, they claimed. This approach eliminated the need to deal with the substance of my arguments – I *and my arguments* could be summarily dismissed. It sent a very powerful warning to all those who might happen to share my views – or any other non-politically correct views – that they should not speak them publicly for fear of the same kind of treatment.

The protestors demanded that the university withdraw its offer of the honorary degree, and they set up a website with an online poll, on which protests could be recorded. The university committee which had recommended me for the honorary degree put out a press release stating that "if it had known what kind of person I was, they would never have offered the degree, but that it was too late to withdraw their invitation"[6] – it's somewhat surprising that they didn't know, in view of the large amount of general media publicity my views had previously received. I suppose that you shouldn't trust university people to do their basic research!

The night before the convocation the university booked me into a hotel far from the campus, under another name. A special security car collected me from the hotel next morning and took me to an underground entrance to the convocation hall to avoid protestors outside the hall. I was flanked by bodyguards and joined the academic procession, which had walked through the grounds without me, only at the back of the hall. I'd been asked to wear shoes in which I could run, in case we needed to make a quick escape. It seemed surreal – like a scene out of a James Bond movie. Some of the faculty members in the academic procession were wearing various sized rainbow flags pinned on their academic gowns and carrying rolled up banners.

Inside the hall, at the front, a special section had been cordoned off for TV crews, of which there were many. The hall was packed upstairs and downstairs with a very large crowd of over three hundred graduands and their families and friends.

The citation was read and the chancellor went to place the ceremonial hood over my shoulders. What happened next was completely astonishing. The audience rose to its feet and thunderous applause rang out. I'm told that at the same time about a third of the platform party, which was behind me on the stage so I couldn't see them, stood and turned their backs to me and the audience, and many unrolled protest banners and rainbow flags. The applause continued unabated. After a considerable period, I signalled to the audience to stop and take their seats and eventually they did. As I walked to the podium to deliver the convocation speech, a single voice rang out from the back of the auditorium. "You should be ashamed of yourself!" a man shouted. A collective very loud "Shhh!" gathered volume as it swept from one side of the hall to the other.

In the silence that ensued, I began my convocation speech as follows:

> To begin, let me say that despite the very public roller coaster ride this convocation has engendered over the last ten days, I am honoured to be standing here today. In that context, an ethics concept, to which I've been giving increasing attention in the last year or two, merits mention. It's called "moral regret." What it requires is that when, for reasons of ethics, something we do or stand for hurts others, even though ethics requires that we do or stand for that, we should still regret the hurt it causes. As we all know, some people are hurt by some of my views. I want say that, although I believe that I must stand by those views, I genuinely regret the hurt that causes to them.

I then greeted each of the 310 graduates as they came to the stage. Many said something kind or complimentary about my degree or the convocation speech – only two refused to shake hands, and one shook hands, but grimaced.

The president of Ryerson University, Sheldon Levy, said that of all the possible responses he'd anticipated, this was the only one he could never have predicted.

So, was the protest against me a "one off" situation in our universities? I do not believe so. One current, very worrying example is the suppression of pro-life groups and pro-life speech on Canadian university campuses – which even the *Globe and Mail*, a strong supporter of "progressive values" such as pro-choice, decried in an editorial.

Whatever our views on abortion, we should all be worried about such developments. Pro-choice students are trying to stop pro-life students from participating in the collective conversation on abortion that should take place. In fact, they don't want any conversation, alleging that to question whether we should have any law on abortion is, in itself, unacceptable. In fact, I have been consulted on several occasions by students applying to medical school or by their parents, who were distressed at being questioned in admission interviews as to whether they had any objections to abortion.

Outside the academy, in some instances some people are going even further: they want to force physicians to act against their conscience and compel them to refer for or carry out abortions under threat of being in breach of human rights or subject to professional disciplinary procedures for refusing to do so. At one point the Ontario Human Rights Commission advised the College of Physicians and Surgeons of Ontario to this effect, in words that could be summarized as "Park your values with your car outside the surgery."

These are examples of political correctness being used as a sword (a weapon) not a shield. It is being used to try to impose certain views and even actions that breach rights to freedom of conscience; to shut down free speech; and to contravene academic freedom. I do not need to emphasize the dangers of this in universities, no matter how worthy one's motives in promoting one's cause. The most fundamental precept on which a university is founded is openness to ideas and knowledge from all sources.

As well, since the Ryerson protests I've been expressly dis-invited from three events – that is, I have accepted an invitation to speak and agreed on all the terms and conditions, then some time later been told the invitation was being withdrawn. That has never happened before in my nearly thirty years of speaking engagements. And, probably uniquely, the withdrawals came from opposite ends of the values spectrum.

One withdrawal was because my views were seen as not being pro-life, and in another case as not being pro-choice. In these two cases, only a speech that would be preaching to the converted was seen as acceptable.

In the third case, a diplomatic explanation was given, but my hunch is that the university administrators, fund-raisers, and public relations professionals involved were frightened of facing protests for having invited me – it's easier to sidestep controversial speakers. No one knows how many comparable invitations are not issued because of fear of controversy.

The cumulative effect is a silencing. And such "silence is golden" in more than a metaphorical sense – potential donors are not offended.

Ryerson University received many calls from people saying they would never donate to the university again, if they conferred the honorary degree on me. A past principal at McGill received similar calls in relation to another controversial issue – the ethics of infant male circumcision – on which I spoke publicly, demanding that I be fired or the callers would never again donate.

Moreover, I was told that in the 2009–10 academic year some law students who were members of McGill OutLaw, a club for gay, lesbian, bisexual, transgender, and allied students, based in the Faculty of Law, had proposed asking other law students not to enrol in any of my classes as a means of public protest against my views on same-sex marriage, but changed their minds because that might have "made them look bad," especially as law students who should be defenders of rights such as free speech.

One of my classes was invaded by students, with TV cameras filming them, and had to be abandoned as they carried out a mock same-sex marriage. I've received very large amounts of hate mail and, as I've explained, been the subject of an online protest petition, as well as needing security precautions when speaking in public, all because I believe all children – including those who are gay as adults – need a mother and a father, which opposite-sex marriage gives them and same-sex marriage takes away.

And if that is how I'm treated, imagine how students, or even junior faculty, who hold views that are seen as not politically correct or, sometimes, just too conservative, feel. They are fearful of speaking out and feel intimidated. Whatever our own views on these matters in dispute – whether professionally, as academics, or personally – this is a situation that we should seek to remedy.

Furthermore, in the context of discussing political correctness in the public square one must not overlook politicians. They, perhaps more than anyone, want to avoid these social-ethical-values issues that are too hot to handle and create "no win" situations, because politicians lose votes whichever side they take on them.

The further deep concern is that this conflict within our universities, and dealing with it by shutting down freedom of speech, might be a micro-example of a much larger problem outside the universities. We might be at risk of annihilating some of our most important shared values, and that creates a situation that threatens society itself.

We cannot hold a society together in the long term without shared values, that is, without a societal-cultural paradigm: as I explained previously, the story about ourselves that supports our most important principles, values, attitudes, and beliefs, one that we tell each other and all buy into in order to form the glue that holds us together. Tolerance alone – especially unbalanced by other important values – is nowhere near enough to found that story. To ensure our story does not disintegrate and continues to be enriched, we must engage in mutually respectful conversation. And the public needs public intellectuals to help them to engage in that conversation.

Among many requirements for their being able to do that, academics must be able to speak freely – and respectfully, openly, honestly, and without threat of repercussions – about contentious but important societal problems. That requires respect for freedom of thought, freedom of speech, freedom of association, and academic freedom – the latter of which is meant primarily for the benefit of the public by allowing academics to feel they can speak the truth, as they see it, to power. The Ryerson University events were in breach of all those freedoms.

Our universities should be models for the larger society of crossing the divides that separate us, not of widening them as currently seems to be happening. And in the much larger context than the university, that of our contemporary multicultural, pluralistic democracies, we must engage in mutually respectful conversation across those divides.

One of the major current societal divides is between religion and secularism, which raises the thorny issue of what role religion should or should not play in the public square. And that, in turn, raises the question of the role of ethicists, as public intellectuals, in this debate.

Religion in the Public Square

Some politicians interpret the doctrine of separation of church and state to mean that their own personal views on what is and is not moral or ethical have no place in politics, often in order to avoid standing up for what they purportedly believe is morally or ethically right when they think that will lose them votes. That means they believe, as Michael Cook, editor of Mercatornet.com puts it, "that morality and politics have little to do with each other. In fact, political expediency should trump moral truths." Surely, this is not a position that should be reassuring to the citizens whom these politicians represent, including as decision makers about issues that will affect our most important shared values. One crucial task of ethicists as public intellectuals might be to hold politicians' feet to the fire – to remind them and the public that this approach is, at best, questionable and probably unacceptable.

It's true that the proper role of religion, if any, in the public square is a contentious issue. Religious people claim, rightly in my view, that in a democratic society all voices including theirs have a right to be heard. Secularists adamantly disagree. They argue that religious voices have no valid role.

We form society through a journey of the collective human imagination. We used to take that journey through a shared religion, but that is no longer possible, yet we still need to take that journey. I believe one role of public-intellectual ethicists is to help the people taking this journey to ask themselves as many of the "right" questions as possible, because it is through such questioning that we can map an ethical path and form shared values in the process. But that role of ethicists needs to be distinguished from another possibility. It is sometimes said that ethicists have replaced clergy as the spokespersons for moral considerations in the public square. I do not agree, or at least that should not be the case. Everyone, including clergy, has a right to speak in the public square.

In an article in the *Globe and Mail*, journalist Michael Valpy quotes American political scientist Benedict Anderson to the effect that "a nation is an imagined community."[7] Valpy points out that we have to understand our fellow citizens with whom we interact, and "share values, community knowledge and mythology," if we are to hear and understand each other. And doing that is "what enables Canadians to live together with sufficient levels of trust and security and to conduct their democracy under the rubric of having a common purpose and serving the common good." The problems are that we can no longer assume a shared knowledge – "the cohesive core of common information is shrinking" – and that we are becoming more polarized in our attitudes, and that is undermining social cohesion. Might it be one task of ethicists in the public square to help people to see where they can agree, even though there is much that they disagree about? Finding where we do have consensus is important not just in relation to the issues involved, but also, as I explained previously, because it provides us with the experience of belonging to the same moral community, and that can help us to find some "shared ethics" at a more general level.[8]

We might need to bind together to experience transcendence – the feeling of belonging to something larger than ourselves – which we might need to experience to find meaning in life. Values surveys have found that a longing for transcendence is a rapidly escalating phenomenon in our intensely individualistic Western societies.

But today, much more than in the past, we humans need to bind together across our differences to form a society. Doing that is a major challenge even just within our local or national societies in the West, as they become more and more internally diverse. One response could be the emergence of what my colleagues Katherine Young and Paul Nathanson have called "secular religions."[9] And it may be that contemporary applied ethics is a form of secular religion, which, if true, gives some support to the criticism of ethicists that they are the "new priesthood" or "moral police."

Secular Religions[10]

It's indisputably true that humanism and atheism function as secular religions binding their adherents through common belief and ideology.

Science can also function as a secular religion and does so when it becomes scientism. The same is true, I believe, of sport, when it becomes *sportism*, especially when that is combined with another powerful "ism," *nationalism*.

And environmentalism is at least a secondary religion for more and more people – but even that has its disbelievers and critics! It's also true of ethics, when it becomes moralism. In short, we are witnessing the emergence of a very large number and range of secular religions.

None of these "isms" is harmful in itself, but they are harmful to finding a shared ethics when they are promoted – as, for instance, Richard Dawkins and other fundamentalist neo-atheists do with scientism – to deny any space for spirituality and traditional religion in the public square and replace those with *secularism*, the most encompassing secular religion that functions as a basket holding all the others.

In other words, I am arguing that it's a mistake to accept that secularism is neutral, as its advocates claim – it's not. It too is a belief system used to bind people together. And if, despite being a belief system, secularism is not excluded from the public square, then religious voices should not be excluded on that basis. The mistake is in taking a disjunctive (either secularism or religion) approach to a situation that requires a conjunctive (both this and that, secularism and religion) approach. We need all voices to be heard in the democratic public square and one hopes that ethicists in their role of public intellectuals can help to ensure that they are.

Mainstream Media

The media play not just *a* central role, but *the* central role in ethics in the public square, in the sense of determining which topics and arguments are and which are not presented, and often how they are presented. That means the media play a central role in determining the opportunities which will and will not be afforded to an ethicist to contribute to and participate in societal debates as a public intellectual.

My own personal experience in this regard, over three decades of working with all forms of media, has been almost entirely a very happy one that I'm deeply grateful to have had the privilege of experiencing. I have enormous respect for journalists, I find they are dedicated, highly intelligent, well-informed or ready to admit when they are not and to learn, usually want to present both sides of an argument, seek accuracy, are often deeply concerned about the issues on which they are reporting, and for the most part try to be fair and balanced. And I'm not speaking from a base of a few fortunate encounters. I don't have statistics, but I've done many thousands of interviews in all forms of media. My experience with editorial, comment, and letters-page editors and with radio and television producers is, with one or two exceptions, the same. Although they may strongly disagree with the arguments I'm putting forward and challenge me to clarify them, they still are willing to print my articles and include me in the programs they produce.

Others tell me, however, that they do not have the same experience. Most often that seems to be because those others are identified as being religious and their views influenced by their religious beliefs, and they are summarily dismissed on that basis. I have written elsewhere about the wrongs that entails and that it is anti-democratic.[11] To repeat: All voices have a right to be heard in the democratic public square.

And it is true that the media can be hostile to religious people and religious voices. Canadian theologian Michael Higgins reports that Roger Alton, the editor of the *Independent*, speaks of the hostility in the media to religion and growing level of intolerance. "The ceiling of respect has been breached."[12] Many journalists are highly individualistic, reject authority and what they see as paternalism, and are often hostile to religion for those reasons. They identify opposition to, for example abortion, euthanasia, or same-sex marriage, as a religious, "right wing," "anti-choice," conservative view, all characteristics from which they personally disidentify.

Conclusion

Being identified as a public intellectual and an ethicist is not an easy role to fulfil and is one I would never have contemplated in my wildest dreams that I would ever have the opportunity to pursue. There are times when it seems just all too much, too hard, impossible to achieve what needs to be done. But almost without exception, I wake each morning wondering what exciting events will unfold before me today, what I will learn, whom I will meet, what challenges I will face, what outcomes we will arrive at? It's an enormous privilege to have those opportunities and I often still view them with wonder and amazement that they are, indeed, mine and such an important part of my life.

APPENDIX

**Selected Print Media Articles on Ryerson University's Award
of an Honorary Degree to Margaret Somerville**

Toronto Star, 8 June 2006: Daniel Girard (education reporter), "Ryerson to honour gay-marriage critic / Degree to come at start of Pride Week / Ethicist says she's pro-child, not anti-gay."

Toronto Star, 9 June 2006, Letter to the editor: Sheila Austin, "Wrong to honour gay-marriage critic" (Re: "Ryerson to honour gay-marriage critic," 8 June 2006).

Ottawa Sun, Geoff Matthews, "Some might like to disagree," 9 June 2006.

Christianity.ca, 14 June 2006: "The New Prejudice: Protests against those receiving honorary doctorates show a growing intolerance of anyone expressing opposition to celebration of homosexuality" (compiled by Janet Epp Buckingham).

Toronto Star, 15 June 2006: Daniel Girard (education reporter), "Ryerson sticks by award for ethicist / Panel says it respects academic freedom / School union, gay groups plan protests."

Canadian Press (Ottawa), 15 June 2006: Dennis Bueckert, "What was supposed to be an honour bestowed by Ryerson University on renowned ethicist Margaret Somerville has turned into an ordeal that she says has left her in a state of shock."

Globe and Mail, 17 June 2006: Editorial, "How Ryerson failed Margaret Somerville."

Globe and Mail, 17 June 2006: Margaret Wente, "Campus diversity – yeah, and I'm Queen of the May."

Le Devoir (Montreal), 19 June 2006: Jean-Claude Leclerc (editorial), "L'homophobie et l'université: Qui donc verse dans la haine et
 l'intolérance?"
National Post, 19 June 2006: Lorne Gunter, "Spineless and rude: Ryerson University shows how not to grant an honorary degree."
Macleans.ca, 19 June 2006: Erin Atack, "Protests as ethicist Margaret Somerville awarded honorary degree by Ryerson."
Christianity.ca, 19 June 2006: Al Hiebert, "Propaganda or Facts – Defeating
 Defeatism: The participation of churches in politics is part of their mission,
 but their engagement must be within a broader mandate under the sovereignty of God and the Lordship of Christ" (originally published in *Carillion*,
 week of 19 June 19).
Toronto Star, 21 June 2006: Editorial, "Ryerson U's duty to combat 'chill.'"
Inside Higher Ed, 22 June 2006: Scott Jaschik, "Honorary Degrees, Tolerance
 and Ethics: Margaret Somerville plans to pick up her honorary degree today
 at Ryerson University, in Toronto, whether protests materialize or not,"
 http://www.insidehighered.com/news/2006/06/19/ryerson.
Globe and Mail, 24 June 24: John Fraser, "Three for thought: what you need to
 read about … academic intolerance / The toxic tower: In the aftermath of
 a flap over the awarding of an honorary degree to a prominent scholar, …
 political correctness remains a scourge of campus life today."
Globe and Mail, 24 June 2006: Rex Murphy, "Conduct most unbecoming of
 Ryerson."
Macleans.ca, 28 June 2006: Brian Bethune, "Q&A with pioneering ethicist
 Margaret Somerville: On the Ryerson fiasco, children's rights and same-
 sex marriage," http://www.macleans.ca/culture/people/article.jsp?
 content=20060701_130175_130175#.

NOTES

1 Jeffrey Simpson, "On truth, fear and broken political promises," *Globe and
  Mail*, 9 Sept. 2009, A15.
2 In order to document the events I describe, I have included some examples
  of the press coverage of them as an appendix.
3 See, for example, Margaret Somerville, "What about the Children?" in
  Daniel Cere and Douglas Farrow, eds, *Divorcing Marriage* (Montreal: McGill-
  Queen's University Press, 2004), 63–78.
4 I want to make it clear that in this section I am generalizing and speaking
  of situations that I have encountered. Not all people who support same-sex
  marriage are moral relativists, although the vast majority of those with

whom I have come in contact are. Likewise, the strategies I describe as being used to prevent any law to govern abortion or to promote same-sex marriage are not used by all advocates, but again are tactics that I have encountered.

5 See, for a more general and in-depth discussion of this issue, Margaret Somerville, "Children's Human Rights to Natural Biological Origins and Family Structure," HeinOnline IJJF Library, 2011, http://heinonline.org/HOL/Page?handle=hein.journals/ijjf1&id=1&collection=journals; *International Journal of the Jurisprudence of the Family* 1 (2010), 35ff.

6 See *Globe and Mail* editorial, posted on 17 June 2006, "How Ryerson failed Margaret Somerville," http://www.theglobeandmail.com/commentary/how-ryerson-failed-margaret-somerville/article730161.

7 Michael Valpy, "Is this the end of the age of our social cohesion?" *Globe and Mail*, 29 Aug. 2009, A17; http://www.theglobeandmail.com/commentary/is-this-the-end-of-the-age-of-our-social-cohesion/article4306947/?page=all.

8 See Margaret Somerville, *The Ethical Imagination: Journeys of the Human Spirit*, 2006 CBC Massey Lectures (Toronto: House of Anansi Press, 2006).

9 Paul Nathanson and Katherine K. Young, *Spreading Misandry: The Teaching of Contempt for Men in Popular Culture* (Montreal: McGill-Queen's University Press, 2001), 209–10.

10 Adapted from Margaret Somerville, "Searching for a Shared Ethics – Challenging Richard Dawkins' 'The God Delusion,'" in Anne Henderson, ed., *The Sydney Papers* (The Sydney Institute), 19, no. 3 (Winter 2007), 20–35.

11 Margaret Somerville, "Should Religion Be Given a 'Pink Slip' in the Public Square?" McGill Centre for Research on Religion, "Religion and the Public Sphere" lecture series, Montreal, 7 October 2009.

12 Michael Higgins, "Why the English don't like to mix the spiritual and the temporal," *Globe and Mail*, 31 July 2009, http://www.theglobeandmail.com/commentary/why-the-english-dont-like-to-mix-the-spiritual-and-the-temporal/article1201142/.

Conclusion

No synopsis of these essays could do them justice, and any selection of Canada's past or present public intellectuals is bound to reflect the anthologist's tastes and interests. The bias of this editor's collection, mindful that one person's intellectual or serious public thinker may be another person's self-interested promoter, is unabashedly political and social. The foregoing essays canvass how knowledge is constructed and ideas created, examine Canadian intellectual history and touch on public policy issues. Diverse in their style and subject matter, taken together the authors present a coherent overview of the role and place of Canada's public intellectuals. Some of the contributors make thoughtful philosophical statements, others offer researched empirical studies, and still others present, sometimes passionately, idiosyncratic accounts of their personal experiences in publicizing the ideas that animate them.

Janice Gross Stein reminds us that public intellectuals are human, creatures with passions as well as intellect. Indeed, reason and emotion are inseparable. Being human, public intellectuals do not escape the weaknesses and luring temptations with which everyone struggles. Hopeful, erudite, and uplifting about the public's capacity to tell when a public intellectual has something to offer and is worth listening to, Stein nevertheless discerns some disturbing trends that debase public debate and engagement. She is anxious that democratic institutions, their channels of communications, and the exchange of ideas so essential in a free and open society not wither. Public intellectuals, driven to engage and share their ideas with others, are vital in a democratic polity. This is especially so in an increasingly digitized world of narrowcasting, where vitriolic partisanship shrinks a common public space. Lamentably, this development has gone hand-in-hand with the "dumbing down" of mainstream media. Eager to expand their report-age of lifestyle and human-interest stories, they have gravitated away from covering world affairs.

The public intellectual in Stein's view must resist and push back against the negative drifts that have fed distrust of politicians and the political process. If the public intellectual expects the public to tune in to her message, however, she must listen, be modest, pay respectful atten-tion to her audience, and avoid hiding behind jargon. Feeling obliged to contribute to public debate in a democracy in matters in which she has some expertise, the public intellectual should not confuse analysis with advocacy. Stein's own style is to expand ideas, stretch their contradic-tions, note their complexities, and steer clear of any rush to judgment.

For Stein's inspiring yin, there is Hugh Segal's sobering yang. His analysis, a model of moderation in its balance and insights, explores the limited dimensions of the public intellectual's influence in public affairs and its battleground of competing political agendas. Like Stein, he emphasizes the importance of transcending narrow partisanship. As a public policy practitioner, he observes that if a public intellectual re-peatedly and predictably advocates the same policy options, those in power discount her and typecast her views. Segal offers Dalton Camp and Michael Kirby, figures from opposing sides of Canada's partisan divide, as examples of political figures who have played important roles as public intellectuals.

The nub of Segal's argument is that the public intellectual must not become captive of the ephemeral high-intensity skirmishes that typ-ify the shallow conflict-driven orientation of today's media with their disdain for exposition. Economics and competitive markets motivate the media to seek out cheap plentiful content, while, at the same time, politicians' desires to mould public opinion in their favour has them and the media in a mutually exploitive relationship that only debili-tates public discourse. (Mark Kingwell also singles out television as a negative influence on public dialogue.) True intellectuals rise above the momentary political fray and escape the enticements of the media and their insistence for "opinions du jour"; these only fulfil the first law of commercial television: providing viewers with so many "jolts per min-ute."[1] Like Stein, Segal points both to the foibles to which intellectuals may fall prey and the distinction between advocacy and analysis. And, like Pierre Fortin and Doug Saunders, he notes the relatively stronger influence in the United States than in Canada of public intellectuals who labour in policy institutes and think tanks, as well as universities, in public policy making.

The proximity and size of the United States figure prominently in a number of chapters, including those by Stephen Clarkson and Saunders. For Saunders, size and geography matter. Public thought in Canada, its very ability to exist, is constrained by the country's under-population and sparseness. He praises the ingenuity of a number of individual Canadians, but laments that, compared to the United States and Europe, Canada suffers a shortage of publishing outlets for public intellectuals because of its limited market. The country's think tanks and policy institutes are insufficiently large to fulfil the policy formulation functions that their American counterparts discharge for the American political parties and administrations. Because public thought is rooted in vibrant institutions that bond thinkers and specific audiences in communications networks, this renders Canada "unable to think," in his estimation. Size, however, does not necessarily dictate a lack of intellectual weight or influence. Ottawa's North-South Institute was ranked first in the University of Pennsylvania's 2011 global ranking of small-budget think tanks – based on a survey of over 1500 peer institutions and experts – and Canadian institutes led by Vancouver's Fraser Institute, according to the same survey, held eight of the ten top spots in a region that included Canada, Mexico, and the Caribbean.[2]

Clever, playful, and humorous, Mark Kingwell skilfully deploys a dialogue format to portray and throw brickbats at a range of personalities who could conceivably qualify as public intellectuals. Flippant and funny, illuminating and at times perplexing, he entertains with his perceptive assessment of the various poses of the public intellectual. Kingwell summons some major philosophical figures – among others, Plato, Lao Tzu, Karl Popper, and Northrop Frye (especially) pop up – after running through a brief candidates' list of Canadian public intellectuals. It includes Frye, Marshall McLuhan, Harold Innis, George Grant, George Woodcock, Jane Jacobs, Margaret Atwood, Charles Taylor, and Michael Ignatieff. Kingwell's dialogical method permits him to "toss ideas around" without being committed to them as he would be in an ordinary essay. Disputing that Canadians are any less anti-intellectual than Americans are, he cites (as does Tom Flanagan in his essay) a newspaper poll which anointed Don Cherry as the country's favourite public intellectual.

Kingwell identifies four types of public intellectuals: the fast-thinking, fast-talking shrewd media tutor, the pretentious and reductionist political pundit with a contrarian bent or ideological agenda, the defender of the status quo à la Julian Benda's treasonous clerks (capitalism is that villainous status quo for Kingwell), and the persistent xenocyst, Kingwell's favourite and for which he plumps. "Xenocyst," foreign to most dictionaries, refers to an entity alien to and indigestible by its environment. Simultaneously misanthropic and hopeful, a cynical tone emerges in Kingwell's parody of himself and other public intellectuals. He is, however, not without a progressive message and it belies jaded disparagement: the best public intellectuals can hope for is to be good citizens. Kingwell concludes by championing the welfare of the underclasses. Those on top, including intellectuals, can take care of themselves.

Nelson Wiseman steps back to identify some of Canada's most prominent public intellectuals in the twentieth century, a period that witnessed the evolution of Canada from beseeching colony to independent self-governing nation. Canada, where the most popular bar song at the time of the First World War was "White Canada Forever," underwent a demographic metamorphosis and a constitutional revolution. Canadians became a sovereign people who re-imagined themselves as a society constitutionally committed to "the preservation and enhancement" of their multinational, multiracial, and poly-ethnic heritage.[3]

Using the dominant ideological "isms" of the twentieth century – conservatism, liberalism, and socialism – as lenses through which to peer at public intellectuals, Wiseman identifies and organizes their ideas across the century's four quarters. He sketches the rough but steady march of a conservative, imperial subaltern Canada in which preachers informed politics, through the Depression, the eclipse of British power, and the rise of secularism. After mid-century, Marshall McLuhan built on but also shifted attention from Harold Innis's meditations about the trade routes of the world to his own map of the trade routes of the mind. At the same time, liberals and conservatives adopted social democratic welfare-state policies and Pierre Trudeau lambasted the "New Treason of the [Quebec] Intellectuals." In the millennium's final decades, neoconservatism overshadowed Canada's historic Tory conservative tradition, new accents and surnames appeared, and identity politics came to the fore.

Intimacy among francophone Quebeckers, occasioned by their relatively few numbers and their concentration in two large cities, means that Quebec's intellectuals are more likely commonly schooled and acquainted with one another's families than are intellectuals in larger societies. "All read Le Devoir," according to Gregory Baum, and this leads him to shine light on the century-old newspaper and its primacy of place for the exchange of ideas in Quebec. Conveying the passionate engagement of Quebec's public intellectuals with their society's identity issues, a theme shared with Alain-G. Gagnon, Baum, like Gagnon, also notes the more subdued role of Quebec's intellectuals and a general decline of social idealism in the aftermath of flustered constitutional ambitions. Like Maude Barlow, Baum points to the energetic activities of Quebec civil society organizations and remarks that *Le Devoir*, in contrast to the English Canadian media, has taken such organizations and their objectives much more seriously. *Le Devoir* has offered a welcoming platform for intellectuals with starkly different positions to plumb issues seriously. This speaks, once again, to the contrasts between the media, as well as the political cultures, in the two solitudes. What Baum does not address is the ideological and political transformation of *Le Devoir* and other Quebec newspapers; during the Second World War, they had been pro-Vichy, anti-Semitic as well as anti-British, and opposed to Charles de Gaulle, whom they cheered during his provocative visit to Quebec in 1967.

Baum sets Quebec's model of interculturalism – which accentuates the exchanges between different cultural groups in a *société d'acceuil* (a receiving society which itself is under pressure) – in opposition to English Canada's multicultural trope, something Quebec has repeatedly rejected. He addresses the debate regarding *la laïcité* – the space between religion and the state – an issue causing particular unease in contemporary Quebec. Protagonists in the debate lie on both sides of the federalist-separatist and left-right divides. The debate, also touched on by Gagnon, is of special interest to Baum as a student of theology and an active social justice advocate. We learn that the report by Charles Taylor and Gérard Bouchard's government-appointed Commission on Accommodation Practices Related to Cultural Differences had a more favourable reception in Europe than in Quebec, a comment on the influence of Canadians' ideas abroad.

Alain-G. Gagnon's study of Quebec's intellectuals is a salutary admonition to think about Canada bi-nationally and it complements Wiseman's anglo-centric history. Two languages and two cultures make for two hearts, two brains, and two intellectual traditions, with public intellectuals oriented differently in the two solitudes; the *Québécois* have participated in debating the reconstitution of their society, the English-speaking Canadians have presented themselves as experts shaping policy. Where the *Québécois* have wrestled with existential issues and engaged with the "high politics" of constitutional futures, English Canadians have grappled with building the central federal state and the "low politics" of public policy and administration that reinforce the constitutional status quo. However, the tarnished lustre of Quebec's intellectuals in the upshot of the constitutional imbroglios and the failure of three referenda in the 1980s and 1990s resulted in some convergence, if not alignment, in the orientations of public intellectuals in the two societies.

Both societies witnessed the decline of the public intellectual as an independent social critic. Many Quebec intellectuals drifted from philosophical and existentialist concerns to embracing the techniques and applications of the social sciences, from imagining an independent Quebec or a redefined Canada to building the extant Quebec state. Called on to serve less as "men of ideas" and more as public servants, the provincial state finessed the issue by co-opting Taylor and Bouchard to study the accommodation of cultural minority practices. Less preoccupied with mobilizing their society and more concerned with managing its tensions, Quebec's public intellectuals are nevertheless still active in defining their society and they continue to be more influential and enjoy a higher status than public intellectuals in most other Western democracies.

Like Gagnon and Baum, who point to the declining status of public intellectuals in Quebec, Sylvia Bashevkin notes the waning of social-movement activism among women. All three associate these developments with Canadians' exhausting exertions in past constitutional battles. Bashevkin critically analyses the space claimed by women public intellectuals, internationally and domestically. Otherwise, women are referred to as public intellectuals only fleetingly by Wiseman in the Introduction, indirectly by Kingwell, who notes men's dominance as media pundits, and by Baum, who singles out *Le Devoir* editor Lise Bissonnette and makes brief mention of the Federation of the Women of Quebec. Bashevkin's historical overview, which traces the ebb and flow of women's visibility as public intellectuals, addresses the factors limiting women's contributions to public affairs. She speculates: will the new social media advance women as "purveyors of public wisdom?" and she pointedly observes that universities, in which female students now outnumber male students in many faculties, have lost their edge as centres of inquiry. This is partly because profit-oriented agencies within the academy and private investors have redirected scholarship and undermined older understandings of the meaning of "knowledge."

Ursula Franklin, Irshad Manji, and Naomi Klein – three figures Bashevkin highlights – are of dramatically different social backgrounds and intellectual interests, but each has been a public force and each has exhibited the courage and creativity that marks the public intellectual. Manji's relocation to the United States provides anecdotal evidence for Saunders's point about the gravitational cultural pull of larger societies; Klein's command of a substantial international following speaks to the Canadian public intellectual's ability to stay put in her home and native land and still exert an effective sway on global public opinion.

In moving from philosophic statements and empirical studies, the contributions of a number of authors reflect on their experiences as practitioners. Tom Flanagan, like Kingwell, presents the public intellectual as fourfold. His reference points, however, are not to others but to himself. As a doctrinaire libertarian acolyte of conservative icons Friedrich Hayek and Milton Friedman, Flanagan served as Preston Manning's director of policy for the fledgling Reform Party and as a campaign director for Stephen Harper. Flanagan relates his experiences as a pundit, as a writer ambitious to influence public opinion by taking polemical positions that gore sacred cows, as an expert government witness in litigation, and as a warrior in the political trenches. He contrasts insightfully the authoritative character of the academic teacher's role with the adversarial nature of the political, judicial, and media arenas.

Flanagan came to realize that getting things right philosophically was quite different from getting them done politically. That requires building coalitions, so he graduated from being an academic intolerant of political compromises and naive about the political process to becoming a sophisticated partisan operative at the most senior levels of the Reform, Canadian Alliance, and Conservative parties. In the employ of Harper, Flanagan came to look at many policy issues as weapons of political combat. He feels his major contribution was to help make Canadian politics more competitive by helping to knock the Liberals off their governing perch.

Flanagan derived much satisfaction from his experience as an expert court witness on Aboriginal issues, which are also addressed by Adams and Richards. He found the legal scrutiny to which he and his ideas were subjected much more rigorous than the academic peer-review process and the experience instilled in him a respectful admiration for the judicial system's adversarial process. As a pundit, freed from the restraints imposed by accountability to a political master, he now responds to reporters whenever they call, something about which Segal cautions. Flanagan finds that dealing with reporters is a two-way street; he learns from them as they query him. Like Segal, Stein, and

Kingwell, he recognizes that the media are more in the entertainment than the information business. However chaotic and superficial the media's Tower of Babel may be, he feels privileged to be given a voice in it. Sounding now more like a Burkean gradualist than a proselytizing libertarian, Flanagan sees policy options as necessarily constrained by conventional wisdom.

Stephen Clarkson's personal chronicle traces the intellectual evolution of Canada's academic world over the past half-century. He contrasts the spirited efforts of the professors in the Toronto-based University League for Social Reform of the 1960s with what he considers is the relatively quiescent role that academics have come to play in critical public policy issues, offering the 1980s Canada-US free trade debate as an example. During the optimism and creative possibilities in the 1960s, when the influence of figures such as McLuhan and Grant was at its peak, the term "public intellectual" had not yet entered the lexicon. Clarkson sees the emergence of the public intellectual "star system"– he cites John Ralston Saul and Maude Barlow as examples – as a response to the shortage of ideas emanating from academics. He speculates, as do others in this collection, that the new media environment, with its blogs, social networks, and vehicles such as YouTube, may break down this syndrome of public intellectual luminaries.

Critical of the current academic environment, as is Bashevkin, Clarkson points to another source for its shortcomings. He notes the shift among Canada's institutions of higher learning from their older British stamp to a fashionable American mould. The United States, unfortunately in his view, began to set the standards for English Canada's universities as a result of the influx of American professors and a new adherence to American academic benchmarks as Canadian governments expanded their stable of post-secondary institutions in the 1960s. To his dismay – here he shares something of Bashevkin's perspective – these publicly subsidized institutions now serve governments and private corporate interests more than they serve the community. The marginalization of academics in public debates and the lurch to a more unjust society saddens Clarkson, an apostle of Trudeau. He thinks professional norms and the structure of incentives for academics penalize those who participate in the public square, but he does acknowledge that university administrators, keen to raise their university's profile, now aggressively encourage their faculty to interact with the media. While Baum extols the contribution of Le Devoir to intellectual discourse in Quebec, Clarkson belittles Canada's self-proclaimed national newspaper, the *Globe and Mail*, for its paltry contribution to public thought in English Canada.

Strikingly, Michael Adams suggests that the oft-dismissed, easily pilloried work of the public opinion researcher represents a public intellectual presence in democratic society. Sound data generated by public opinion research has more than mere commercial value or public policy application. By identifying the collective voices of distinct social groups, surveys that report on values may foster empathy and introspective self-examination among citizens of Canada's diverse democratic society. Survey research on values is therefore worthwhile and its dissemination, in Adams's judgment, enhances the quality of civic life. Unlike most of the authors in this collection, Adams is interested in the psycho-demographics of Canadians as well as their heterogeneous social and cultural backgrounds. Recognizing, however, that survey researchers are no more qualified to think of themselves as public intellectuals than are meteorologists, he makes the case that what pollsters do is offer the public a mirror – a metaphor he repeatedly summons – of its collective thinking. And the public is keenly curious to learn about itself. Public intellectuals should be no less eager to see what the public mirror reflects; it may nourish some of their Big Ideas. The mirror metaphor, however, is flawed. Because the pollster's survey questionnaire frames and channels opinions, his mirror cannot offer a pure reflection of something that is already "there."

Adams set out to find whether the self-anointed spokespeople and heads of organizations nominally representing groups such as Muslims and urban Aboriginals accurately reflect the views of members of those groups. One of the experts he consulted in his survey design regarding Aboriginals was Richards, whose contribution to this collection deals with the role of intellectuals such as Flanagan in Aboriginal policy. Like Segal, Adams regrets the demise of Canada's long-form census, which facilitated the rigorous use of data-based methodologies including his own for studying Aboriginals' attitudes. He concludes by quoting Leibniz: "Let us calculate, without further ado, to see who is right." A sceptic could cite Einstein's retort: "Not everything that can be counted counts and not everything that counts can be counted."

Maude Barlow picks up some of Adams's themes. Her public intellectuals are populist tribunes who give voice to those relegated to the edges of public discourse, the ordinary citizens in Adams's surveys. Social activists such as Barlow are a genus of public intellectual suspicious of elites' agendas. These intellectuals are troubled, as Kingwell suggests he is, about the marginalized and powerless, for they have little access to traditional public arenas such as the mainstream media which are controlled by private commercial interests pushing corporate agendas. For Barlow, a healthy democracy requires participation, inclusion, and re-skilled and well-tooled broad civil society movements that are not hoodwinked by the legalese and bafflegab of "experts" serving a small, privileged, hegemonic cadre of mandarins, select politicians, and the corporate titans who make up the Canadian Council of Chief Executives. An egalitarian committed to social and environmental justice, Barlow has faith in the capabilities of non-experts and pledges herself to provide citizens with accessible research that demystifies complicated public policy issues.

Like Flanagan, Barlow considers the building of broad coalitions of groups and individuals as prerequisites for policy change, but she parts sharply with Flanagan's neoliberal conservatism. Her alliances are with groups such as the Canadian Auto Workers, and she relates her experiences fighting the Canada-US Free Trade Agreement in the 1980s (an issue about which Clarkson feels academics were too quiescent), the Multilateral Agreement on Investment in the 1990s and, more recently, the Security and Prosperity Partnership for North America. She counts the late American civil rights and peace activist Howard Zinn as one of her public intellectual heroes and lists more than a dozen Canadians – freshwater scientist David Schindler, political economist Jim Laxer, muckraking journalist Linda McQuaig, corporate globalization critic Naomi Klein (see Bashevkin's essay), David Suzuki, Tony Clarke of the Polaris Institute, Barry Campbell of the Canadian Centre for Policy Alternatives, and physician Danielle Martin of Canadian Doctors for Medicare among them – as fellow-traveller public intellectuals.

The United States, conspicuous in the life of Canada and therefore in many of the chapters, stands out as well in Pierre Fortin's look at economists as public intellectuals. Buttressing points made by Saunders and Segal, Fortin observes that there are relatively few exchanges of economists between universities and governments in Canada, unlike the case south of the border. He bemoans the decline of economic history and the sociology of economic behaviour and the ascendancy of formalism and mathematical problem solving in the discipline. Professional advancement is largely dependent on publishing in international journals, most of which are American and have little interest in their northern neighbour. This deters Canadian economists from investing in the study of Canada's economy and Canadian public policy; their research focus has shifted towards mathematized abstract theory and foreign economies, especially that of the United States.

Proportionately fewer economists in Canada than in the United States are recognized as public intellectuals. Nevertheless, some Canadian economists such as Tom Courchene and Jack Mintz have considerable influence in public affairs and policy debates. Drawing on his experience, Fortin stresses the importance of retaining one's independence as a thinker, maintaining one's reputation through publication in academic forums, and respecting the public's intelligence. Essential are precision, clarity, conciseness, concrete prescriptions, and restricting oneself to matters in which one is expert.

John Richards offers some intriguing generic observations about public intellectuals in his case study of public intellectuals and Aboriginal policy. He adroitly skewers John Ralston Saul's romantic attribution of Canada's collectivist traditions to the country's alleged Aboriginal roots.[4] Like Segal and Fortin, Richards offers his own public intellectual exemplars – MP Stéphane Dion, Conrad Black, and former Parti Québécois cabinet minister Joseph Facal. He thinks Facal may accomplish more in advancing his policy proposals now that he is no longer at the cabinet table because he is free to champion them in print as a public intellectual unencumbered by the exigencies that limited him as a politician. Like Flanagan and Barlow, Richards notes that coalition building motivates politicians and, like Margaret Somerville, he addresses political correctness. Silenced by fear of charges of racism, few politicians will address issues such as violence against women on First Nations reserves.

Richards, working with Michael Adams's Environics Institute and two policy think tanks – the C.D. Howe Institute (with which he is affiliated) and the Caledon Institute of Social Policy – argues that public intellectuals have hyperventilated the high politics and philosophical discourses underpinning the constitution's provisions for Aboriginal treaty rights (also a subject of Flanagan's expertise). They have devoted insufficient attention to the dramatic rural-to-cities movement of Aboriginals and their conditions on and off reserves. The media reflect these biases, alert as they are to the activities and pronouncements of the Assembly of First Nations, which speaks for on-reserve Indians, other organizations that represent the majority of Aboriginals, those living off reserves, get scant notice.

Margaret Somerville reminds us of how the academy's older contemptuous view of their professors' appearances in the media has shifted in a few short decades. She echoes Clarkson's observation that universities, seeking to raise their profile and define popular exposure as a contribution to their community, now assiduously court the media and urge their professors to engage with them. A student of the relatively new field of bioethics, Somerville struggles with the implications of society's cornerstone values for life-and-death issues such as the treatment of seriously disabled newborn and "designer" babies, euthanasia, and the allocation of scarce health-care resources. These are the feedstock for polarizing "culture wars," and while majority positions in ethics controversies may have a democratic imprimatur, they are not necessarily ethically sound. Somerville, committed to contributing to the public's informed engagement in "ethics talk," does not subscribe to the idea that professional ethicists are or should be the moral police of an increasingly secularized society. What are, she asks, the "shared ethics" which could bond Canada's pluralistic, multi-religious, and secular postmodern society?

For Somerville, as for Stein, a willingness to listen respectfully to others' ideas, to all voices in the public arena, is essential. But attentive listening must not be at the expense of fearlessly expressing one's own truth, something politicians may shirk in their pursuit of the coalitions needed to gain and sustain power. In a frontal assault on political correctness as an intensely narrow-minded and intolerant plague, she revisits the furore ignited when Ryerson University decided to award her an honorary degree, and the institution's shameful response to the uproar. In her view, the moral relativism of postmodernism – "the equality of all values" and its paradigm of no grounded truths – hijacks fundamental democratic values such as freedom of association, speech, and conscience. Political correctness, wielded as a weapon to silence certain voices such as Somerville's in opposition to same-sex marriage, is perversely hypocritical in that it incites a form of proselytizing fundamentalism. Insistent on black and white, defining issues in the disjunctive (either/or), rejecting the conjunctive (both/and), political correctness chills debate and its many shades of grey. Dogmatic secularism in Somerville's view is not neutral but itself religious because it is ultimately faith-based. Like Flanagan, she thinks journalists are well informed, dedicated, and highly intelligent, but she has qualms, as do many others in this collection, about their employers, the media.

While there is no single concern or consensus in these essays, common thematic threads emerge: anxieties regarding the pace and logic of the media, the transformation of universities and the new expectations of its professoriate, the influential pull of American soft power, the enduring cultural divide between English Canada and Quebec, the rise of think tanks and of public-policy advocacy by public intellectuals. To some readers, the focus on such issues will suggest that the interests of Canada's public intellectuals have lagged behind their society's transformation as Aboriginals, women, and visible minorities have moved from the periphery into the mainstream of Canada's cultural and political life. With the exception, however, of the four female contributors (in a stable of fifteen authors), these newer voices are absent here. Excepting the contributions of Michael Adams and Nelson Wiseman, there are relatively few references to Canadians of non-British, non-French, ethnic origins, and only Sylvia Bashevkin directly addresses the place of women in public thought. Canada's Aboriginal peoples are referred to in a number of chapters, most notably those by John Richards, Tom Flanagan, and Adams, but not the perspectives of Aboriginal thinkers themselves. As these essays collectively reflect them, the faces and preoccupations of Canada's public intellectuals have not changed as rapidly as have the faces and concerns of Canada's evolving society.

There are both affinities and disparities in the ruminations of the creative thinkers assembled here about how public intellectuals fare in Canada and their proper place in contemporary society. Most of the authors address modes of public intellectualizing and some discuss how building coalitions contributes to operationalizing Big Ideas. Others point to Canada's ideological traditions, past and present. Many identify challenges facing Canadian public intellectuals as independent social critics. Some also identify the opportunities that new media offer public intellectuals. Some are cautious and leery about public intellectuals' exposure in the mainstream media, while others welcome it. A common theme is that public intellectuals whose influence resonates across Canada's partisan divides are not victims of the fleetingly fashionable; they know that standing up for what they think and believe may lead to rebuke as well as respect.

NOTES

1 Morris Wolfe, *Jolts: The TV Wasteland and the Canadian Oasis* (Toronto: Lorimer, 1985), 114–16.

2 *The Global Go To Think Tank Report, 2011*, http://www.gotothinktank.com/
wp-content/uploads/2012/01/2011GlobalGoToThinkTanksReport-UN
EditionWITHOUTLETTER.pdf.

3 Peter Russell, *Constitutional Odyssey: Can Canadians Become a Sovereign
People?* 3rd ed. (Toronto: University of Toronto Press, 2004); the quote is
from the Constitution Act, 1982, section 27.

4 John Ralston Saul, *A Fair Country: Telling Truths about Canada* (Toronto:
Viking, 2008).

Contributors

A Fellow of the Marketing Research and Intelligence Association – the highest honour bestowed upon a member – **Michael Adams** is the president of the Environics group of research and communications consulting companies, which he co-founded in 1970. The author of four Canadian best-sellers, his book *Fire and Ice* won the 2003 Donner Prize for the best book on Canadian public policy and was selected in 2005 by the *Literary Review of Canada* as one of the 100 most important books ever published in the country. His book *Unlikely Utopia: The Surprising Triumph of Canadian Pluralism* focuses on the promise and challenge of Canadian multiculturalism. His Environics Institute released a major research project on urban Aboriginal life in Canada in 2010. The recipient of an honorary doctor of letters from Ryerson University, he inaugurated a writing scholarship, which awards a student at his former high school first-year tuition at an Ontario post-secondary institution for the best personal essay written.

Maude Barlow, the national chairperson of the 65,000-member Council of Canadians and founder of the Blue Planet Project, is senior adviser on water to the president of the 63rd session of the United Nations General Assembly. She chairs the board of Washington-based Food and Water Watch, is an executive member of the San Francisco–based International Forum on Globalization, and is a councillor with the Hamburg-based World Future Council. The recipient of ten honorary doctorates and the 2005 Right Livelihood Award (known as the "Alternative Nobel Prize"), she has authored or co-authored sixteen books, including the international best-seller *Blue Covenant: The Global Water Crisis and the Coming Battle for the Right to Water*.

The first female principal of University College at the University of Toronto and a fellow of the Royal Society of Canada, **Sylvia Bashevkin** is a past president of the Canadian Political Science Association and of the women and politics research section of the American Political Science Association. She is the author of many books, including *Women, Power, Politics: The Hidden Story of Canada's Unfinished Democracy* and *Welfare Hot Buttons: Women, Work and Social Policy Reform*. Her interests include probing the obstacles as well as the opportunities that face women who seek to become more involved in politics and how to enhance both the quality and quantity of citizen engagement in Canada.

Gregory Baum is a student of the interaction of religion and society. Born a Jew and raised as a Protestant in Berlin, he converted to Catholicism and was the long-time editor of *The Ecumenist*. He has taught at the University of Toronto and at McGill University, holds seven honorary degrees, and was selected a *peritus* by Pope John XXIII during the period leading up to the Second Vatican Council. A member of the Order of Canada, he is currently associated with Montreal's *Le Centre justice et foi*, a centre for adult education and advocate for refugees and immigrants. Among his recent books are *Religion and Alienation: A Theological Reading of Sociology*, *The Theology of Tariq Ramadan: A Catholic Perspective*, and *Signs of the Times: Religious Pluralism and Economic Injustice*.

A Rhodes Scholar with a doctorate from the Sorbonne, **Stephen Clarkson**, teaches political economy at the University of Toronto. His book *Canada and the Reagan Challenge* won the John Porter prize, and his two-volume biography *Trudeau and Our Times* (co-authored with Christina McCall) was awarded the Governor General's award. More recently, he authored *The Big Red Machine* on the Liberal Party's electoral performance. His 2010 book (written with Stepan Wood) *A Perilous Imbalance: The Globalization of Canadian Law and Governance* examined the contradictory dilemmas confronting Canada through its engagement in global governance. His primary research and teaching focus remains the political economy of North America, on which he has published a trilogy over the last ten years. *Uncle Sam and Us* (2002) analysed the impact of globalization and neo-conservatism on Canada. *Does North America Exist?* (2008) looked at how the continent has been "governed" since NAFTA and 9/11. His latest book, *Dependent America?* (2011), assessed the extent to which the United States derives its extraordinary power from the economic, military, and diplomatic support it receives from its two neighbours. Clarkson has been elected a fellow of the Royal Society of Canada and was appointed to the Order of Canada in 2011.

Born in Ottawa, Illinois, **Tom Flanagan** has taught at the University of Calgary since 1968 and was elected a fellow of the Royal Society of Canada in 1996. His book *First Nations? Second Thoughts* received both the prestigious Donner Prize in 2000 and the Canadian Political Science Association's Donald Smiley Prize for the best book on Canadian politics published in 2000. A consultant and expert witness for the Crown in a number of Aboriginal and treaty-rights cases, his most recent book, *Beyond the Indian Act: Restoring Aboriginal Property Rights*, explains how private property rights may be introduced onto First Nations lands. A former adviser to Preston Manning and the Reform Party, Flanagan managed Stephen Harper's leadership campaign for the Conservative Party and directed the party's national election campaign in 2004. His experiences in the Conservative war room during the party's successful 2005–6 election campaign are described in his book *Harper's Team: Behind the Scenes in the Conservative Rise to Power*.

Pierre Fortin, a Governor General's award medallist, has published some 10 books, 40 reports, and 200 scholarly articles in Canada and abroad. A fellow of the Royal Society of Canada, a board member of the Canadian Institute for Advanced Research, and a past president of the Canadian Economics Association, he served as chief economic adviser to the premier of Quebec. In 1995 the members of the Association of Quebec Economists selected him as "the most distinguished Quebec economist of the last decade." He has twice won the Gold Award of the National Magazine Awards Foundation for "the best regular column in a Canadian magazine." Among his degrees, he holds a BA in classical humanities from the Jesuit College in Quebec City.

Alain-G. Gagnon has influenced researchers on federalism in Belgium, the United Kingdom, and Spain, where the Universidad Carlos III de Madrid recently honoured him for his research and where he received the Josep Maria Vilaseca i Marcet award from the Generalitat de Catalonia in 2007. A fellow of the Royal Society of Canada and a Trudeau fellow, from 1982 to 2003 he taught at Queen's, Carleton, and McGill universities. Since then, he has held the Canada Research Chair in Quebec and Canadian Studies at l'Université du Québec à Montréal (UQAM). He is the founding director of the Centre de recherche interdisciplinaire sur la diversité au Québec (CRIDAQ) and the director of the Groupe de recherche sur les sociétés plurinationales (GRSP). His book *Contemporary Canadian Federalism* has been translated into Catalan, Spanish, and German.

Mark Kingwell, who won an Outstanding Teaching Award at the University of Toronto where he is a professor of philosophy, has lectured extensively in Canada, the United States, Europe, the Middle East, and Australia. A contributing editor of *Harper's* and the author of fifteen books on political, cultural, and aesthetic theory, including the national best-sellers *Better Living* (1998), *The World We Want* (2000), *Concrete Reveries* (2008), and *Glenn Gould* (2009), his articles on politics, architecture, and art have appeared in, among other places, the *New York Times*, *Utne Reader*, *Bookforum*, and *Queen's Quarterly*. A recipient of the Spitz Prize in political theory, he was awarded an honorary DFA degree from the Nova Scotia College of Art & Design for his contributions to theory and criticism. He is currently at work on a book about twenty-first-century democracy.

Trained as an economist, **John Richards** emigrated from Britain to Saskatchewan where he served as an NDP, and then Independent Socialist, MLA in the 1970s. He holds the Roger Phillips chair in social policy at the C.D. Howe Institute, is the co-editor of the Canadian public policy journal *Inroads*, and teaches in the Graduate Public Policy School at Simon Fraser University, where he received the President's Award for service to the university through media and public relations in 2005. Over the past two decades, he has also taught and conducted research in Bangladesh and heads the Centre for Policy Research at the International University of Business Agriculture and Technology in Dhaka.

Honoured as the best columnist in Canada in 2006, **Doug Saunders** has no academic degrees, but his penetrating, educated writing has won him the National Newspaper Award, Canada's equivalent of the Pulitzer Prize, on four separate occasions. As the *Globe and Mail*'s European bureau chief, he interviewed many of the world's leading politicians and intellectuals. A prolific student of the larger themes and intellectual concepts that drive international affairs, his recent book, *Arrival City: The Final Migration and Our Next World*, draws on his visits to twenty locations on five continents where he studied the effects of the final wave of rural-urban migration on the world's cities. It has been published in the United States, Britain, Germany, the Netherlands, Finland, Spain, Australia, New Zealand, and China and shortlisted for the Writers' Trust of Canada's Shaughnessy Cohen Prize for political writing.

Hugh Segal, an unstinting champion of Canada's red Tory conservative tradition and critic of "American fast-food conservatism" as selfish and directionless, placed second to former prime minister Joe Clark in the 1998 Progressive Conservative leadership race. He currently serves as the chair of the Special Senate Committee on Anti-Terrorism, and is a former chair and present member of the Senate Committee on Foreign Affairs. A former associate cabinet secretary in Ontario, chief of staff to the Prime Minister Brian Mulroney, and past-president of the Institute for Research on Public Policy, he sits on the Council of the International Institute for Democratic and Electoral Assistance (Stockholm), is a member of the Order of Canada, and, in 2010, was appointed to the Eminent Persons Group to advise Commonwealth heads of government on how to increase the Commonwealth's salience and influence.

As the founding director of the McGill Centre for Medicine, Ethics and Law, **Margaret Somerville** has played an active role in the world-wide development of applied ethics, in particular the study of the wider ethical and legal aspects of medicine and science. Elected a fellow of the Royal Society of Canada in 1991, she is the recipient of eight honorary degrees and many awards including the Distinguished Service Award of the American Society of Law and Medicine, the *Pax Orbis ex Jure* Gold Medal of the World Jurist Association, the Order of Australia, and the UNESCO Avicenna Prize for Ethics in Science. A keynote speaker at UNESCO conferences in Paris, Barcelona, and Tehran, she has been a consultant to the United Nations Human Rights Commission in Geneva and law reform commissions in Canada and Australia.

Janice Gross Stein, the Massey Lecturer in 2001, holds honorary degrees from three universities, is a fellow of the Royal Society of Canada, and a member of both the Order of Canada and the Order of Ontario. Her co-authored *The Unexpected War: Canada in Kandahar* won the Writers' Trust of Canada's Shaughnessy Cohen Prize in 2008 for political writing and she was awarded the Molson Prize by the Canada Council for her outstanding contribution to public debate. An honorary foreign member of the American Academy of Arts and Science, she is an internationally recognized authority on conflict management and has lectured at many venues including the NATO Defence College in Rome.

Born in Bucharest, **Nelson Wiseman** is an associate professor at the University of Toronto where he specializes in Canadian government and politics. In 2009 *Choice* selected his book *In Search of Canadian Political Culture* as an Outstanding Academic Title. He has served as a consultant to departments of the Canadian, Ontario, and Manitoba governments and as an invited witness at House of Commons and Senate committees. In 2010 he authored an invited submission for the UK House of Lords Select Committee on the Constitution. A columnist for the *Hill Times*, he appears frequently in the media to comment on Canadian politics. International media where his comments have appeared include the *New York Times*, *Rzeczpospolita* (Warsaw), *Diario El Nacional* (Venezuela), *Izvestia* (Moscow), *Al Jazeera*, the BBC, *Yomiuri Shimbun* (Japan), the *Australian* (Sydney), *Xinhua* (China), *Berlingske Tidende* (Denmark), *Liberazione* (Italy), the *Financial Times*, the *Wall Street Journal*, and Radio France International.